All biblical verses are used as reflected in the New International Version (NIV) of the Christian Bible unless otherwise noted.

Published by Simple Truths, an imprint of Sourcebooks, Inc.
P.O. Box 4410, Naperville, Illinois 60567-4410
(630) 961-3900
Fax: (630) 961-2168
www.sourcebooks.com

Printed and bound in China.

QL 10 9 8 7 6 5 4 3 2 1

CONTENTS

What a Difference a Day Makes

An apple a day keeps the doctor away.

The power of a daily habit is woven throughout our common-sense prescriptions for a better life. I don't know if an apple a day really keeps the doctor away, though I'm pretty certain that eating ten apples in one day is missing the point of the proverb. Some medicine does its work all at once, in one dose. But most of the important things in life—a marriage, a child, a career, a reputation—require daily attention.

No wonder the power of our daily habits is woven throughout God's Word.

God's mercies are new every single day.
—LAMENTATIONS 3:23

God's strength is provided for us each day to meet the challenges of that particular day.
—DEUTERONOMY 3:25

We are advised to put each of our days in proper order.
—PSALM 90:12

Jesus calls us to follow Him daily.
—LUKE 9:23

If we were to list all the verses that talk about the importance of a single day and our daily activities, that list alone would fill up this book. That's why I'm so certain that spending time each day with God—in His Word, in prayer, in reflection of His love and plans for you—will make a tremendous positive difference in your life and spirit. Day by day.

My prayer is that these Bible verses, short devotions, and prayer starters will be a special part of your time with God each day. And every day of the year.

January
Faith and Growing Faith

Being a Christian is more than just an instantaneous conversion—it is a daily process whereby you grow to be more and more like Christ.
—BILLY GRAHAM

New Year, New You

*Now faith is confidence in what we hope for and
assurance about what we do not see.*

—HEBREWS 11:1

I t's a new year, and that means it's time for a fresh, new start. When the calendar turns over, it's always a great time to take stock of where you are in life and make plans to grow and move forward with a renewed spirit of faith and optimism.

Are you excited about all that is to come? Or are you discouraged because not everything worked out the way you wanted last year? Maybe in the past you have made New Year's resolutions and commitments that you weren't able to keep.

You may be thinking about better health, habits, relationships, and an assortment of other worthy goals today. Go for it! But don't forget about the most important issue of all: your spiritual life, your relationship with God.

Where do you begin? Time in God's Word, time in prayer, time in expressing love, and time in serving others are all part of the mix. But laying the only sure foundation for anything that you do, great or small, begins with faith.

Heavenly Father, I bring you my faith and ask you to strengthen and make it grow in me in all the days to follow.

His Faithfulness

He is the faithful God, keeping His covenant of love to a thousand generations of those who love Him and keep His commandments.

—DEUTERONOMY 7:9

I'm ready for a fresh start. But my faith doesn't feel very strong right now. I'm just not sure I'm strong enough to walk the walk God has for me.

Here's some good news to hold onto tightly. Your faith doesn't have to be strong and huge at this moment in time. In fact, it can be as small as a mustard seed, and you can still move mountains. How? Because of God's faithfulness to you! His strength is sufficient even in your weakness. All He asks is that you exercise the faith you have right now and trust in Him.

That's all He is asking of me?

If your faith is in God and His faithfulness, it becomes the basis for a confidence and an assurance that is greater than any situations life throws your way. Your simple first steps of faith allow you to experience God's presence and grace in the ups and downs of daily living. Even when you fail; even if your faith waivers.

Step boldly into your new year. God has great plans for you. Even if you can't "see" how great this year can be, your simple faith will feed you with a hope to accomplish more than you ever thought was possible!

Faithful God, thank you for meeting me right where I am in my spiritual journey and giving me strength to live for you.

An Overcomer

*Who is it that overcomes the world? Only the one
who believes that Jesus is the Son of God.*

—1 JOHN 5:5

S ome of our challenges are caused by others. Some can't be blamed on people but seem to be the results of circumstances—"bad luck." Some of our biggest problems, if we're honest, are brought on by the person we see each morning in the mirror.

When you determine in your heart to draw closer to God and grow spiritually, you may discover a season of life where you don't have *fewer* problems but, in fact, *more* challenges and hardships.

Satan doesn't spend much time tempting and harassing those who just go along with the flow and have little concern for spiritual matters. He wants to derail those who are ready to make a difference for God in the world.

That doesn't sound very encouraging until you ponder the Words of Jesus—His presence in your life gives you all the strength you need to be victorious in even the toughest of times.

Are you struggling with temptation? Are there some tough days ahead at work or in your home? Don't lose heart! Your faith makes you an overcomer!

Jesus, I do believe in you and find strength in your presence.

Age Doesn't Matter

*Don't let anyone look down on you because you are
young, but set an example for the believers in speech,
in conduct, in love, in faith, and in purity.*

—1 TIMOTHY 4:12

When it comes to standing as an example of Godly faith, age is not an issue throughout Biblical history. Moses led the children of Israel to the Promised Land at the age of 120! Abraham and Sarah became first-time parents over ninety! But youth was served as well. The prophet Samuel was called by God to restore purity to the Temple at eleven or twelve. David became King of Israel when he was about the same age. David would not have been old enough to get a driver's license in our day and age when he slayed the giant and gained an amazing victory against the enemies of God's people.

Do you feel your age is a hindrance to growing closer to God and being a positive witness of His love and goodness? Whether you are in your senior years and have served God for decades, or you are a youth who has just started walking with God, what matters is your faith. With God inside of you, you have everything you need to make a difference in your world!

Gracious God, thank you for working in and through me right where I am in life.

No Doubt

*But when you ask, you must believe and not
doubt, because the one who doubts is like a wave
of the sea, blown and tossed by the wind.*

—JAMES 1:6

I s it possible to walk with God and have absolutely no doubts? To live every moment in absolute confidence that God is in control?

The Apostle James tells us to bring requests to our Heavenly Father with belief and to "not doubt"—the literal translation would be to "not waver."

Consider two kings. Saul was the first king of Israel, a gifted leader who began his reign with tremendous victory. But the latter years of his rule were tragic, as his doubts led him on a path of compromise and disobedience.

David faced the very same challenges, fears, and doubts. The difference was that David brought his doubts and fears to God. His faith in God was so strong that he stood fast when the waves and winds of life buffeted him.

Do you have doubts? You haven't lost your faith. The question is what you are going to do about your doubts and fears. Like David, turn your heart toward the God who loves you. With faith, you can stand strong and stable in the midst of the storm.

Dear Lord, thank you for loving me so much that you allow me to bring my doubts to you and for renewing my strength.

A Child of God

Yet to all who did receive Him, to those who believed in His name, He gave the right to become children of God—children born not of natural descent, nor of human decision or a husband's will, but born of God.

—JOHN 1:12

A first-grade teacher asked her students to draw a picture of their families. One little boy showed his picture and generated some curiosity because he had a different hair color from his other family members. One boy asked if his hair was different because he was adopted. Before the teacher could respond, a little girl exclaimed, "I know all about adoptions because I was adopted!"

"What does it mean to be adopted?" asked the teacher.

"It means," said the girl, "that you grew in your mommy's heart instead of her tummy."

What a powerful and delightful glimpse into what it means to be part of God's family. God has adopted us not out of a sense of pity or obligation. He has called each of us His child because of His incredible love for us and our eternal destiny. We grew in His heart.

Do you ever suffer from feelings of not belonging? Do you sometimes feel insecure? Bring those feelings to God, but most of all, pause to consider the amazing reality that you are His beloved child!

Thank you, loving Father, for adopting me into your family and for loving me so much.

What a Treasure

For God so loved the world that He gave His one and only Son, that whoever believes in Him shall not perish but have eternal life.

—JOHN 3:16

A CLASSIC DEVOTION FROM CHARLES SPURGEON (NINETEENTH CENTURY)

God gives to every man that believes in Christ everlasting life. The moment you believe, there trembles into your bosom a vital spark of heavenly flame that never shall be quenched. In that same moment when you cast yourself on Christ, Christ comes to you in the living and incorruptible Word that lives and abides forever.

When I first received everlasting life, I had no idea what a treasure had come to me. I knew that I had obtained something very extraordinary, but of its superlative value I was not aware. I looked to Jesus, He looked on me, and we were one forever. That moment my joy surpassed all bounds, just as my sorrow had aforetime driven me to an extreme of grief. I was perfectly at rest in Christ, satisfied with Him, and my heart was glad. But I did not know that this grace was everlasting life until I began to read in the Scriptures, and to know more fully the value of the jewel that God had given me.

Heavenly Father, thank you for the gift of salvation for today—and for all eternity.

Never Hungry Again

Then Jesus declared, "I am the bread of life.
Whoever comes to me will never go hungry, and
whoever believes in me will never be thirsty."

—JOHN 6:35

Hunger and thirst are realities and necessities of life. Just as we crave physical nourishment, we likewise experience a hunger and thirst in the spiritual realm. We are not physical beings trying to be spiritual; we are spiritual beings who have a physical life.

Look at the people around you, and it is obvious the world is chasing down various paths to find meaning. Some look inside themselves for answers to the meaning of life, striving to be successful according to the wrong values. Some people give up pursuing spiritual fulfillment and medicate themselves with drugs, alcohol, or sensual pleasures.

As C. S. Lewis, said: "There is a God-shaped vacuum in the heart of every man which cannot be filled by any created thing, but only by God, the Creator, made known through Jesus."

As you continue to draw near to God each day, have you affirmed that spiritual growth and every spiritual gift come from God and God alone? Put your trust in God and savor the bread and water that flow from His life into yours.

Lord, thank you for the spiritual nourishment you give me each day.

Living Water

*Whoever believes in me, as Scripture has said, rivers
of living water will flow from within them.*

—JOHN 7:38

When Jesus promised rivers—not streams, not creeks, not rivulets, but rivers—of living water that flow not just *into* a believer but *from* a believer, His hearers must have thought this was an offer that was simply too good to be true. In a desert land, how would it be possible to pour forth rivers from within?

Jesus, of course, is promising a spiritual life force that spills over from the abundance of His presence inside of us. His grace is given in such great measure that it flows in, through, and yes, even from us.

When you think of your own spiritual vitality, do you recognize the abundance of grace that is ready to flow out from you? If you've been underestimating the riches you have in and through Christ, now is the time to let your faith grow in all that you have been gifted.

Wonderful Savior, thank you for the spiritual riches that are mine through knowing you.

Whatever You Ask

Therefore I tell you, whatever you ask for in prayer,
believe that you have received it, and it will be yours.

—MARK 11:24

I can pray for anything and receive it? Just because I asked? Anything?

It is obviously possible to ask God for things that are based on selfish or misguided thoughts and attitudes. But before you assume that you should be careful what you ask God for, don't forget His invitation for you to come before His throne with boldness; don't ignore His teaching that we are to bring our daily needs before Him; don't disobey His command to rely on Him with our utmost trust and faith for both our needs and desires.

Yes, some people ask God for the wrong things, but it is quite possible that the greater spiritual danger, in our self-sufficient culture, is that we don't ask enough!

Begin your prayers each day with praise and thanksgiving to God. Don't forget to ask that God forgive you of any shortcomings in thought, word, and deed. Pray for others. But then pray for yourself and your needs with the utmost confidence that the God who knows everything you need is ready to bless you both materially and spiritually.

Thank you, gracious Father, for being the giver of everything I need now and in eternity.

11

Seeing the Glory

*Then Jesus said, "Did I not tell you that if you
believe, you will see the glory of God?"*

—JOHN 11:40

What do you see when you think of human glory? Do you see someone who has done something that merits our attention and amazement? Consider, then, that celebrities are often glorified just because they are famous, not for something that they have accomplished. Human glory isn't always that amazing!

God's glory, on the other hand, is more than amazing. The original Hebrew word for "glory" could be translated "weight." In other words, God's glory is something substantial. It's not just smoke and mirrors, but something of real weight.

When we believe in Jesus Christ, we are given the privilege of seeing the glory of God without fear of death or injury. It is a beautiful invitation to more fully gaze closely at the One who created and sustains the world by the power of His Word. This is not some vague spiritual feeling, but standing in the presence of the Almighty.

Your life will change for eternity not by looking at yourself and others more closely, but when you open your eyes wide to the glory of the Creator.

Creator God, I praise you and worship your majesty and glory. Your greatness is beyond description.

Choose Life

*I have chosen the way of faithfulness; I
have set my heart on your laws.*

—PSALM 119:30

M any scholars and critics agree that "The Road Not Taken"
by Robert Frost is one of the best known examples of
American poetry. Frost's closing thought tells us: "I took the
one less traveled by, / And that has made all the difference."

Jesus tells us there is a broad road and a narrow road. The
broad road is for the masses who want to go with the flow
and not take seriously God's call to faith and repentance. The
narrow road is for those who say yes to God and His will.

In Psalm 119, the great poet and warrior, King David, shows
why God said he was "a man after my own heart" (Acts 13:22).
He chose faithfulness. He set his heart on God's ways. In other
words, he committed his heart, soul, and body to the road less
traveled. It made all the difference in the world for him.

Is it time for you to confirm and affirm what spiritual road
you are on?

**Dear God, I choose you and your ways! Thank you for
walking with me on the journey of life.**

Say It

For it is with your heart that you believe and are justified, and it is with your mouth that you profess your faith and are saved.

—ROMANS 10:10

A wife's husband never said he loved her. When she confronted him, his answer was: "I told you I loved you on the day we got married, thirty years ago. Nothing's changed; why repeat myself?"

While thrilled he loved her then and now, she longed to hear what was in his heart again.

Salvation is a matter of the heart: forgiveness. And it is a matter of action: repentance. But it is also a matter of our words: confession.

We speak the words on the day that we receive Jesus Christ into our hearts, but we must continue to confess what God has done and is doing in our lives as we grow in our faith. Even a simple statement to coworkers or neighbors, such as "I've been so blessed by God," can open the doors to deeper spiritual conversations at God-appointed moments.

Confession is a wonderful and powerful way to grow spiritually—and to bless others. Our words tell others—and ourselves—what is in our heart. What are you telling the world is in your heart?

Loving Father, with my words, I declare you are my Lord and Savior.

Though He Slay Me

"Because you have so little faith. Truly I tell you, if you have faith as small as a mustard seed, you can say to this mountain, 'Move from here to there,' and it will move. Nothing will be impossible for you."

—MATTHEW 17:20

A CLASSIC DEVOTION FROM OSWALD CHAMBERS (TWENTIETH CENTURY)

Faith by its very nature must be tested and tried. And the real trial of faith is not that we find it difficult to trust God, but that God's character must be proven as trustworthy in our own minds. Faith being worked out into reality must experience times of unbroken isolation. Never confuse the trial of faith with the ordinary discipline of life, because a great deal of what we call the trial of faith is the inevitable result of being alive. Faith, as the Bible teaches it, is faith in God coming against everything that contradicts Him—a faith that says, "I will remain true to God's character whatever He may do." The highest and the greatest expression of faith in the whole Bible is: "Though He slay me, yet will I hope in Him" (Job 13:15).

Dear God, thank you for the gift of faith in my life. Take the spark that is in my spirit and turn it into a roaring fire.

Accepting Others

Accept the one whose faith is weak, without
quarreling over disputable matters.

—ROMANS 14:1

I f you hired a carpenter to build shelves for your family room
and returned home to find a new toolshed in your backyard,
what would your response be?

God has given every single believer a huge job. He wants us
to be witnesses in our world. He wants us to tell others about
what He is doing in and through our lives. A common temptation and problem is that instead of witnessing—telling our
story in God—we take on the job of judging and convicting
others. Do you have a friend who is doing wrong? Your job is
to witness to your friend, but not to convince them that they
are a sinner. That is God's job, and He does this through the
Holy Spirit. If your friend comes to you and asks for counsel
and help, by all means, provide counsel and help. But trust God
to bring conviction to your friend's heart.

God has given you a job. Be His witness. He hasn't asked you
to build a toolshed. So until He does, finish the shelves!

**Father of peace, help me to bring peace, not strife, to those
in my life.**

Overflowing Joy

May the God of hope fill you with all the joy and
peace as you trust in Him, so that you may overflow
with hope by the power of the Holy Spirit.

—ROMANS 15:13

W e live in an interconnected world that is brought together, in large measure, by the Internet and social media. What a great way to share family pictures and stay in touch with friends that are scattered across the country and globe! One of the most fascinating dynamics of social media is when a post "goes viral."

People are drawn to the love of God through our consistent witness that God is at work in our lives. But nothing is more contagious than an overflowing joy. A joyful heart will go viral more powerfully and quickly than anything else we offer to the world.

Jesus loved parties, told jokes, enjoyed His friends, and He drew crowds. He went viral! Sometimes believers have the reputation for being too serious and somber about everything. They are not fun to be around. They don't smile enough.

Has your heart been so filled with joy that it overflows and splashes others? Paul has prayed that God Himself will fill you with overflowing joy. Make that your prayer as well.

Loving Father, fill me with a contagious joy!

Even in the Dark

For we live by faith, not by sight.

—2 CORINTHIANS 5:7

A mother was tucking her daughter in when the daughter announced she was scared of the dark. The mother told her that God would always watch over her. The girl looked out and saw the moon and stars. She asked if that was God's night-light. Her mother answered that yes, it was, and that God never slept, even when it was totally dark. The daughter finally smiled and said, "Well, as long as God's light is on, we might as well go to sleep."

Fear of darkness is instinctive. We don't like to walk in the dark, not knowing what is around us. There are moments and even seasons of life when all that is visible to us is the very next step. Nothing else is clear or illuminated.

Paul tells the Corinthian church—and us—to have confidence and courage. The believer walks with certainty by faith, not sight.

Are you ever afraid of the dark? Be assured that it is safer to walk with God in the dark than to walk alone in the light of a noonday sun!

Almighty God, thank you that you walk with me each step of my journey, whether it is day or night.

You've Got the Power

*I pray that out of His glorious riches He may strengthen
you with power through His Spirit in your inner being, so
that Christ may dwell in your hearts through faith.*

—EPHESIANS 3:16–17

A little boy came face-to-face with a bully on the playground. Instead of backing down, he stood tall and smiled. Both mad and confused, the bully yelled at him, "Don't you know I'm going to pound you and there's nothing you can do to stop me?"

The little boy pointed at an older, larger kid across the playground and said, "That's my brother. If you lay a hand on me, you're the crazy one."

No force in the universe is more powerful than God. That means we have the ultimate "big brother." But the Apostle Paul prays that we may receive a power that stands in contrast to our typical definitions of strength. He prays that, through our faith, we fully appreciate and accept an inner strength that resides in our heart.

Do you consider yourself to be a person of power and strength? If you have even the slightest doubt, pray along with Paul that you receive a unique internal power that resides inside of you and permeates every fiber of your being.

Father, from your glorious riches, grant me the strength to face any challenge or temptation that I might face in life.

Contagious Encouragement

*Therefore, brothers and sisters, in all our distress and persecution
we were encouraged about you because of your faith.*

—1 THESSALONIANS 3:7

When we think of heroes of the faith, it is hard to find anyone more determined, enthusiastic, and zealous than the Apostle Paul. When he was put in prison, he sang and wrote about joy. Whether shipwrecked or persecuted, he thanked God for the special grace that came to him through challenges and hardships. What a role model for courage and strength under fire!

Can others let us down? Yes. Can we depend on the faith of others for our own faith? No. But within the church, which is made up of imperfect people—like you and me—God has created a safe place where we can be encouraged by others and, just as importantly, we can encourage others.

All of us need someone mature and strong whom we can look up to; each of us also needs someone younger, someone newer in the faith, who can look up to us. That is a big responsibility, but also a reminder to stay true to our calling to walk with Jesus Christ all the days of our lives.

Heavenly Father, give me the grace to be a faithful encouragement to others who follow you.

Draw Near

Let us draw near to God with a sincere heart and with the full assurance that faith brings, having our hearts sprinkled to cleanse us from a guilty conscience and having our bodies washed with pure water.

—HEBREWS 10:22

When faced with temptation, both Adam and Eve fell in disobedience. When God came to visit the couple, He had to call out to them because in their guilt and shame they hid from Him.

The good news for each of us is that God still calls out to us—even if we have fallen through sin and disobedience. Because of God's never-ending love for us, He seeks us even when we have hidden ourselves in shame.

But God knows my shame. He knows my failings. I am not worthy to stand in His presence.

The good news continues. With a sincere heart filled with faith, He cleanses us of the burdens of shame and guilt so that we can approach with Him a purity we longed for, but didn't think was possible. His forgiving, cleansing, loving power—His grace—provides us everything we need to come before His throne with both humility and boldness.

What are you waiting for? Are you still hiding? Now is the time to draw near to God!

Almighty God, I walk into your presence because of your gracious invitation and your cleansing power.

Love is the Greatest

If I have the gift of prophecy and can fathom all mysteries
and all knowledge, and if I have a faith that can move
mountains, but do not have love, I am nothing.

—1 CORINTHIANS 13:2

A CLASSIC DEVOTION FROM HENRY DRUMMOND
(NINETEENTH CENTURY)

Everyone has asked himself the great question of the modern world: What is the summum bonum—the supreme good?

We have been accustomed to be told that the greatest thing in the religious world is faith. That great word has been the keynote for centuries of the popular religion, and we have easily learned to look upon it as the greatest thing in the world. Well, we are wrong. In the 13th chapter of 1 Corinthians, Paul takes us to Christianity at its source, and there we see, "The greatest of these is love." It is not an oversight. Paul was speaking of faith just a moment before. He says, "If I have a faith that can move mountains, but do not have love, I am nothing." So far from forgetting, he deliberately contrasts them, "Now abideth faith, hope, love," and without a moment's hesitation, "The greatest of these is love."

You remember the profound remark that Paul makes elsewhere, "Love is the fulfilling of the law." Christ's one secret of actually living the Christian life is love.

Loving Father, let my life be marked by the love I show to you and to others.

Perseverance

You know that the testing of your faith produces perseverance.

—JAMES 1:3

Perseverance is not a passive attitude where we sigh and say, "Oh well, I hope this burden goes away someday." It is a confident and resilient spirit that says, "I will stand, no matter what the burden." It is a declaration of faith that God works out all situations, even the toughest circumstances, for our good, both now and in eternity.

Note that James does not say that trials produce faith. Trials actually reveal what faith we already have. But when trials are faced with faith, that steadfast belief in the character of God, we do receive the gift of patience and perseverance.

Are you under fire in your life? Don't lose heart. Let your faith well up inside of you to face the challenge with grace and poise. Then you will discover a strength you never knew you possessed!

Dear God, whatever I face in life, help me to exercise the faith you have gifted me with confidence, joy, and patience.

Be on Guard

Be on your guard; stand firm in the faith; be courageous; be strong.

—1 CORINTHIANS 16:13

There is a reason we lock our doors at night. Have we locked the appropriate doors to safeguard our faith?

We know that there is an enemy of our soul who would like nothing more than to see us fall from our faith and stumble into thoughts, attitudes, and deeds that lead to spiritual destruction. Sometimes Satan comes to us as a "roaring lion." But most often he comes to us as an "angel of light" who seduces us from the path of righteousness. Sometimes he doesn't have to show up at all, as we are assaulted every day by words and images that seek to draw us from our spiritual commitment to God.

Are you on your guard spiritually? Or have you carelessly opened your ears and eyes and heart to seductive messages that would shipwreck your faith? Have you taken a stand to secure your heart and home from the siren call of a sinful society?

You have a spiritual enemy. Are you on guard?

Heavenly Father, protect me from the distractions and temptations of this age so I can stand strong in my faith.

Sing!

But I will sing of your strength, in the morning I will sing of your love; for you are my fortress, my refuge in times of trouble.

—PSALM 59:16

A variety of popular, long-running television shows showcase musical talent. We love to listen to great singers, and if we are honest, most of us love to sing and wish we had the talent to entertain millions of listeners.

King David was unique in his combination of skills. He was a fighter. As a young man, he led thousands to victory time after time, often against impossible odds. But he wasn't just a good fighter; he was a poet, songwriter, musician, and singer. David composed and compiled the majority of Psalms in the Bible. What better place is there to go to experience the joy of worship?

Whether you have a wonderful voice or can barely hold a tune, David reminds you to sing for joy before the Lord. We are to make a joyful noise in order to worship God!

If you need a little accompaniment, put some worship music into a playlist and sing along. Make a joyful noise today!

Father God, you are worthy of all my praise. I lift my voice in song to worship you!

Time with God

And without faith it is impossible to please God, because
anyone who comes to Him must believe that He exists
and that He rewards those who earnestly seek Him.

—HEBREWS 11:6

The vast majority of people in America express at least a vague belief that God exists. It is common for even the least religious of individuals to say, "You're in my prayers," when a tragedy strikes someone close to them—even if they never pray! An active faith understands that the ultimate purpose of humans is to know and glorify God. God desires an intimate, loving relationship with us—and it pleases Him greatly when we reciprocate.

Do you want to please God? Believe He exists and *seek Him*. That means getting to know Him through time in His Word. But don't do these things as a list of obligations that must be fulfilled. Recognize that God is present in His Word, in our prayer, and in Christian fellowship. Realize and affirm that you are not spending time in religious activities, but you are in reality spending time with God.

If you love someone and want to know them, you spend time with them. If you love God and want to draw closer to Him, then spend time with Him.

Dear Lord, it is my pleasure to please you in earnest faith.

Genuine Faith

These have come so that the proven genuineness of your faith—of greater worth than gold, which perishes even though refined by fire— may result in praise, glory, and honor when Jesus Christ is revealed.

—1 PETER 1:7

The Apostle Peter was not always known as a man who stood strong under pressure. Early in his time with Jesus, Peter was great on making promises but weak on following through. But as he grew in his faith, Peter became the head of the church and boldly preached the name of Jesus in the face of opposition.

How did a man who once denied Christ become a model of faith?

Peter's words put trials and sufferings in perspective: "He has given us new birth into a living hope through the resurrection of Jesus Christ from the dead, and into an inheritance that can never perish, spoil, or fade. This inheritance is kept in heaven for you, who through faith are shielded by God's power until the coming of the salvation that is ready to be revealed in the last time. In all this you greatly rejoice, though now for a little while you may have had to suffer grief in all kinds of trials" (1 Peter 1:3–6).

Peter's faith gave him strength to stand under pressure.

Father God, when I face temptations and trials, help me to reveal my genuine faith in you.

27

Speak It

I do not hide your righteousness in my heart; I speak of your faithfulness and your saving help. I do not conceal your love and your faithfulness from the great assembly.

—PSALM 40:10

An old adage tells us actions speak louder than words. One quote, often attributed to St. Francis of Assisi, is "Preach Jesus, and if necessary, use words." We must express the love of God through the way we live: our compassion, our faithfulness, our servanthood.

But the words that come out of our mouth matter too. We speak for the glory of God, but the world needs to hear our words of grace and blessing as well. Desperately.

Do your words build others up or tear them down? Do you encourage or discourage? Are you positive or negative? Most importantly, do your words lift up the goodness of God? The question isn't whether you stand on a soapbox and preach, it is whether there is a steady flow of words from your mouth that naturally let others know you believe God is good.

When you speak positive words that reveal a God of love, you stand in contrast to a society that speaks with cynicism, arrogance, and profanity. When you speak words of life, everyone who hears you is blessed!

May the words of my mouth be a blessing to you and others, O Lord, my strength and my redeemer.

Pray On

Rejoice always, pray continually, give thanks in all circumstances; for this is God's will for you in Christ Jesus.

—1 THESSALONIANS 5:16–18

A CLASSIC DEVOTION FROM E. M. BOUNDS (NINETEENTH CENTURY)

Much time spent with God is the secret of all successful praying. Prayer which is felt as a mighty force is the mediate or immediate product of much time spent with God. Our short prayers owe their point and efficiency to the long ones that have preceded them.

The short prevailing prayer cannot be prayed by one who has not prevailed with God in a mightier struggle of long continuance. Jacob's victory of faith could not have been gained without that all-night wrestling. Much time with God alone is the secret of knowing Him and of influence with Him. He bestows His richest gifts upon those who declare their desire for and appreciation of those gifts by the constancy as well as earnestness of their importunity. Christ, who in this as well as other things is our example, spent many whole nights in prayer. Many long seasons of praying make up His history and character. Paul prayed day and night. David's morning, noon, and night praying were doubtless on many occasions very protracted.

Almighty God, thank you for the gracious invitation to enter your presence in prayer.

Limitless Love—Unlimited Future

Your love, Lord, reaches to the heavens, your faithfulness to the skies.

—PSALM 36:5

When was the last time you sat down to consider the love of God? Today's verse tells us that it reaches to the heavens.

Do you realize that there is nothing you have done, no sin or mistake so great, that God's love can't reach that far to forgive and redeem?

We are tempted to look at our past mistakes and get stuck there. Some of us dwell in a past filled with regrets. We can certainly learn from our past—and God Himself tells us to look backward to remember His faithfulness. But let's not forget that God's love and faithfulness allow us to look forward with hope, confidence, and optimism.

It's too late for me. I've made too many mistakes.

It's never too late to walk in faith. Because of God's limitless love, we are not trapped in our past. We can walk boldly into the future with the full knowledge that God will be with us every step of the way. His love covers our past, present, and future.

Loving Father, I receive your love; I let go of past failings, and today I walk boldly in faith.

Start with the Heart

But the Lord said to Samuel, "Do not consider his appearance or his height, for I have rejected him. The Lord does not look at the things people look at. People look at the outward appearance, but the Lord looks at the heart."

—1 SAMUEL 16:7

When God chose a king, He didn't use a typical human checklist. David wasn't born into an influential family. He wasn't an impressive physical presence like his predecessor, King Saul. As the youngest son, David was an afterthought even within his own family. When Samuel began the selection process for a new king, he had received clear instructions from God on who was worthy to be named king: start with the heart.

As you think about where you are currently and where you are going in life, it is easy to focus on externals. How much money do I make? How big is my house? Do I drive a nice car? Do I have the latest gadgets?

That's not God's starting point for how He sees you, and it shouldn't be yours. The real question comes down to your heart. Do you love God? Do you love others? Do you exhibit patience, kindness, and generosity?

Where are you at in your life today? Where are you heading? Start with your heart!

Heavenly Father, renew my heart that I might love you and others more and more each day.

A Prayer for Endurance

*Let us throw off everything that hinders and the
sin that so easily entangles. And let us run with
perseverance the race marked out for us.*

—HEBREWS 12:1

God of strength,
I know a relationship with you is not like a hundred-meter sprint: one quick burst and it's finished. You desire a relationship with me that is like a marathon, covering every day of my life. I confess that my endurance is lacking right now, God. I get distracted too easily. I get discouraged. I take things for granted and forget to be thankful—especially to you.

You know the unhealthy dynamics that I have allowed to accumulate in my life, slowing my pace and causing me to stumble. I ask that you grant me the resolve and the grace to rid myself of habits and attitudes that keep me from fully serving and loving you. I pray that you give me an undefeatable spirit that learns to run long distances without grumbling, ready and willing to go as far and long as you ask of me.

Thank you, gracious Father, that you await me at the ultimate finish line of life with an embrace and crown that will last forever!

In Jesus's blessed name. Amen.

February

Love and
Relationships

Love means loving the unlovable—
or it is no virtue at all.

—UNKNOWN

Make Things Right

Any man or woman who wrongs another in any way and so is unfaithful to the Lord is guilty and must confess the sin they have committed.

—NUMBERS 5:6-7

If you grew up attending church, maybe you remember singing a song about Zacchaeus:

Zacchaeus was a wee little man,

And a wee little man was he.

So he climbed up in a sycamore tree,

For the Lord he wanted to see.

We don't know a lot about Zacchaeus, but we do know he was a small man—and what was truly small was his heart. A corrupt tax collector, he stole from his own people on behalf of the Romans.

But Zacchaeus wanted something more—something bigger. That all became possible when Jesus entered his life. He opened his home to Jesus and those he had once despised. Unlike the ruler who loved money more than people, Zacchaeus also opened his pocketbook and paid back more than he had stolen.

This "wee" man is still a model of restitution. An encounter with God leads to a desire to make things right with people you have hurt. It's not easy, but it's worth it to know that our lives reflect God's presence in our hearts.

God of peace, give me the grace and strength to make peace with others in my life.

Practical Love

Therefore, as we have opportunity, let us do good to all people,
especially to those who belong to the family of believers.

—GALATIANS 6:10

In Galatians, Paul sets out some of the most practical principles for expressing love for one another. First, he tells us that we should be redemptive people, helping restore those who have been caught in a sin (6:1). He cautions you that, as you reach out to help someone, you should be extra careful not to get trapped in sin yourself.

Second, Paul urges us to help carry the "excessive weights" that others are forced to bear (6:2). He challenges us to love others unconditionally, without judgment and comparisons (6:4). Competition can be friendly and healthy, but when it consumes our relationships, the inevitable result is conflict.

Third, Paul points out that we aren't required to do everything for others (6:5). But when someone has burdens that are bigger than any one person should handle alone, we should step in and help.

Finally, Paul reminds us not to give up on loving others (6:9). Some people are difficult to love, but our steadfast persistence may help allow them to receive God's forgiveness and peace.

Father God, so many people have loved and blessed me; help me to share your love in my world.

Love Beyond Reason

You did not choose me, but I chose you.

—JOHN 15:16

Throughout the Old Testament, God spoke to His people through prophets. Some of the prophets delivered fiery speeches. Others, like Hosea, communicated truth about God through describing dramatic events in people's lives. In Hosea's case, he spoke on how he was married to a highly promiscuous and unfaithful wife. She had children—but they were the sons of other men. He still loved her, but finally she left him and lived as a prostitute. When she lost her beauty and charm and was sold into slavery, what did Hosea do? He acted like God.

He went to the market to redeem her. He bought her, not as a slave, but to make her his wife once again. In this act of commitment and mercy, Hosea showed God's people that God still loved them, even though they were not faithful to Him and had chased after other gods.

No matter where we've been, He loves us the same way too! He chose us because He loves us.

Heavenly Father, your love never fails. Thank you for redeeming me when I was not faithful to you.

Show Love

But you will receive power when the Holy Spirit comes on you; and you will be my witnesses in Jerusalem, and in all Judea and Samaria, and to the ends of the earth.

—ACTS 1:8

Peter wrote, "Always be prepared to give an answer to everyone who asks you to give the reason for the hope that you have" (1 Peter 3:15). That means that all of us should be prepared to tell others how we know God is real and has made us into a new person through Jesus Christ. Are you prepared to witness through your love?

Jesus tells His disciples that the easiest way people will know that they have a real and powerful relationship with God is by how they love one another. In 1 Corinthians 13, Paul says: "Love is patient, love is kind. It does not envy, it does not boast, it is not proud. It does not dishonor others, it is not self-seeking, it is not easily angered, it keeps no record of wrongs" (4–5).

How about you? Do you show love to your family through your words and your actions? To your friends? Are you helping the people around you draw closer to God?

Loving Father, help others to draw near to you because they see your love in me.

Love Is a Verb

Dear children, let us not love with words or
speech but with actions and in truth.

—1 JOHN 3:18

If love is only an emotion, then love for a spouse, a child, or even God would depend on how we feel about them at a given moment. Feelings are fickle—what if, every time we got sick, we felt like rejecting faith and love? As crazy as that sounds, that is exactly how many people treat their relationships. No wonder people fall in and out of love so much. They are treating love as an emotion rather than what it really is: an active verb.

God demonstrated His love for us by sending His Son to redeem us. That's no emotion, but an act that demonstrates love. Jesus demonstrated His love through action—He did go to the Cross to die for our sins.

Ultimately, we too love God and those around us when we actively demonstrate it.

Do you want to get better at loving others? Then get busy and do something loving. Have you shown someone you love them today?

Dear God, I marvel at how much you love me and at how you came to redeem me. Help me to love as you do, with actions as well as words.

A Beloved Bride

And so we know and rely on the love God has for us.

—1 JOHN 4:16

Evangelist and philanthropist George Mueller once said that not once in his marriage did he pass his wife or see her enter a room without love filling his heart. He always saw her as a gift from God, and his love intensified each time they were near each other. The kind of love between Mueller and his wife is perhaps rare, but still stands as a marker, a reminder, of what God intends between spouses.

But what's even more amazing is that the Bible refers to Christ's church as His bride. He loves us more tenderly, deeply, and devotedly than the best husband on earth could ever cherish his beloved bride.

Life becomes more wonderful when we live with the knowledge that we are as precious to God as a bride. It's not surprising, then, that when we are filled up with God's love, we are able to love the people in our world all the better: spouse, children, parents, friends, and colleagues.

Are you struggling to express love? Start at the beginning and realize how loved you are.

Thank you, Lord, for your love for me, your child. Help me allow your love to fill my life with joy, and help me spread that joy everywhere I go.

Calvary Love

If I speak in the tongues of men or of angels, but do not have love, I am only a resounding gong or a clanging cymbal.

—1 CORINTHIANS 13:1

A CLASSIC DEVOTION FROM AMY CARMICHAEL (TWENTIETH CENTURY)

IF...I have not compassion on my fellow servant, even as my Lord had pity on me, then I know nothing of Calvary love.

IF...I belittle those whom I am called to serve; if I adopt a superior attitude, then I know nothing of Calvary love.

IF...I can enjoy a joke at the expense of another; if I can in any way slight another, then I know nothing of Calvary love.

IF...I can speak an unkind word or think an unkind thought without grief and shame, then I know nothing of Calvary love.

IF...I slip into the place that can be filled by Christ alone, making myself the first necessity to a soul instead of leading it to fasten upon Him, then I know nothing of Calvary love.

IF...the burdens of others are not my burdens too, and their joys mine, then I know nothing of Calvary love.

IF...the burden my Lord asks me to bear be not the burden of my heart's choice, and I do not welcome His will, then I know nothing of Calvary love.

Father, forgive me for times when I have been insensitive and unkind to others. Renew a heart of love in me.

From the Beginning of Time

For God so loved the world that He gave His one and only Son, that
whoever believes in Him shall not perish but have eternal life.

—JOHN 3:16

P arents love their children before they are even born. Why
else would they have names picked out? And the rooms
brightly painted? And clothes neatly folded? And books picked
out to read? Rarely does a parent need to be told to love their
newborn infant. Even during the terrible twos and the tumultuous teens, parents steadfastly love their children.

God has loved us—has loved you—from the foundation of
the world. You are no mere accident or an unexpected surprise
to Him. He loved you even before you were in your mother's
womb just as much as He loves you today. He wasn't forced
to love you. He didn't watch you to see if there was anything
you did that would make you more lovable. He just loved and
loves you.

We like to debate whether it is possible to fall in love at first
sight. When it comes to God's love for us, it happened before
first sight. He has loved us throughout all of eternity.

Heavenly Father, I stand in awe of your love for me. Thank
you for your never-ending love.

9

A Love that Never Fails

Your love, Lord, reaches to the heavens, your faithfulness to the skies.

—PSALM 36:5

A woman sobbed as she told her friends about the divorce she had gone through years before. Remarried and in love, she had never been treated better in her life. Her new husband gave her no reasons to distrust him. But she could not get over feelings of abandonment from her first marriage and lived in constant fear that someone she loved would leave her.

Healing began when another woman said to her: "I can't promise you that your husband will be faithful to you and never leave you. I can't even promise you that I'll always be here for you. Humans are not always true. But God will never leave you. When you know how much God loves you, you'll stop worrying about your husband. Everything else will fall into place."

Are you living in fear? Do you worry about your relationships? Begin with trusting God, then let Him help you learn to trust others. Your relationships will improve as your spirit finds total peace and confidence in God.

Thank you, Lord, for your faithful love, the anchor of my life. May my entire day be a song of gratitude for your loving-kindness.

Love Sweet Love

Therefore go and make disciples of all nations, baptizing them
in the name of the Father and of the Son and of the Holy Spirit,
and teaching them to obey everything I have commanded you.
And surely I am with you always, to the very end of the age.

—MATTHEW 28:19–20

The song was a huge pop hit in the 1960s sung by Jackie DeShannon, and was a huge hit again in the 1970s as remixed by Tom Clay. The lyrics asserted, "What the world needs now is love, sweet love—no, not just for some, but for everyone."

We live in a lost and hurting world. People run to addictions and entertainment to numb their pain. But the heartfelt cry of every human heart is to be loved.

How is God's love shared? From the heart, words, and service of His people. Do you love others enough to share the Gospel with them? In some cases, the best starting point is to invite others to a special service at your church. But it always begins with an authentic relationship and a listening ear. If we hear the hearts of others, we'll know exactly when to talk to them about God's gift of salvation.

And when that happens, Heaven rejoices, and everyone experiences "love, sweet love."

Lord, please give me a heart that longs to reach others with your love.

Love Sees No Color

*Then Peter began to speak: "I now realize how true
it is that God does not show favoritism."*

—ACTS 10:34

As far as we've come as a nation, all of us still have room to grow in our love for those who are superficially different from us. God makes no distinction among colors, races, or nationalities. God loves all types of people, and He has given everyone on earth the opportunity to experience salvation.

Jesus commanded us to love as He loves. The only way to love as Christ loves is to love without barriers. It might take a little extra effort to get to know people of other backgrounds and love them, but the rewards are rich.

In the wise words of Martin Luther King Jr.: "I have a dream that my four little children will one day live in a nation where they will not be judged by the color of their skin, but by the content of their character."

We are blessed when we reach out to others in our community with the love of Jesus, seeing them through His eyes. That may make us uncomfortable, but it is a demonstration of active faith and love.

Lord, help me to love everyone with your love, and give me courage to build bridges in my sphere of influence.

Tough Love

My son, do not despise the Lord's discipline and do
not resent His rebuke, because the Lord disciplines
those He loves, as a father the son he delights in.

—PROVERBS 3:11–12

Discipline is a somewhat lost concept in our culture. Nowhere is that more evident than in how we raise our children. Those of us who are a little older can remember Dad—or even a teacher—getting out the "board of education" when we got in trouble. It was far from pleasant, but it certainly got the point across.

Discipline yourself—or leave it to someone else to do that for you. Even if a boss, parent, spouse, friend, or customer won't step up and hold us accountable for our decisions, the good news is we have a Heavenly Father who cares too much about our actions and the state of our heart to just ignore things we do wrong. That's His tough love.

Do you show love to your children by providing them with fair and godly discipline? Don't stop there. Consider your own life. Have you experienced God's chastening? Do you resist and respond with resentment or with an open heart? Love wants what is best for everyone. Oftentimes, that means discipline!

Dear God, I don't like to experience discipline in my life, and I too easily get resentful. Help me to learn what you have to teach me in moments of correction.

The Language of Love

Carry each other's burdens, and in this way
you will fulfill the law of Christ.

—GALATIANS 6:2

Author Leo Buscaglia was asked to judge a contest to find the most caring child. The winner was a four-year-old whose elderly neighbor had recently lost his wife. Upon seeing the man cry, the little boy went into the gentleman's yard, climbed onto his lap, and just sat there. When his mother asked him what he had said to the neighbor, the little boy said, "Nothing, I just helped him cry."

The Bible tells us to mourn with those who mourn and rejoice with those who rejoice (Romans 12:15). One of the ways God helps us bear burdens is to send us the loving comfort of other people. If you want to experience and live out God's love for you, make your heart available both to receive love and companionship from others and to be a loving presence in someone else's life.

Do you want more love in your life? Give more love. Be there for others. Even if you don't have adequate words of comfort, know that your presence will make the biggest difference.

Father, thank you for the gift of love that you bring through others. Send me to someone I can encourage today.

Valentine's Day

*See what great love the Father has lavished on us, that we
should be called children of God! And that is what we are! The
reason the world does not know us is that it did not know Him.*

—1 JOHN 3:1

Plush teddy bears, extravagant flower arrangements, greeting cards—the signs of Valentine's Day are inescapable in the middle of February. Some think that this holiday is a completely secular and commercial occasion. But if God is love, and if love is a sign of His work, then maybe we should put even more emphasis on a holiday meant for celebrating love.

Of course, the love proclaimed on Valentine's Day can stray far from the pure love of God. But if you get creative and ask for help from God, you just might find ways to share His unending love with those around you.

At the heart of the matter, never forget that you can give without loving, but you cannot love without giving. That doesn't require expensive gifts. That means committing your heart and life to others.

Do the people in your family and community know how much you love them? Don't limit Valentine's Day to romance, but use it as a reminder that we are to show love to everyone we come in contact with.

**Lord, help me to spread joy and light in my world, sharing
your love with others.**

FEBRUARY

15

Show Love

*But love your enemies, do good to them, and lend to them
without expecting to get anything back. Then your reward
will be great, and you will be children of the Most High,
because He is kind to the ungrateful and wicked.*

—LUKE 6:35

A CLASSIC DEVOTION FROM JOHN CHRYSOSTOM (FOURTH CENTURY)

Let us show forth a new kind of life. Let us make earth, heaven; let us hereby show the world of how great blessings they are deprived. For when they behold in us good conversation, they will look upon the very face of the kingdom of heaven. Yea, when they see us gentle, pure from wrath, from evil desire, from envy, from covetousness, rightly fulfilling all our other duties, they will say, "If the Christians are become angels here, what will they be after their departure hence? If where they are strangers they shine so bright, how great will they become when they shall have won their native land!"

Thus they too will be reformed, and the world of godliness "will have free course," not less than in the apostles' times. For if they, being twelve, converted entire cities and countries; were we all to become teachers by our careful conduct, imagine how high our cause will be exalted.

Compassionate Father, let me show the world my faith by the way I live my life.

Be Reconciled

*If you forgive anyone's sins, their sins are forgiven; if
you do not forgive them, they are not forgiven.*

—JOHN 20:23

One of the most important matters in God's eyes is reconciliation. Just as He sent His son Jesus into the world to reconcile people to Him, so He gives us the mandate to be peacemakers, to be reconciled even to our enemies.

You alone cannot control the process of reconciliation. That's why we are told to keep peace "as far as it depends on you" (Romans 12:18). But before dismissing the call to reconciliation as too hard, we need to remember:

- Reconciliation is God's idea and His way of doing things (Romans 5:8–10).
- As we forgive others, we are forgiven by God (Luke 6:37).
- One of the blessings of walking with God is peace (Galatians 5:22).

Are you ready to be a peacemaker? Reconciliation does not always happen all at once, so don't get discouraged or give up because of a lack of results. And reconciliation does not mean submission to other's abuse, cruelty, or lack of response. But what is in our power, let us do!

Lord, make me an instrument of your peace in reconciling the world to you.

Loving My Family

Dear friends, since God so loved us, we
also ought to love one another.

—1 JOHN 4:11

H ave you ever noticed that we tend to be at our very best with casual acquaintances and even complete strangers? And we act our absolute worst with those who are closest to us? We fall into the trap of taking for granted those who love us the most. The good news is that there are two simple steps that will cure the majority of family conflicts—and make any family stronger.

First, cultivate a spirit of gratitude. When was the last time you felt thankful for the people in your home—and said thank you? *Doesn't that get redundant? Isn't that a bit of overkill?* Think about your own life. Do you ever get tired of people being grateful to you or appreciating you?

Second, demonstrate your love. Children often spell the word "love" with four different letters: T-I-M-E. Are you eager to spend time with them? Do you make it a point to enjoy things that they enjoy?

The Apostle James said that faith without work is dead (James 2:17), and in the same way, love without actions is empty.

Heavenly Father, thank you for my family. Help me to express the love I truly have for them.

Train up a Child

Start children off on the way they should go, and even
when they are old they will not turn from it.

—PROVERBS 22:6

I n Deuteronomy 6, after the children of Israel were delivered from slavery in Egypt, a great challenge was given to the fathers by Moses that would bless their lives and the lives of their children and grandchildren.

- Be obedient: Obey all His rules and commands I give you so that you will live a long time (6:1–2).
- Pursue God's truth: Listen, Israel, and carefully obey these laws. Then all will go well for you (6:3–4).
- Love God: Love the Lord your God with all your heart, all your soul, and all your strength (6:5–6).
- Teach God's Word: Teach them to your children, and talk about them when you sit at home and walk along the road, when you lie down and when you get up (6:7–9).
- Don't follow false gods: Do not forget the Lord, who brought you out of the land of Egypt where you were slaves (6:10–19).

Raising children certainly isn't easy. But with time, patience, and a complete trust in God, you can bless your children beyond your imagination.

Father God, let me be a model of faith to my own children and all those who know me.

A Loving Touch

Jesus was indignant. He reached out His hand and touched the man.

—MARK 1:41

For many of us, God is more an idea than He is a person. No wonder we forget that God loves us not in principle, but actively! Think back to childhood, to climbing up on your father's lap and experiencing the warmth of his arms as he held you and read to you or asked about your day at school. Even if that wasn't your exact experience, you get the picture. How lovely to know that our Heavenly Father cares that much.

There are many stories throughout the Gospels about people being touched by the Lord: Jesus feeding the five thousand and calming the storm, Jesus healing a boy who was paralyzed, and Jesus healing the blind man. The examples of Him reaching out and touching people demonstrate His personality and passion.

In the same way, God wants our love for Him and others to be active. Receive His touch—and pass it on in your world today!

Lord Jesus, how blessed I am to have a Savior who came down from Heaven and walked among His people. Thank you for being available to me, for loving me in so many practical ways. I love you.

For God So Loved You

For God so loved the world that He gave His one and only Son, that whoever believes in Him shall not perish but have eternal life.

—JOHN 3:16

Very few people question that God is loving. But many of these very same people question whether God truly loves them. They are certain God hears the prayers of others, forgives others, and is patient and loving with others—but not with them.

How about you? Do you know not only that God loves the world but also that He loves you?

One simple activity that might bring that point home is to write out John 3:16, but in place of the phrase "the world," insert your own name. Then read the verse out loud several times today—and tomorrow. In fact, you might try that right now. Then put the verse where you will be reminded of the truth often.

This is not a matter of arrogance or self-aggrandizement. This is taking to heart what God Himself says to us.

Our life changes when we experience for ourselves the reality that God loves the world—and each individual in it. Including you! Saint Augustine said it beautifully: "God loves each of us as if there was only one of us."

Thank you, Heavenly Father, for loving me so much that if I were the only lost person in the world, you would still die for me.

21

The Mark of a Christian

By this everyone will know that you are my
disciples, if you love one another.

—JOHN 13:35

A CLASSIC DEVOTION FROM FRANCIS SCHAEFFER
(TWENTIETH CENTURY)

Through the centuries men have displayed many different symbols to show that they are Christians. They have worn marks in the lapels of their coats, hung chains about their necks, even had special haircuts.

Of course, there is nothing wrong with any of this, if one feels it is his calling. But there is a much better sign. It is a universal mark that is to last through all the ages of the church until Jesus comes back.

What is this mark?

"A new command I give you: Love one another. As I have loved you, so you must love one another. By this everyone will know that you are my disciples, if you love one another" (John 13:34–35).

This passage reveals the mark that Jesus gives to label a Christian, not just in one era or in one locality, but at all times and all places until Jesus returns. If we expect non-Christians to know that we are Christians, we must show the mark.

Father of love, I pray the world will recognize me as your child because of the love I show.

22

——— *Love Always Wins* ———

But I tell you, love your enemies and pray
for those who persecute you.

—MATTHEW 5:44

David Wilkerson's bestselling book *The Cross and the Switchblade* is the account of his dramatic and sometimes traumatic encounters with Nicky Cruz, leader of a notorious New York City gang.

One night, when Cruz threatened to use his knife to cut up Wilkerson, he was shocked to hear the preacher tell him that if he did, every piece of his body would scream out how much God and Reverend Wilkerson loved him. That message of love would not leave the heart and mind of Cruz.

And now, for over fifty years, he has walked with God, serving in ministry, telling thousands about the power of God's love and how it can transform even the wickedest of sinners.

Nature teaches us to love our friends. But it is God who teaches and enables us to love our enemies. With God's help, we can love everyone—even those we don't very much like. But when we allow God to work through us to love the unlovable, miracles happen and lives are changed.

Hate is powerful and destructive. But love is the winner.

Lord, your love can transform anyone—and I'm grateful that it has transformed me. Help me be a conduit of your love in someone's life this week.

I Am Third

*Make my joy complete by being like-minded, having
the same love, being one in spirit and of one mind. Do
nothing out of selfish ambition or vain conceit.*

—PHILIPPIANS 2:2-3

There is no magical formula that will improve your marriage quickly. Only when both spouses begin to practice the biblical principle of submitting to one another can love and a marriage soar. Submission simply means: I love you so much, I will look out for your interests before I look out for my own.

God's plan for your life includes personal fulfillment, success, and happiness. But He also asks His children to be strong enough to take the initiative in loving and serving others. Even your spouse! And if you're not married, there are still many people in your life whom you can serve in love.

Love is the most poignant and powerful force in the world. So whether your marriage is healthy and thriving, in need of some fine-tuning, or in a serious crisis, express to your spouse the love that God has so generously lavished on you—and watch God rekindle the flames of love and romance.

No, the formula for loving relationships hasn't changed: God first, others second, me third.

Lord, you love the church—your children—as a husband loves his bride. Help me to love those closest to me with your love.

Keep It Simple

Love the Lord your God with all your heart and
with all your soul and with all your mind.

—MATTHEW 22:37

Some people claim to love God but have a strong aversion to "religion" and going to church. *Too many rules. Too much judging. It's not very fun. It's controlling.*

But we are called to be part of the body of Christ, so an isolated faith isn't part of God's plan for us. However, the desire to keep things simple isn't such a bad impulse. It is something Jesus did. When the religious leaders of His day asked Him what matters most, He was able to summarize the Ten Commandments and the entire body of religious law into two simple commands:

- Love God with all your heart.
- Love your neighbor as yourself.

What more is there? It doesn't get any simpler than that. But don't mistake "simple" for "easy." Jesus Himself showed us the true cost of loving God and others!

When faith seems too complicated and you begin to wonder what really matters most, don't get lost in theory or duties. Keep it simple, and remember your faith is to be in love with God and others.

Dear God, I do love you with all my heart. Help me to love my neighbors as you love them.

God Still Speaks

My sheep listen to my voice; I know them, and they follow me.

—JOHN 10:27

Throughout the Bible, God interacts intimately with those who seek Him. He whispered to the prophet Samuel as a young boy. He spoke directly through the prophets like Isaiah and Daniel. He wrestled with Jacob until he was finally willing to submit to God's will. He greeted Mary as someone "highly favored." And in Jesus, God walked among us, just as He did with Adam and Eve in the Garden of Eden.

Thousands of years later, God is still speaking. He longs to hear from us in prayer, and He wants to speak back to us. Relationships thrive on communication—regular, high-quality communication. Through prayer and listening to God through reading his Word, we can experience a loving, thriving relationship with none other than God Himself.

The clearest indicator of a healthy relationship is the quality of the communication shared. Are you on speaking terms with God? Do you bring your needs and requests to Him? Do you lift up His name with words of praise and thanksgiving? Do you quiet your heart to hear what He has to say to you?

Lord, thank you that you speak to us and seek us out. Thank you for knowing me. Teach me to listen to and follow you.

26

The Greatest Is Love

And now these three remain: faith, hope and
love. But the greatest of these is love.

—1 CORINTHIANS 13:13

The focus of the devotions for February has been love. What better way to wrap up the month than to read from the famous "love chapter" from the Apostle Paul:

> **If I give all I possess to the poor and give over my body to hardship that I may boast, but do not have love, I gain nothing.**
>
> **Love is patient, love is kind. It does not envy, it does not boast, it is not proud. It does not dishonor others, it is not self-seeking, it is not easily angered, it keeps no record of wrongs. Love does not delight in evil but rejoices with the truth. It always protects, always trusts, always hopes, always perseveres. (1 Corinthians 13:3–7)**

How would your life be different if 1 Corinthians 13 became a checklist of how you treated others? You would truly live a life of love.

Dear God, thank you for all the talents and gifts you have given me. But thank you most of all for love. Help love to grow in me every day.

Why I Love God

We love because He first loved us.

—1 JOHN 4:19

A CLASSIC DEVOTION FROM BERNARD OF CLAIRVAUX (TWELFTH CENTURY)

You want me to tell you why God is to be loved and how much. I answer, the reason for loving God is God Himself; and the love due to Him is immeasurable. We are to love God for Himself, for two reasons: nothing is more reasonable, nothing more profitable.

Could any reason be greater than this, that He gave Himself for us unworthy wretches? And being God, what better gift could He offer than Himself?

Ought He not to be loved in return, when we think who loved, whom He loved, and how much He loved? For it was God who loved us, freely, and loved us while we were yet enemies.

Who is it that gives food to all flesh, air to all that breathe? These are not God's best or only gifts, but they are essential to bodily life. Man must seek for the highest gifts—dignity, wisdom, and virtue. And virtue impels man to seek eagerly for Him who is man's source, and to lay fast hold on Him when He has been found.

Dear God, I express to you that I love you with all my heart.

A Prayer for Love

*"You have heard that it was said, 'Love your neighbor and
hate your enemy.' But I tell you, love your enemies and pray
for those who persecute you, that you may be children of your
Father in heaven. He causes His sun to rise on the evil and the
good, and sends rain on the righteous and the unrighteous."*

—MATTHEW 5:43-45

Dear God,
   I know that there are many things happening in the
world today that break your heart—and that anger you.

As I see reports of violence, cruelty, exploitation, and negli-
gence, I too get sad and angry—and oftentimes judgmental.
There are individuals and groups and even countries I don't
feel love for. Help me to never make excuses for governments,
leaders, and organizations that do what is evil, but do remind
me that if your purpose for sending Jesus is not to condemn
the world, then that can't be my focus either.

I ask that you help me to be redemptive—to see the world
through your eyes of love and compassion. When I begin to
condemn others, help me to pray for the salvation of the wicked
instead. Show me ways I can support ministries and organizations that act redemptively in the world—and to participate
directly as you provide me opportunity.

In the loving name of Jesus. Amen.

March
Money, Generosity, and Charity

I have found that among its other benefits,
giving liberates the soul of the giver.
— MAYA ANGELOU

Our Generous Father

*And my God will meet all your needs according
to the riches of His glory in Christ Jesus.*

—PHILIPPIANS 4:19

F or St. Paul, the issue of provision was simple. He had an unshakable confidence that God would provide for his every need. Why? Because Jesus taught His disciples: "Therefore I tell you, do not worry about your life, what you will eat or drink; or about your body, what you will wear. Is not life more than food, and the body more than clothes?" (Matthew 6:25). Everything they needed was provided by the Heavenly Father.

But that's not what I'm worried about. I have too many bills and not enough income. My kids need braces and the car is making funny noises.

The line between want and need is blurred in our modern consumer culture. And we should probably step back and ask ourselves if our spending habits are making our lives more complicated than they need to be. But you are where you are. God promises to meet you there and provide for you. He wants you to acknowledge your condition of need and to open your heart to Him in trust. He will take care of the rest.

Almighty God, thank you for providing me with all the grace, wisdom, and resources I need for life.

The Gift of Giving

Be openhanded and freely lend them whatever they need.

—DEUTERONOMY 15:7-8

One true test of our character is what we do with our money. God calls us to give a portion of our income to Him through ministry and to also give special sacrificial offerings to meet special needs as we feel directed in our hearts.

When we are generous with our money above and beyond expectations, a number of healthy emotional and spiritual dynamics are fostered in our lives:

- We clutch less tightly to what we can generate and become more aware that all good gifts come from God: "Every good and perfect gift is from above, coming down from the Father of the heavenly lights, who does not change like shifting shadows" (James 1:17).
- We learn to trust and serve God with a pure heart: "You cannot serve both God and money" (Matthew 6:24).
- We receive the joy that comes from helping someone in need (Matthew 25:23).
- We become better stewards in all areas of our finances; there is a strange paradox that the more we give the more we seem to have (Matthew 19:29).

Provider God, teach me to become a gracious steward of all you have put in my care.

Money Won't Make You Happy

Better a little with the fear of the Lord
than great wealth with turmoil.

—PROVERBS 15:16

Benjamin Franklin wrote about money often, usually advising readers to be more frugal. His belief was simple: "Money never made a man happy yet, nor will it. There is nothing in its nature to produce happiness. The more a man has, the more he wants. Instead of its filling a vacuum, it makes one."

It's hard to be content in our materialistic culture, where so much of a person's worth is derived from how much money and how many things they have. We want others to respect and hold us in high esteem.

In Romans 12:2, Paul reminds us that we are not to "conform to the pattern of this world," but we are to be "transformed by the renewing of your mind." We are to offer our bodies as living sacrifices to God. In other words, we give Him everything we have and everything we are.

Franklin claimed his advice was sound and told us to "rely on it." Committing ourselves to God and experiencing a renewed mind is even better counsel. Rely on it!

Lord, thank you for the provisions you give us to meet our physical needs. It's good to have money and the things it can buy. But remind me to enjoy peace over things.

Not for Sale

Peter answered: "May your money perish with you, because
you thought you could buy the gift of God with money!"

–ACTS 8:20

In this affluent world we live in, anything can be bought with the swipe of a card or a click of a button. But the most important things in life cannot be bought.

In Samaria, a man named Simon had the reputation of being a wizard and possessing supernatural powers. He made a lot of money off that reputation. When he saw the power of the Apostles bring healing by laying their hands on the afflicted, Simon wanted a piece of the action. He was willing to invest a sizable chunk of money to get the power. Peter's rebuke is strong and clear: you can't buy the gifts of God, and you will perish for thinking you could.

God's gifts are free to those who receive. They can't be bought. What truly matters to God comes from receiving the Holy Spirit into our hearts: love, faith, integrity, compassion, peace, kindness, generosity, hope, joy.

Rejoice that He gives you all the spiritual riches you need through faith in Him and His love for you.

O Father, protect me from the pervasive materialism of our world. Grant me a thirst for righteousness and the things money can't buy.

The Love of Money

The love of money is a root of all kinds of evil.

—1 TIMOTHY 6:10

Some Christians use this verse to chastise the rich. But before we heap scorn on the financially wealthy, let's revisit the verse and note that Paul doesn't say money is the root of all evil, nor is our need for money. It's the *love* of money that's problematic.

There was a family with whom we attended church. Though both were college-educated, they were in a constant state of financial distress. The big reason was that the husband could not keep a job. He didn't make it a secret that he just didn't like to keep regular hours.

When asked how they got by, they reported that they survived on government assistance, food pantries, and gifts from our church or individuals. But most of all by trusting God to meet all their needs.

In the case of this couple, they were right to trust God to meet all their needs, but at the same time, one or both of them needed to have enough appreciation of money (not love of money!) to work for it.

Father, let me never slide into a love for money where it becomes more important than people and you. But give me the opportunities, ambition, and energy to take care of my family.

A Small Gift Can Become Huge

But a poor widow came and put in two very small copper
coins, worth only a few cents. Calling His disciples to
Him, Jesus said, "Truly I tell you, this poor widow has
put more into the treasury than all the others."

—MARK 12:42–43

It was only a couple of pennies, but her gift continues to give through the centuries as a model of humble and extravagant sharing. She gave straight from her heart out of love and honor for God and His call for us to be generous. God made something tiny grow into something large and beautiful that caught the attention of Jesus and filled Him with awe for her.

A young boy shared two loaves of barley bread and five fish, and Jesus used His gift to feed five thousand hungry people. (See John 6.)

God knows how to multiply! You might not have much money or influence; you may not have tremendous talents or gifts; you might feel like you're out of energy right now. But if you give something, anything, out of a loving heart, God can take something small and turn it into something great.

The smallest things become great when given out of a heart full of love for God. Our gifts are so appreciated and admired by God. They serve to unite us with Him eternally.

Dear God, thank you for taking what I bring to the table and making something great out of it.

What Is Silver?

Jesus answered, "If you want to be perfect, go, sell
your possessions and give to the poor, and you will
have treasure in heaven. Then come, follow me."

—MATTHEW 19:21

A Classic Devotion from Gregory Palamas (Fourteenth Century)

If you fail to notice your suffering brothers—that is, Christ's brothers—and refuse to share your abundant food, shelter, clothing, and care with the needy, if you withhold your surplus rather than attend to their needs, then listen carefully and groan. Indeed, it is we ourselves who should listen and groan—I who speak these things stand accused. My conscience testifies that I am not entirely free of passion. While some may shiver and go without, I eat well and am nicely clothed. But even more to be mourned are those with treasures beyond their daily needs who cling to them, even seek to expand their holdings. Though commanded to love their neighbor as themselves, they have not loved their neighbor even as much as they have loved dust—for it is gold and silver that they have loved, and what are gold and silver but dust?

Gracious God, help me to share from my abundance with those in need.

Debt

The rich rules over the poor, and the borrower
becomes the lender's slave.

—PROVERBS 22:7

D ebt is dangerous. It puts us under the power of a whole industry of people who make a very good living off the financial distress of those who have experienced a series of unfortunate circumstances or who have never disciplined themselves to live within their means.

If "bad luck" or "bad discipline" applies to you, don't run. Don't hide. Don't pretend you don't have a problem. Stand up, raise your eyes to Heaven, and tell God exactly where you are financially, even if it hurts to say your troubles out loud.

Long before stock market crashes, subprime mortgage schemes, and other financial setbacks, Solomon said in Proverbs 22:26–27: "Do not be the one who shakes hands in pledge or puts up security for debts; if you lack the means to pay, your very bed will be snatched from under you."

If you're in debt, change your spending until you can get out of it. If you're not in debt, be assured many will offer you "cheap money." Run!

Lord, I want your peace more than I want possessions that never deliver what they promise. Help me to get out of and stay out of debt!

Don't Make Promises You Can't Keep

It is better not to make a vow than to make one and not fulfill it.

—ECCLESIASTES 5:5

S ome things happen that are beyond our control. But with our emphasis on buying to the utmost of our abilities, too many of us stretch our credit and sanity, putting ourselves unnecessarily at risk.

Due to some loopholes in the law, there was an extended period of time when mortgage companies made it very easy to buy a house. Millions treated this as an opportunity to buy more than they could afford. It worked out for many, but millions of others lost their homes.

This devotional is not about professional financial advice. But it is about the wisdom of the ages as expressed in God's Word. Solomon warns his son not to get in a speculative leveraged position where there is a solid chance he can't pay what he owes. It is amazing that what Solomon saw almost three millennia ago can still be seen today.

God's Word encourages us to walk in the Spirit. One simple way we can do that is to not make promises that we have tangible worries we can't keep!

Heavenly Father, thank you that you love us so much to give us guidelines to navigate our earthly life. Give us wisdom to seek your Word and live by the principles you have set forth.

The Curse of Oppressing the Poor

*One who oppresses the poor to increase his wealth and
one who gives gifts to the rich—both come to poverty.*

—PROVERBS 22:16

Her life was a series of bad decisions. Her mother was a drug addict and, as a child, Tammie was in and out of foster homes. At the age of sixteen, she dropped out of high school and got into drugs herself. She worked as a prostitute for several years. Ten years later, with no high school degree, no husband, and two young children, she showed up at the food pantry that was an outreach of our church.

Through working with Tammie for several years, including a time she and her boys lived with us, we have seen her dreams come true. But we've also seen a whole network of individuals and businesses who prey on people like Tammie, those who have little to no experience or savvy on financial matters. These businesses charge exorbitant fees and interest rates that amount to usury and make a lot of money off those who can least afford it.

Solomon said the same thing in his day and understood that people who take advantage of the poor will be particularly cursed.

Lord, may I always stand up for and protect the neediest in our society.

Our Daily Bread

Keep falsehood and lies far from me; give me neither
poverty nor riches, but give me only my daily bread.

—PROVERBS 30:8

Jesus calls on us to steer clear of making money and things the highest priority in our lives (Matthew 6:24 and 32–33). When we obsess over money, we encounter numerous problems: We become distracted from God; we don't love others as we should because of greed and envy; and we become unhappy and ungrateful because we focus on what we don't have instead of what we do have.

Outside of the Bible, perhaps the wisest words ever uttered about money come from the great eighteenth-century British evangelist and social reformer, John Wesley: "Make all you can; save all you can; give all you can."

To do those three things requires hard work, self-control, and generosity, three virtues that God rewards—and three virtues that will solve almost all money management problems. As in all areas of life, what matters most is our level of trust in God. As we honor the Lord by asking for His counsel and following His guidelines for money and work, He will give us our daily bread along with wisdom and peace.

Almighty God, I honor you with my money and thank you for the wisdom and peace that flows back into my life.

If It Sounds Too Good to Be True

The simple believe anything, but the prudent
give thought to their steps.

—PROVERBS 14:15

Isn't it obvious that money is a huge issue, both spiritually and in the normal, everyday course of life? Solomon said that the naive believe everything (Proverbs 14:15), including offers of getting rich for just twenty bucks and a prayer. As "theologian" P. T. Barnum famously stated, "There's a sucker born every minute." What makes us naive when it comes to our money?

Combine legitimate needs with illegitimate greed, and we are easily conned into falling for get-rich-quick schemes. Solomon admonished his son: if it seems too good to be true, it probably is.

When once-in-a-lifetime opportunities come, ask yourself a few questions: Am I open to "everything" because I'm feeling desperate? Am I being naive out of greed? Am I looking for a quick fix because I've not budgeted and have gotten myself in trouble?

There is one offer that sounds too good to be true, but really is true. It's God's promise to meet your needs out of the riches of His grace.

Don't be a sucker. Keep your faith in God.

Father, give me maturity of thought and judgment on the opportunities that come my way, always mindful of the advice you give in your Word.

Keep Your Eyes Open

Those who give to the poor will lack nothing, but those who close their eyes to them receive many curses.

—PROVERBS 28:27

The word *philanthropy* is a combination of the two Greeks words for "love" and "man." It simply means love for our fellow humans. This love is a recurring theme in the Scriptures. From those who have much, God expects much. Those who clutch their wealth are judged harshly.

Most of us don't have vast sums of money from which to make vast offerings. We'd like to be incredibly generous, but by the time we pay for our tithe and costs of living, we're relieved we made it to the next paycheck without putting extra on our credit card.

But the Lord honors faithful giving, no matter how large or small. Period.

Give what you can, when you can—don't just wait for special seasons of the year. The poor are poor all year. Not just at Christmas and Thanksgiving.

There are so many needs in the world and in our communities, it is easy to get overloaded to the point where we want to close our eyes to the needs of others. Solomon reminds us to keep our eyes open and give.

Father, thank you for the gifts you have given me. I acknowledge they are all from you. Help me to give more.

His Riches

Rejoice always, pray continually.

—1 THESSALONIANS 5:17

A CLASSIC DEVOTION FROM E. M. BOUNDS (NINETEENTH CENTURY)

Prayer is an ardent and believing cry to God for some specific thing. God's rule is to answer by giving the specific thing asked for. With it may come much of other gifts and graces... But even they come because God hears and answers prayer.

We do but follow the plain letter and spirit of the Bible when we affirm that God answers prayer, and answers by giving us the very things we desire, and that the withholding of that which we desire and the giving of something else is not the rule, but rare and exceptional. When His children cry for bread He gives them bread.

Prayer is no petty invention of man, a fancied relief for fancied ills. Prayer is the contact of a living soul with God... Prayer fills man's emptiness with God's fullness. It fills man's poverty with God's riches. It puts away man's weakness with God's strength. It banishes man's littleness with God's greatness. Prayer is God's plan to supply man's great and continuous need with God's great and continuous abundance.

Thank you, gracious Father, for the riches you bestow on me.

Don't Give Carelessly

Blessed are those who have regard for the weak;
the Lord delivers them in times of trouble.

—PSALM 41:1

To be generous is to reflect the heart of God Himself. It is much more than a token of generosity, but a stance that is central to who we are as Christ followers.

The Lord promises that He will deliver those who care for the poor. God is so very kind. He is always rewarding faithfulness. But the prayer of our hearts needs to be that we never do good deeds to be seen or get something in return. We need to do them because we love; we need to give because we care.

Have you stopped to consider that true success as a Christian is not in being blessed, but in what we do with that blessing?

Jesus reminds us that, ultimately, when we bless the needy with the blessings we have received from God, we bless the very heart of Jesus. He says in a story: "The King will reply, 'Truly I tell you, whatever you did for one of the least of these brothers and sisters of mine, you did for me'" (Matthew 25:40).

Father, all I do and give, I do and give for Jesus.

Check on Your Sheep and Goats

Be sure you know the condition of your flocks, give careful
attention to your herds; for riches do not endure forever.

—PROVERBS 27:23–24

Solomon, with his insights into most areas of life, understood that a person's finances play a large factor in the quality of a person's life. He's not just addressing the wealthy in this verse, but all of us.

Give careful attention to your herds. For us, he is saying that we must keep our eyes on our job and other items of value. His list to us in the twenty-first century might go something like this: go the extra mile at work; make sure your house is well maintained; change your car oil every five thousand miles; go see your IRA adviser and make sure you have your retirement account apportioned correctly.

Being rich or poor is not a sign of God's favor or displeasure. The size of our nest egg does not indicate how spiritual we are. But how we maintain what we have is a very good sign of wisdom, and God wants us to be wise for our own good and for the good of those we love.

How is your herd of sheep doing?

Father, I thank you for all the blessings and opportunities you have brought into my life. Help me to always be faithful to you with the gifts you have given me.

Slow Down a Second

The plans of the diligent lead to profit as surely as haste leads to poverty.

—PROVERBS 21:5

Despite hundreds of commercials on television selling this or that financial service, despite 24/7 business and finance news shows, despite the popularity of call-in radio shows that dispense financial advice, most Americans don't like to seriously talk about their finances.

Can we change the subject? And does this really have anything to do with my spiritual life?

The book of Proverbs covers practical life topics like marriage, parenthood, business, personal integrity, our relationships with God, good reputation, and, quite often, how we handle our finances.

God wants us to live wisely. Because our world is corrupted by sin, challenges and calamities will be part of our sphere of activity. There's nothing we can do but prepare ourselves to ride out the storm. But Solomon advises us to not *be* the source of poverty. Don't do things haphazardly. Don't rush this direction and that. Be diligent. Do some studying. Make a plan.

Nothing can replace a steadfast trust and hope in God for provision today and tomorrow. But what plans have you made based on the gifts God has given you?

God of provision, I come to you with love and worship, asking you to help me be faithful with your gifts in my life.

God's Plans for Your Wealth

*"For I know the plans I have for you," declares
the Lord, "plans to prosper you and not to harm
you, plans to give you hope and a future."*

—JEREMIAH 29:11

Jesus saw wealth as a gift from God to be used in His service. Those who have been blessed with wealth beyond their need have a responsibility to share generously with the poor and avoid the sins of arrogance, dishonesty, and greed.

Paul, in his first letter to Timothy, tells this young pastor to "Command those who are rich in this present world not to be arrogant nor to put their hope in wealth, which is so uncertain, but to put their hope in God, who richly provides us with everything for our enjoyment. Command them to do good, to be rich in good deeds, and to be generous and willing to share. In this way they will lay up treasure for themselves as a firm foundation for the coming age, so that they may take hold of the life that is truly life" (1 Timothy 6:17–19).

God has a plan to use you and your wealth!

Father, keep us ever mindful that life with you is the true life. Protect us from any corrupting influences of this world and its values.

Don't Judge Based on Money

He causes His sun to rise on the evil and the good, and
sends rain on the righteous and the unrighteous.

—MATTHEW 5:45

I n Jesus's time, it was a common belief that great wealth was a sign of God's favor and poverty was punishment for sin. But in the Sermon on the Mount, Jesus says rain falls and sun shines on both the good and the evil, refuting that belief. He stresses this even further in His parable of the rich man and Lazarus (Luke 16:19–31). At least part of the reason the rich man ended up in hell was because of his hard-heartedness toward the beggar Lazarus. Lazarus, though he was as impoverished as a man could be, ended up in heaven.

Despite the Bible's many warnings against judging on appearances, the idea that wealth is a sign of God's favor and that the poor have done something to deserve their condition persists today. Often, this idea is used to justify callous attitudes toward those who are poor.

But we aren't supposed to take on the role of judge, period. Jesus's own thoughts give special emphasis to not judging others based on how little or how much they have financially.

Heavenly Father, help me to see others as you see them, not judging others based on my incomplete knowledge.

Joyful Generosity

Honor the Lord with your wealth, with the first fruits of all your crops.

—PROVERBS 3:9

The word *tithe* is introduced in the Old Testament. The Hebrew word simply means "ten percent." Over time, it took on the added meaning of the religious act of obedience to give ten percent—the first ten percent—of one's yearly income to God.

The Christian is never commanded to tithe, but is still commanded to give. In the Old Testament, a specific amount was proscribed: ten percent. The New Testament proscribes the powerful concept of *joyful generosity*.

Many Christian pastors and scholars still teach the principle of tithing, and many Christians use this as a good guideline for giving, which is fine. In whatever way you decide what to give, don't give sparingly and don't give with a sad or angry heart. Joyful generosity is noticed and rewarded by God. One miracle of giving tithe and offerings is that what you have left always goes further.

If you already give, keep doing so joyfully and generously. If you don't support ministry, begin now to give. You will discover that generosity is always blessed in some way by God.

God, you have given me so much from your heart of generosity and love. Teach me to be a joyful giver.

Warning Signs of Greed

You know we never used flattery, nor did we put on a
mask to cover up greed—God is our witness.

—THESSALONIANS 2:5

A CLASSIC DEVOTION FROM RICHARD BAXTER (SEVENTEENTH CENTURY)

The signs of covetousness are these:

- Not preferring God and our everlasting happiness before the prosperity and pleasure of the flesh; but valuing and loving fleshly prosperity above its worth.
- Desiring more than is needful or useful to further us in our duty.
- When in our trouble and distress we fetch our comfort more from the thoughts of our provisions in the world, or our hopes of supply, than from our trust in God, and our hopes of heaven.
- When we are more thankful to God or man for outward riches, or any gift for the provision of the flesh, than for hopes or helps in order to salvation.

Provider God, thank you for giving me everything I need in life. Grant me a spirit of contentment.

The Reciprocity of Blessing Others

One person gives freely, yet gains even more; another
withholds unduly, but comes to poverty.

—PROVERBS 11:24–25

God wants us to be generous with the money He has given. The Bible sees it as an investment. In Proverbs 19:17, Solomon teaches: "Whoever is kind to the poor lends to the Lord, and He will reward them for what they have done." When you give to someone in need, God says He accepts that as if it were an actual loan to Himself. How amazing!

Sometimes, in hindsight, we question whether or not the money we gave did anything good; we wonder if the recipient really needed our gift or if they squandered it. We do need to be lovingly wise. There is nothing wrong with vetting where our offerings and gifts are going. But then we need to stop worrying over how the money we give is spent.

Our gifts are never truly a waste, for we ourselves are blessed when we obediently give to help those in need. We can never give to God without receiving some distinct blessing in our own lives. That is the reciprocity of blessing others—we always get back!

Father God, you are so kind and loving to me. Thank you for giving me so much. Thank you that even when I try to be generous, you are more generous with me.

Count Your Blessings

Moreover, when God gives someone wealth and possessions, and the ability to enjoy them, to accept their lot and be happy in their toil—this is a gift of God.

—ECCLESIASTES 5:19

What do you have to thank God for? What are the different ways you are blessed? Make a list. As the old hymn advises: "Count your blessings; name them one by one; count your many blessings; see what God has done."

The secret of contentment and happiness in life is to focus on what we have, not on what we don't have. When we lose our spirit of gratitude, our eyes stop seeing the good in our lives but notice everything others have with resentment and jealousy. *Why do they catch all the breaks?* We create reasons to be unhappy. *I never get what I really want.* We manufacture problems that don't even exist. *I just don't have enough to live on.* We nourish negative attitudes when we could be walking with joy. *My life is so miserable.*

When was the last time you counted your blessings? You are undoubtedly richer in the grace of God than you thought you were!

Father, thank you so much for the grace you show even when I don't deserve it. You have blessed me in so many ways. Teach me to use my gifts to honor you and further your kingdom here on earth. You are my God.

Patient Wealth

*The plans of the diligent lead to profit as
surely as haste leads to poverty.*

—PROVERBS 21:5

I f you are trying to get out of debt, don't expect it to happen overnight. The time it takes to fix past misfortunes or mistakes can be very frustrating, but your patience will be rewarded.

Solomon tells us that the wise path is the path of patience. You don't need to buy everything you think you want right now. Wait a while. You might discover you didn't want it that much in the first place.

Wisdom is patient. Maybe you need to consolidate your credit card debt, but make sure you know the terms and what you will really be paying for some instant relief from opening too many bills each month.

There are people who never made much money who are wealthy in their retirement years. How? They lived within their means and invested from the first day they started making money. The number one principle of investing is *time*—money grows over time.

Whether getting out of debt or investing for the future, be patient and disciplined, and give God time to work on your behalf.

Dear God, grant me the patience and perspective I need to make wise decisions in every area of my life, including finances.

The Value of Hard Work

Let us not become weary in doing good, for at the proper
time we will reap a harvest if we do not give up.

—GALATIANS 6:9

There's another principle in the Bible that we shouldn't ignore: the principle of hard work. The book of Proverbs instructs us to look to the ant, who has no "overseer or ruler, yet it stores its provisions in summer and gathers its food at harvest" (6:7–8).

We must also be careful how we speak about work. Do we denigrate the "grind" of work to others, to our children, even to ourselves? Do we make work something bad by how we speak of it? Consider this: for most people in the world, work, even if unpleasant, beats the alternative every time. It is lack of work that leads to poverty and crime. Talk of work as a blessing!

Yes, it's vital that we wait on God and look to Him for provision, but the absolute best thing to do while we're waiting is some hard work. Even if you are laid off and in between jobs right now, don't stop working. Take on a project for yourself or others. That may speed up your next opportunity!

Dear Lord, thank you for the blessings in my life. Give me a spirit of diligence and commitment to the tasks in front of me.

Spend as You Believe

*The wise store up choice food and olive
oil, but fools gulp theirs down.*

—PROVERBS 21:20

Some of us aren't disciplined in our budgeting and simply need to cut up credit cards. Warren, now in his fifties, had experienced many ups and downs financially. He determined to do just that. He cut up his cards and made a commitment to use only cash and a debit card.

It didn't take long for him to get into a healthy pattern. His next project was to set up some automatic monthly drafts with his bank that included a check to his church and one to a small investment account.

"I always wanted to give, and I always wanted to save, but the money was never there at the end of the month. So I started having those checks go out on the first of every month."

The result, over the course of ten years, was the joy of faithfully and consistently giving to his church, no debt, and a surprisingly healthy nest egg. Most of all, Warren began experiencing a peace that had eluded him for years.

Does your spending reflect what you believe in?

Provider God, give me the wisdom to spend my money in ways that reflect your values.

Contentment

I have learned the secret of being content in any and every situation,
whether well fed or hungry, whether living in plenty or in want.

—PHILIPPIANS 4:12

Aspiration, wanting to advance in life, including in one's finances, is certainly not sinful and can be a good impulse. But it can also lead to spiritual problems. It is fine to want more, to strive for more, but don't forget certain principles:

- Contentment: God want us to be happy and thankful for what we have.
- Covetousness: God does not want us to long for things others have; covetousness is the spirit behind robbing, defrauding, and other financial crimes.
- Comparisons: God doesn't want us to determine our self-worth nor establish our lifestyle based on what others have; comparison leads to jealousy.
- Compromise: God doesn't want you to lose sight of eternal values; money is never more important than relationships, integrity, and honoring God.

Paul was driven. He never slowed down unless put in chains in a prison. But even then, he was always at work for the cause of Christ. Drive and ambition are fine as long as Christ always comes first.

Dear Lord, I seek your kingdom and righteousness first, and I am happy with whatever blessings come my way.

Worldly Dependencies

Truly He is my rock and my salvation; He is
my fortress, I will never be shaken.

—PSALM 62:2

A CLASSIC DEVOTION FROM HENRI NOUWEN
(TWENTIETH CENTURY)

In general, we are busy people. Our calendars are filled with appointments, our days and weeks are filled with engagements, and our years filled with plans and projects... Why is this so? Why do we children of the light so easily become conspirators with the darkness?

The answer is quite simple. Our identity, our sense of self, is at stake. Secularity is a way of being dependent on the responses of our milieu. The secular or false self is the self which is fabricated [as Thomas Merton says] by social compulsions. What matters is how I am perceived by my world. If having money is a sign of real freedom, then I must claim my money.

The compulsion manifests itself in the lurking fear of failing and the steady urge to prevent this by gathering more of the same—more work, more money, more friends. These very compulsions are at the basis of the two main enemies of the spiritual life: anger and greed. They are the inner side of a secular life, the sour fruits of our worldly dependencies.

Dear God, let my sense of identity be rooted in loving you, not loving things.

Where Not to Find Joy

Why spend money on what is not bread, and
your labor on what does not satisfy?

—ISAIAH 55:2

People have pursued joy on every path imaginable; some have successfully found it in some measure; others have failed miserably on their pursuit. Words from history teach us that joy cannot be found in certain places:

- Not in pleasure: Lord Byron lived a life of hedonistic pleasure if anyone did. He wrote: "The worm, the canker, and grief are mine alone."
- Not in money: Captain of industry Jay Gould had plenty of money. When dying, he said: "I suppose I am the most miserable man on earth."
- Not in position and fame: Lord Beaconsfield enjoyed more than his share of both. Yet he wrote: "Youth is a mistake; manhood a struggle; old age a regret."
- Not in military glory: Alexander the Great conquered the known world in his day. Having done so, he wept in his tent and said: "There are no more worlds to conquer."

Where do we find joy? What is the best path? Since joy is the most tangible sign of the presence of God, the best place to begin is in pursuing Him and His presence.

Lord, I know that the real joy in life is in Christ alone. Thank you for sending your son, that I might know joy in Him.

Wisdom That Will Pay Off

Some people, eager for money, have wandered from the faith and pierced themselves with many griefs. But you, man of God, flee from all this, and pursue righteousness.

—1 TIMOTHY 6:10-11

"That man is richest whose pleasures are cheapest."

—HENRY DAVID THOREAU

"Money is like love; it kills slowly and painfully the one who withholds it, and enlivens the other who turns it on his fellow man."

—KAHLIL GIBRAN

"Never stand begging for that which you have the power to earn."

—MIGUEL DE CERVANTES

"Empty pockets never held anyone back. Only empty heads and empty hearts can do that."

—NORMAN VINCENT PEALE

"Don't tell me where your priorities are. Show me where you spend your money and I'll tell you what they are."

—JAMES W. FRICK

Father, make me wise in the ways of money, that I can experience more peace and be more generous.

A Prayer for Generosity

*Each of you should give what you have decided in your heart to give,
not reluctantly or under compulsion, for God loves a cheerful giver.
And God is able to bless you abundantly, so that in all things at all
times, having all that you need, you will abound in every good work.*

—2 CORINTHIANS 2:7-8

Dear God of all generosity,
I can never thank you enough for everything you have
given to me. You created a wonderful world for me to live in.
You gave me the breath of life. You have redeemed me when I
was a slave in my sins. You have brought countless blessings
into my life.

I want to be like you. I want to be like Jesus. I want to be a
cheerful giver. But I confess that I struggle to be generous.

God, I pray you will give me a heart like yours. Help me to
see those around me as you do. Give me a love in my heart that
sees giving as the joyful act of worship that it is, not as a painful
sacrifice. I pray that my generosity will not only include giving
from my finances, but spill over into all forms of kindness
and service. Help me to open my eyes to the opportunities to
experience joy through giving to those in need.

In Jesus's blessed name. Amen.

April
Kindness and Compassion

While women weep, as they do now, I'll fight; while children go hungry, as they do now, I'll fight; while men go to prison, in and out, in and out, as they do now, I'll fight; while there is a drunkard left, while there is a poor lost girl upon the streets, while there remains one dark soul without the light of God, I'll fight; I'll fight to the very end!
—GENERAL WILLIAM BOOTH

Wounded Healers

*Praise be to the God and Father of our Lord Jesus Christ, the
Father of compassion and the God of all comfort, who comforts
us in all our troubles, so that we can comfort those in any
trouble with the comfort we ourselves receive from God.*

—2 CORINTHIANS 1:3-4

All of us have witnessed instances when a friend or loved one has made bad choices—or have, through absolutely no choice of their own, simply been confronted with a tough set of circumstances. Whether you are in need of a personal touch from God in your own life or are walking beside someone else who is broken, remember:

- God never forsakes us (Deuteronomy 31:6): Even if our brokenness is of our own making, God is still kind and merciful, and always on our side.
- God can turn tragedy into triumph (Psalm 30:11): Even in the darkest moments of the soul, God provides a supernatural comfort and perspective that allows individuals to experience and exhibit God's love and power.
- God sends helpers (Galatians 6:10): Even though God is all-powerful, more often He sends human helpers, including doctors, to work on His behalf. It is no lack of faith to turn to others for help.

God of comfort, thank you that you are with me in every situation of life, that you bring peace, confidence, and healing.

2

The Towel and Basin Society

Now that I, your Lord and Teacher, have washed your feet,
you also should wash one another's feet. I have set you an
example that you should do as I have done for you.

—JOHN 13:14-15

T wo of the disciples, James and John, asked their mother to help them assume the seats of honor in Jesus's kingdom. Her request to Jesus was: "Grant that one of these two sons of mine may sit at your right and the other at your left in your kingdom" (Matthew 20:21).

Jesus's response was that she didn't know what she was asking. She and her sons were interested in the trappings and benefits of power, but not the sacrifice.

When Jesus taught His disciples the true meaning of greatness, He taught with a towel and basin. He washed their feet—the duty of a house servant. Peter, still unable to comprehend the object lesson, initially refused to let Jesus lower Himself in such a way. We live in a competitive and self-aggrandizing world. Examples of humility, kindness, helpfulness, and caring for others first—servanthood—are hard to find. Great is the reward, the sense of purpose, the self-satisfaction of one who follows the Master's example as a member of the "Towel and Basin Society."

Lord, I offer my life in service to you and to others with a joyful heart.

The Blessing of Being a Blessing

*In everything I did, I showed you that by this kind of hard work
we must help the weak, remembering the words the Lord Jesus
Himself said: "It is more blessed to give than to receive."*

—ACTS 20:35

One of the greatest sources of joy in one's life is bringing joy to others. Despite studies that prove the happiest people in the world are those who serve others, there continues to be a worldwide need for more volunteer support.

Most of us can count the blessings in our own lives...but can we count the ways that we bless others?

In Deuteronomy 16, the children of Israel are reminded to come before the Lord to worship. Three yearly feasts had been established as special times to grow closer to God. Passover was to be celebrated at the beginning of the year to commemorate that God had delivered Israel from oppression and slavery (Exodus 12). What a blessing!

One of the expectations when the people attended the feast was spelled out in Deuteronomy 16:17: "Each of you must bring a gift in proportion to the way the Lord your God has blessed you." Has God answered your prayers? It is wonderful to serve a God who wants to bless you, but let's not forget to bless others in equal measure.

Faithful God, thank you that when I bless others you bless me!

4

Loving the Unlovable

Bear with each other and forgive one another if any of you has a grievance against someone. Forgive as the Lord forgave you.

—COLOSSIANS 3:13

Every living creature has been blessed by God with a way to protect itself. When a sand particle gets inside the oyster's shell, for example, that tiny abrasive becomes life-threatening to the oyster due to the oyster's soft, porous tissue. But the oyster secretes an essence from its own being to create a pearl from the grain of sand.

What would happen if we, like the oyster, didn't try to discard the abrasive and unlovable people from our lives—even when we felt threatened—but rather welcomed them as opportunities for God's love to create something beautiful inside us?

A popular saying states that "love means to love that which is unlovable; or it is no virtue at all." Are you reaching out and showing love to the unlovable? The easy path is to ignore, avoid, and reject certain people. Perhaps there are some individuals who are so harmful to us and our loved ones that we should avoid them. But our first response needs to be compassion and love. Are you demonstrating the fruit of the Holy Spirit by showing kindness, patience, and love?

Lord, I want to allow you to work in my life through any circumstances, even the unpleasant ones. Teach me to love with your love.

Costly Love

My command is this: Love each other as I have loved you.

—JOHN 15:12

The missionary had little, but he knew that the starving Chinese mother he encountered had nothing at all. The woman looked weak from starvation. He wondered if she would live through the night.

He handed the mother all the food he had, a cooked sweet potato. The young mother took a bite of the potato, chewed it carefully. She then did something that amazed him. She pressed the warm food into her baby's mouth. She repeated the process again and again, not keeping a single bite for herself.

His heart was broken when the mother died during the night. But the little girl lived. He realized he had witnessed in human form the love that God has for His children. He died in order that we might live. He demonstrated the ultimate expression of love.

We may never have to die for someone we love. But with God's help, we can learn to love others sacrificially, reflecting His perfect love. True love doesn't stop when it becomes inconvenient. It keeps doing and giving, even when the cost is personally great.

Dear Lord, help me love others the way you have loved me.

Burden Bearers

Carry each other's burdens, and in this way
you will fulfill the law of Christ.

—GALATIANS 6:2

We are not responsible to carry every burden of others. In Galatians 6:5, Paul says that "each one should carry their own load."

But there are some burdens that are excessive. They are too heavy for one person to lift alone. That is the word Paul is using: burdens are staggering weights. Physical disabilities, emotional traumas, and other burdens can crush one's spirit through sheer magnitude. In cases like this, Paul says we can fulfill the law of Christ by helping someone carry the load.

One of the great paradoxes in life is that when we extend a hand to others, we grow stronger. We don't get worn out; we are energized from the inside.

Is there someone in your life who needs you to share the love of Christ with him or her? Is there a friend who is going through an incredibly difficult period of life? Are you willing to help someone carry that weight?

Lord, I pray for eyes to see the needs around me. Help me be a burden bearer, Father God.

Feeding the Hungry

For I was hungry and you gave me something to eat, I was thirsty and you gave me something to drink, ...I needed clothes and you clothed me.

—MATTHEW 25:35-36

A CLASSIC DEVOTION FROM RON SIDER (TWENTIETH CENTURY)

According to Scripture, defending the weak, the stranger, and the oppressed is as much an expression of God's essence as creating the universe.

Only in the Incarnation can we begin to perceive what God's identification with the weak, oppressed, and poor really means. "Though He was rich," Paul says of our Lord Jesus, "yet for your sake He became poor" (2 Corinthians 8:9).

Jesus was born in a small, insignificant province of the Roman Empire. His first visitors, the shepherds, were viewed by Jewish society as thieves. His parents were too poor to bring the normal offering for purification. Since Jewish rabbis received no fees for their teaching, Jesus had no regular income during his public ministry. Nor did he have a home of his own.

When John the Baptist sent messengers to ask him if he were the long-expected Messiah, Jesus simply pointed to his deeds: he was healing the sick and preaching to the poor.

Father God, give me a heart of love and compassion for those who are suffering.

Intercessory Prayer

For the entire law is fulfilled in keeping this one
command: "Love your neighbor as yourself."

—GALATIANS 5:14

James, the head of the early church in Jerusalem, said that if anyone is sick, call for the elders of the church to lay hands on that person and anoint them with oil for their healing (James 5:14). Paul challenges the church in Galatians to "restore" to salvation the person who has fallen away from their Christian walk (Galatians 6:1). Jesus sent all His disciples into the world to make new disciples in His name (Matthew 28:19–20). Throughout the Bible, we read that we really do need each other. Faith is not a solitary journey. The church works like a body, and each part is needed for it to work right (1 Corinthians 12:13–18).

One of the most dynamic expressions of this interrelatedness is intercessory prayer. The good news is Jesus is our intercessor who constantly speaks to God the Father on our behalf (Romans 8:34).

Whatever your need—or the need of your loved one—be assured that your faith united with the faith of others creates miracles!

God of love, I bring the hurts and needs of others before you today.

One Hug to Go, Please

Always strive to do what is good for each other and for everyone else.

—1 THESSALONIANS 5:15

The restaurant was crowded. A handful of waitresses hustled to serve more guests than they had been prepared for. A family made rude remarks regarding the service before the father spoke harshly to his server, demanding their food. In her rush to serve the family, a plate fell from her tray and shattered. After a stunned half-second, she broke down and cried.

From the next table, a woman stood up without a word and gave the waitress a hug. The waitress cried on her shoulder before cleaning up the mess. When the waitress returned, the father, embarrassed, apologized to her. She looked at him gratefully, and a smile returned to her face.

Life doesn't always go smoothly. Sometimes the food comes out slowly, and a host of other petty annoyances bring out our surly side. All of us need to relax, and some of us need a hug. Small gestures of kindness can make a huge difference.

The kind actions of others can bring out the best in people, even during difficult circumstances. Whom can you encourage today?

Lord, help me sow the seeds of peace and kindness in my life.

Serving the Poor

There will always be poor people in the land. Therefore
I command you to be openhanded toward your fellow
Israelites who are poor and needy in your land.

—DEUTERONOMY 15:11

T he motto "Give a man a fish and he will eat for a day; teach a man to fish and he will eat for a lifetime," forms a foundation for the work of many charities and ministries as they strive to help the people they serve grow progressively self-sufficient. So many of the poor in our midst need not just food for today, but encouragement, compassion, and a mentor to help them meet their challenges for a brighter tomorrow. So, as we try to follow the Bible's command to look after the poor, it might be a good idea to pray for wisdom about ways we might best help someone move toward a new level in life.

That doesn't mean we should stop writing checks for immediate needs. But don't be afraid to get your hands a little dirty, to get creative with your giving. Whatever you do, ask God to help you meet the deepest needs of those around you.

Mother Teresa reminds us: "We cannot do great things on this earth, only small things with great love."

Father, I'm in awe of your compassion for the poor. Show me how to reach out to others with your compassion and love this month.

You Are Gifted

His master replied, "Well done, good and faithful servant! You
have been faithful with a few things; I will put you in charge
of many things. Come and share your master's happiness!"

—MATTHEW 25:23

Albert Schweitzer, winner of the Nobel Peace Prize in 1952, was a biblical scholar, a medical doctor, a missionary, and a celebrated musician. However, in the eyes of God, Schweitzer was no greater than anyone else who uses their talents to their utmost in the service of others.

Jesus's parable of gold gives us some perspective. The master gave each of his servants a different amount of bags of gold, "each according to his ability" (Matthew 25:15). The ones who multiplied their gold were rewarded, but the servant who simply buried his gold faced punishment. We will be judged on how well we use our abilities. Even if we have fewer talents than someone else, we must always put what we have to use. Are you using what God has given you?

In the great orchestra we call life, you have an instrument and a song, and you owe it to God to play them to the very best of your ability.

Lord, help me to know what my gifts are, and show me how to use them for you.

Always Enough

*Taking the five loaves and the two fish and looking up to
heaven, He gave thanks and broke the loaves. Then He gave
them to the disciples, and the disciples gave them to the people.
They all ate and were satisfied, and the disciples picked up
twelve basketfuls of broken pieces that were left over.*

—MATTHEW 14:19–20

In the nineteenth century, evangelist George Mueller founded
many homes throughout England to care for kids orphaned
by war. With so many mouths to feed, he prayed daily for provision for even the most basic needs of the children.

Not long after he prayed, his wife came in and announced,
"A man I'd never seen before came to the back door. He said, 'I
know you're trying to feed some orphans. God bless you for it.
This is to help you in that good work.' And George, he gave me
a huge bag of oats, and look—molasses!"

"Praise God!" said Mueller. "Today I will tell the story of how
Jesus fed the five thousand."

Maybe you're feeling a little low on resources today, unsure
of how to help those around you. Remember that for every great
need, there is a great God. There's always enough!

**Father, thank you for always providing for me. Help me
share from my abundance.**

Paid in Full

And God is able to bless you abundantly, so that in all things at all times, having all that you need, you will abound in every good work.

—2 CORINTHIANS 9:8

A long with many others, the Litt family suffered during the Great Depression. To keep food on the table, Mr. Litt opened an account with their grocer that, despite working to pay off, he could never seem to catch up to. Having unpaid bills pained the proud father—what if his family were cut off from the credit line?

When she turned sixteen, Kathryn Litt went to work at the five-and-dime store to help with family expenses. Due to the many sacrifices her father had made, she wanted to repay him. After receiving her first paycheck, she handed him a carefully wrapped present. He couldn't hide his tears at the neat stack of receipts from the grocer, all marked "paid in full."

During times of trouble, it's tempting to turn to selfishness. However, ask instead what the Lord would have you do.

Is there a friend or family member who you know is in the midst of difficult financial circumstances? Pay a bill or perform some other simple act of kindness. Don't hesitate to do what God puts on your heart.

Lord, help me to trust you so much that I am able to give freely to others even in the midst of my own troubles.

Offer Love Freely

Dear friends, let us love one another, for love comes from God.
Everyone who loves has been born of God and knows God.

—1 JOHN 4:7

A CLASSIC DEVOTION FROM ISAAC OF NINEVEH (EIGHTH CENTURY)

Do not demand love from your neighbor, because you will suffer if you don't receive it; but better still, indicate your love toward your neighbor and you will settle down. In this way, you will lead your neighbor toward love.

Do not distinguish the worthy from the unworthy. Let everyone be equal to you for good deeds, so that you may be able to also attract the unworthy toward goodness, because through outside acts, the soul quickly learns to be reverent before God.

He who shows kindness toward the poor has God as his guardian, and he who becomes poor for the sake of God will acquire abundant treasures. God is pleased when He sees people showing concern for others for His sake. When someone asks you for something, don't think: "Just in case I might need it, I shall leave it for myself, and God—through other people—will give that person what he requires." These types of thoughts are peculiar to people that are iniquitous and do not know God.

Lord, plant mercy, kindness, compassion, and love deep in my heart.

15

A Shoulder to Cry On

Come to me, all you who are weary and
burdened, and I will give you rest.

—MATTHEW 11:28

After the loss of her husband, a widow received a call from a friend who said, "I have no idea what you are feeling now, but I want you to know that even though I don't understand, I am here for you. If all I can do is listen to you cry, or even cry with you, that is what I will do." So together they cried.

This went on for weeks until the moment came that they could laugh together. This opened up opportunities for the widow to talk about the incredible memories she had of her husband. She began to heal.

We worry about having words of wisdom or the ability to give grand gifts. Maybe you can do those things for others who are trapped in a rough spot. But eloquence and wealth are not required. What is most precious and rare for those walking through days of sorrow is someone to simply be there and listen.

Are your ears open to the hurts around you?

Father, you are the burden bearer. Thank you for inviting me to cast my cares upon you. Help me to ease the burden for someone else today, God.

APRIL

16

True Greatness

*Whoever wants to become great among you must be your
servant, and whoever wants to be first must be your slave—
just as the Son of Man did not come to be served, but to
serve, and to give His life as a ransom for many.*

—MATTHEW 20:26-28

In his classic little novel, *Journey to the East*, Hermann Hesse
tells of a band of rich and powerful men who are recruited
for an adventure that promises great wealth and glory. Their
only information comes through a humble servant, Leo, who
prepares their food, polishes their boots, and plays the guitar
and sings to them each night as they fall to sleep.

The sojourners bicker among themselves about who should
be the leader, while no one but Leo accepts the mantle of
serving the group. One by one, the men desert the party to
return home, all but broken. One of the men, bitter and angry,
determines that he will find the mysterious sponsor for peace
of mind. He eventually discovers that the great patron was Leo,
the humble servant. In explaining why the expedition failed,
Leo explains: great tasks require great servants.

Do you aspire to do great things? Then become a servant.
You will influence the direction of your family, church, and
community by serving others.

**Lord, you humbled yourself on the Cross; strengthen me to
humble myself in service to you and others.**

Hospitality

Do not forget to entertain strangers, for by so doing some people have entertained angels without knowing it.

—**HEBREWS 13:2**

Throughout Scripture, an act of hospitality becomes the opportunity for a holy moment. Abraham serves a meal for three strangers—who turn out to be God, delivering His prophecy about Abraham and Sarah's future (Genesis 18:1–15). The widow at Zarephath makes a cake of bread for Elijah out of the very last of her flour and oil, and miraculously she never runs out of food supplies during a time of famine (1 Kings 17:7–15). Peter's mother serves Jesus and the disciples after He heals her from a fever (Matthew 8:14–15).

In our modern day, hospitality can be something no less holy. God blesses us for receiving others into our homes. And when we take the time to demonstrate care for someone else, we realize that we are merely returning the love God gives to us.

Have you invited the new neighbors over yet? When was the last time you served Sunday dinner to friends at church? The traditional proverb says it beautifully: "When there is room in the heart, there is room in the house."

Thank you for the people you've given me to love, Heavenly Father. Be with me as I plan to show hospitality this week.

New Shoes

As a father has compassion on his children, so the
Lord has compassion on those who fear Him.

—PSALM 103:13

I n New York City during the Great Depression, a little boy was standing before a shoe store, barefoot, peering through the window. A woman approached and asked, "My little fellow, why are you looking so earnestly in that window?"

"I was asking God to give me a pair of shoes," was his answer.

She took him by the hand and went inside. After washing and drying his feet, she tucked them into a pair of warm socks and new shoes. As she turned to go, the boy caught her by the hand, and looking up at her with tears in his eyes, asked: "Are you God's wife?"

No question, life is hard. But sometimes we lose sight of the truth that God is good and that it is in His nature to give. God's goodness is the root of all goodness.

You may never be asked if you are God's wife, but they will recognize you are His child.

God, you have made my life so good. Help me to bring some of your goodness into the lives of others.

Happy to Give

*And do not forget to do good and to share with
others, for with such sacrifices God is pleased.*

—HEBREWS 13:16

As a Christmas present, Michael received a brand-new car from a close friend who had just inherited a very large sum of money. Michael couldn't believe his good fortune. Weeks later, as Michael left the office to go home, a shabbily dressed man stood near his parking spot, admiring his new wheels. "Hey man, is this your car?" the man asked.

Michael nodded. "My friend gave it to me for Christmas."

The homeless man was astonished. "You mean, it cost you nothing?"

Michael nodded sheepishly.

The man said, "Man, I wish..." When Michael looked alarmed, the man held up his hand to keep him from saying anything. "I wish," the man continued, "that I could be a friend like that."

Michael was amazed. And his statement was amazing. But think about it. Would you rather always be the receiver, or would you like to have so much you could be the giver?

What can you bless someone with today? Maybe you can't afford a brand-new car! But is there something small?

Dear Lord, whether I have a lot or a little, you have given me something I can share. Show me someone I can bless today.

Loving the Whole World

*Therefore go and make disciples of all nations, baptizing them
in the name of the Father and of the Son and of the Holy Spirit.*

—MATTHEW 28:19

A s a young man, William Carey worked as a shoemaker living in London. However, he was fascinated by those who traveled to foreign lands. Later in life, he became a missionary to India and shared the message and love of Christ to thousands upon thousands.

We live in a fallen world that is filled with war and strife. It is easy to harbor hatred for other countries and the millions of souls living in places that are in conflict with our own nation. Jesus tells us we are to love our enemies. It doesn't mean we aren't loyal and patriotic to our own country when war is justified, but we are still called for God's love to break through to the uttermost parts of the globe. Like William Carey, we need to pray over other peoples.

Whether or not you serve on an overseas mission field, God has given each of us a calling to love, serve, and evangelize others.

What mission field has God called you to serve in?

Lord, show me what I can do to serve you by serving others. I pray you give me joy in doing whatever you call me to accomplish.

A Higher Purpose

For it is God's will that by doing good you should
silence the ignorant talk of foolish people.

—1 PETER 2:15

A CLASSIC DEVOTION FROM PHILLIPS BROOKS (NINETEENTH CENTURY)

The purpose and result of freedom is service. It sounds to us at first like a contradiction, like a paradox. Great truths very often present themselves to us in the first place as paradoxes, and it is only when we come to combine the two different terms of which they are composed and see how it is only by their meeting that the truth does reveal itself to us, that the truth does become known.

It is by this same truth that God frees our souls, not from service, not from duty, but into service and into duty, and he who mistakes the purpose of his freedom mistakes the character of his freedom. He who thinks that he is being released from the work, and not set free in order that he may accomplish that work, mistakes the Christ from whom the freedom comes, mistakes the condition into which his soul is invited to enter.

Lord, give me the heart of a servant.

Divine Appointments

*Paul and his companions traveled throughout the region of
Phrygia and Galatia, having been kept by the Holy Spirit
from preaching the word in the province of Asia.*

— ACTS 16:6

One thing to watch for is when your well-laid-out plans get waylaid. Instead of grumbling and getting frustrated, consider the possibility that God is up to something.

- A missed flight connection puts you in a seat next to someone dealing with spiritual issues.
- A wrong turn takes you by an outreach center you had never heard of.
- A conflict with a neighbor becomes the open door for a new relationship.
- A canceled meeting frees you up to take one of your children out for a long and overdue discussion.

Paul had plans to minister in Bithynia. But God had plans for him to minister in Macedonia and introduce the Good News to a whole new continent (Acts 16:6–10). He was led by the Spirit in a dream and told to change his plans immediately. He did and embarked on a period of remarkable ministry. The same Spirit of God will lead you too. Keep your heart and eyes open!

God, thank you for your spirit to guide and direct my steps and work.

God's Gift of Rest

*By the seventh day God had finished the work He had been
doing; so on the seventh day He rested from all His work.*

—GENESIS 2:2

A ccording to Genesis 2:2, even God rested after creating the universe. And unlike God, we get tired. When our bodies and brains are tired, they don't function as they were created to do. We need the renewal that comes from rest. But just as much as we need physical rest, we need to recharge our spirits as well. We need to take a moment at the end of the day to simply take a deep breath and say a short prayer of praise and thanksgiving in order to take care of our souls.

Sometimes we run the risk of burning ourselves out, even in serving God. Don't wait until the point of exhaustion to take time to slow down, thank God for His love and support, and ask Him for His help and grace.

Jesus knows we must step apart from the rush and rest a while, or else we may just plain come apart.

Dear Lord, I need your refreshing, renewing grace to keep me going.

The Lion's Den

"Daniel, servant of the living God, has your God, whom
you serve continually, been able to rescue you from the
lions?" Daniel answered, "May the king live forever!"

—DANIEL 6:20-21

Who said serving God was easy? It's definitely not for the faint of heart. Sometimes it even gets dangerous.

When you serve God, you might get intimidated. And that's OK, as long as you keep going. What's important to remember is that God is always with you.

Remember Daniel in the lion's den? He was kept overnight in a sealed pit with hungry lions, but when morning came, he shouted from the bottom, "My God sent His angel, and He shut the mouths of the lions. They have not hurt me, because I was found innocent in His sight" (Daniel 6:22).

You probably won't be thrown into a literal pit of lions, but you might find yourself under pressure as you serve God. Whatever happens, know that He is near you, pleased with you, helping you, and turning a lion's den into a sanctuary of praise.

Do not let Satan deceive you into being afraid of God's plans for your life.

Lord, sometimes I get scared. I feel unable to meet the challenges in front of me. Help me remember that you are working in and through me.

In God's Arms

But He said to me, "My grace is sufficient for you, for my power is made perfect in weakness." Therefore I will boast all the more gladly about my weaknesses, so that Christ's power may rest on me.

—2 CORINTHIANS 12:9

A father and his young son returned home after a trip to the grocery store. The son loved being with his dad and "helping" him. On this occasion, he wanted to help his dad finish the chore by helping him carry in groceries. In fact, he wanted to carry the largest bag—which was much too heavy for him. The father came up with a quick and simple solution. He put the bag in his son's arms, and then wrapped his arms around him and the bag and carried both inside.

When the mighty king and all his soldiers shrank back in fear, a young shepherd boy stepped forward and declared he would face the giant (see 1 Samuel 17). They tried to put the king's armor on him, but it was much too large and cumbersome. But he was nimble and good with a slingshot. That's all God needed to help David win a mighty battle.

Do all you can—but humbly and gratefully realize it is God's power working through you that makes all the difference.

Dear God, I can accomplish great things with you working in and through me.

Love in Deed

If anyone has material possessions and sees a
brother or sister in need but has no pity on him,
how can the love of God be in that person?

—1 JOHN 3:17

A ctions speak louder than words. We all know this common bit of wisdom. But how many of us still struggle to implement this principle in our lifestyles? How many of us rationalize our lack of love in action on the basis of our fine intentions and words?

Perhaps we have blended in with a self-serving, me-first, materialistic, egocentric culture. Since that is the world we live in, it shouldn't surprise us when we discover we have conformed to the world. That is the prevailing message we hear day and night.

But when the light of God brings conviction to our heart, it's time to act. Is God's love in you being choked off because it is bottled up?

We stem the input of His grace when we put a dam in front of the output. How do you reactivate the flow of God's love in your life? He will do it for you. Your job is simply to meet a need right in front of your eyes. Even if you can't feed a hundred people, feed at least one.

Dear God, thank you for the opportunities you put before me to share your love.

Your Little Secret

When you give to the needy, do not let your left hand know what your right hand is doing, so that your giving may be in secret. Then your Father, who sees what is done in secret, will reward you.

—MATTHEW 6:3–4

The art of self-promotion is alive and well. We have photographers, publicists, and brand specialists to shape wonderful impressions of the good things we do. We blog and tweet and update Facebook about our every act of kindness. If our gift to a poor family didn't get a hundred likes on Facebook, did it really happen?

All of us need to check our own hearts and motives on why we do what we do. Is it for the praise and admiration of others, or is it out of love for people and the desire to honor God?

If you serve others for the reward of their admiration and gratitude, then your reward will be fleeting and ultimately dissatisfying. If you serve others for the reward of bringing pleasure to your Father God's heart as you work side by side with Him, then you will gain eternal rewards.

Some acts of service need to be a well-kept secret between you and God.

Lord, I want to love others and honor you in my words and deeds.

28

A Costly Love

Jesus looked at him and loved him. "One thing you lack," He said. "Go, sell everything you have and give to the poor, and you will have treasure in heaven. Then come, follow me."

—MARK 10:21

A CLASSIC DEVOTION FROM MOTHER TERESA (TWENTIETH CENTURY)

We are reminded that Jesus came to bring the good news to the poor. He had told us what good news is when He said: "My peace I leave with you, my peace I give unto you." He came not to give the peace of the world, which is only that we don't bother each other. He came to give the peace of heart, which comes from loving—from doing good to others.

Jesus gave His life to love us, and He tells us that we also have to give whatever it takes to do good to one another. And in the Gospel Jesus says very clearly: "Love as I have loved you."

It is not enough to say: "I love God," but I also have to love my neighbor. ...And so it is very important for us to realize that love, to be true, has to hurt. I must be willing to give whatever it takes not to harm other people and, in fact, to do good to them.

God of love, give me the courage and love to bless others, even though it may cause me pain.

Sacrifice and Service

But even if I am being poured out like a drink offering
on the sacrifice and service coming from your
faith, I am glad and rejoice with all of you.

—PHILIPPIANS 2:17

I n the New Testament, Paul stands as an icon of sacrificial service. He endured beatings and floggings (2 Corinthians 11:25), he wept over wayward and hurtful congregations (2 Corinthians 2:4), and he frequently went without the basic necessities of life (Philippians 4:12). Yet he affirmed, "I can do all this through Him who gives me strength" (Philippians 4:13).

God does not call us all to face such danger and hardship. But all of us are called to voluntary humility and sacrifice. Paul told the Philippian church to "have the same mindset as Christ Jesus: Who, being in very nature God, did not consider equality with God something to be used to His own advantage; rather, He made Himself nothing" (Philippians 2:5–7).

It can be painful to serve God and others to the point of sacrifice. But as Paul discovered, God supplies our every need along the way.

The cost of true greatness is humble, selfless, sacrificial service.

Thank you, God, for so many examples in Scripture and in my life of people who serve you faithfully. Create in me a heart that beats to do your will.

A Prayer for Compassion

Do not forget to do good and to share with others,
for with such sacrifices God is pleased.

—HEBREWS 13:16

Merciful God,

You are an awesome God, full of compassion and kindness. Your love and mercy know no bounds. Your heart is always turned toward those who are hurting and who have serious needs. You are the father of the orphan and the husband of the widow. You give sight to the blind. You have a special place in your heart for the poor.

I want to do good deeds and help others. I know that my family needs me. But I also know how much it pleases you when I reach out to others who are in need. I ask that you renew in me a heart of compassion and give me the strength to do something about it.

As I share with the needy with both my finances and my time, I will remember to praise you for the many blessings you have given me. Open my eyes to the need around the world—and across the street.

In Jesus's name. Amen.

May

Hope

Never, never, never give up.
—WINSTON CHURCHILL

A Reason to Hope

"For I know the plans I have for you," declares
the Lord, "plans to prosper you and not to harm
you, plans to give you hope and a future."

—JEREMIAH 29:11

J eremiah is known as the "weeping prophet." Imagine losing absolutely everything you hold dear—your family, home, country, church, and all your possessions.

In the midst of this hopelessness, the young prophet, Jeremiah, called to speak for God at an early age, dried his eyes and boldly proclaimed a new promise—that God had a future filled with hope for these people. That promise did come true for the Hebrew children, and the same promise still echoes and holds true today, no matter what the situation in which you find yourself.

Do things look bleak in your life right now? Are you flooded with insecurity about the future? Just as God had a plan for His people thousands of years ago, He has a plan for you—a good, pleasing, and perfect plan. And He is trustworthy to make that plan happen.

God, you know all things, including my future. Thank you for the good plans you have made for me.

A Bright, Shining Future

"What no eye has seen, what no ear has heard, and
what no human mind has conceived"—the things
God has prepared for those who love Him.

—1 CORINTHIANS 2:9

N o one knows the future. Oh, some economists are better than others at predicting tomorrow's economic conditions; some technology experts are better at predicting what tools we will be using in the days to come. But no one really knows the future.

Except for God. And He knows the plans He has for you. Some of which are greater and more exciting than you can imagine today. Could Abraham truly fathom that God was going to bring forth a great nation from his lineage? Could David really comprehend that God was going to unite and expand a loose confederation of tribes into a nation under his kingship? Could Paul have understood that he would travel from the Middle East to Asia Minor and into Europe to share the Gospel?

What lies ahead? You already know the answer. When you have an open and obedient heart, the future holds great works and great moments that God has planned specially just for you! For those who love God, the future is as bright as the promises of God.

Dear God, thank you for your promise of a bright, meaningful, and surprising future.

Nothing to Fear

I sought the Lord, and He answered me; He
delivered me from all my fears.

—PSALM 34:4

A little boy was admitted to the hospital for surgery. When his parents briefly left him in the room alone for the first time, his nurse, who knew that he was alone, called his name over the intercom to ask him how he was doing. This was decades before the wireless age, and even something as simple as an intercom system was new to him. The wide-eyed child sat up in his bed and responded, "Is that you, Lord?!"

Even when we feel all alone and afraid, we can know that God is near to us, leading and protecting and comforting us, sometimes in mysterious ways we don't recognize. All that's required for us to experience His divine presence is the simple belief that He is real, that He is always near, and that His eyes are always watching over us. Do you have that much faith?

God walks with us. He scoops us up in His arms or simply sits with us in silent strength until we cannot avoid the awesome recognition that yes, even now, He is here.

Lord, thank you for your nearness. Thank you for hearing my prayers. Give me an open heart to hear you and see your hand in my life.

Pressed, Not Crushed

We are hard pressed on every side, but not crushed; perplexed, but not in despair, persecuted, but not abandoned; struck down, but not destroyed. We always carry around in our body the death of Jesus, so that the life of Jesus may also be revealed in our body.

—2 CORINTHIANS 4:8–10

Jerry, a beloved husband and father, died from cancer after years of chemotherapy and radiation, suffering in horrible ways from the effects of both. During that time, he clung to 2 Corinthians 4:8–10 as a source of hope.

How would the Apostle Paul describe this brave man? Jerry was perplexed, but not in despair. He was not forsaken and not destroyed, because he knew that come what may, the end result would be the same: he would be with Jesus and experience the glorious full manifestation of all His promises!

Jerry's peace and poise under pressure became the touchstone for his family's faith after he was gone.

The good news is that we too can experience the same kind of peace and hope that Jerry did. No matter what is pressing down on you, God will preserve you and give you strength. You will not be crushed. Your life is secure in eternity.

Dear God, with you on my side, nothing can destroy or crush me. Thank you for your work in my life.

Praying Hands

He has made everything beautiful in its time.

—ECCLESIASTES 3:11

Albrecht and Franz, both very poor, but both artists, made a deal: they would draw lots; the winner would continue in art school, while the other worked to support both of them. Once the winner was an artist, he would in turn support the other.

Albrecht won the drawing and went on to have a wildly successful career as an artist. Tragically, however, Franz could no longer be an artist—his fingers were stiff and twisted from years of crushing labor. A true friend, Franz was not bitter, but thrilled for Albrecht's success.

Albrecht welcomed Franz into his home. One day Albrecht found Franz kneeling, his hands intertwined in prayer. Struck by inspiration, he grabbed his sketchpad. Five hundred years later, few of Albrecht Dürer's works are more famous or beloved than the *Praying Hands*.

Do you feel left behind? Have you wondered why things work out so well for others but not for you? Have you let go of the dreams and hopes you once held so tightly?

God can make a work of art out of any circumstances.

Father God, teach me to remain faithful to you and keep my eyes open for miracles.

Finish Strong

*I have fought the good fight, I have finished
the race, I have kept the faith.*

—2 TIMOTHY 4:7

A fast start is no guarantee of future success, whether the endeavor is big or small.

- Too many couples fall madly in love, but later let the flames of romance, friendship, and commitment dampen and die out.
- We go on a diet, lose ten pounds, and then celebrate with a piece of rich, buttery cake.
- A golfer hits par on every hole on the front nine, but then falls apart and double bogeys a couple of holes down the home stretch.

It was a battle for Paul to accept Jesus as the Son of God and his personal savior. But when he did, he was on fire to share the love of God with the entire world. Despite significant seasons of persecution, hardship, betrayal, and even opposition from fellow believers, he never lost his passion to live for Christ.

You're off to a tremendous start in growing closer to God than ever before. Don't stop now. Keep kindling the flames of your faith. Finish strong. Commit to walking in faith today and all the days to follow.

Loving Father, I commit myself again to walking with you every day for the rest of my life.

Be Patient

The end of a matter is better than its beginning,
and patience is better than pride.

—ECCLESIASTES 7:8

A CLASSIC DEVOTION FROM CATHERINE OF SIENA (FOURTEENTH CENTURY)

There is no sin nor wrong that gives a man such a foretaste of hell in this life as anger and impatience. It is hated by God, it holds its neighbor in aversion, and has neither knowledge nor desire to bear and forbear with its faults. And whatever is said or done to it, it poisons quickly, and its impulses blow about like a leaf in the wind.

It becomes unendurable to itself, for perverted will is always gnawing at it, and it craves what it cannot have; it is discordant with the will of God and with the rational part of its own soul. And all this comes from the tree of Pride, from which oozes out the sap of anger and impatience. The man becomes an incarnate demon, and it is much worse to fight with these visible demons than with the invisible. Surely, then, every reasonable being ought to flee this sin.

Heavenly Father, grant me patience so that I can treat others with grace and kindness.

8

Wishing on Stars

He who began a good work in you will carry it on
to completion until the day of Christ Jesus.

—PHILIPPIANS 1:6

Jiminy Cricket told us that we should wish upon a falling star. Peter Pan asked us to believe in fairies and to clap our hands. Most fairy tales end with a kiss and happily ever after—but in real life things are rarely as simple.

We know that we can't make the kind of wishes that happen in fairy tales. But sometimes we do seem a bit naive—maybe even childlike—in the things on which we set our hope. Jesus warns us against building our houses on sand (Matthew 7:24–27).

There is only one sure foundation we can build our life on, and that is a relationship with God and His faithfulness. Pastor Rick Warren shares this insight: "What gives me the most hope every day is God's grace; knowing that His grace is going to give me the strength for whatever I face, knowing that nothing is a surprise to God."

Fairy tales are charming and can point to the power of faith. But true hope is only found in the love and power of God.

Lord, thank you for walking beside me every step of my journey. Thank you for your daily grace that makes all the difference in my life.

9

A Courageous Hope

Be strong and take heart, all you who hope in the Lord.

—PSALM 31:24

What keeps us from attempting—let alone accomplishing— great things in life? Nothing sabotages our dreams and purpose and calling like fear! No wonder the phrase "fear not" is found more than six hundred times throughout the Bible. The opposite of fear is courage. But how do you get courage if you're afraid? It's not like we can follow the Yellow Brick Road with Dorothy and Toto to see if a wizard will bestow courage on us.

Can we ever walk without even a trace of fear in our life? No, but we can walk with the courage and faith to overcome fear. The source of that courage is hope.

When the children of Israel crossed the Jordan River to enter the Promised Land, the waters did not part until they took their first step. The same is true for us today. With a total confidence in God and His plans for our life, we have to take the first step to experience His miraculous power to open the path before us.

Are you ready to take the first step?

Oh Lord, I do put my hope in you this day. Give me courage and strengthen my heart so I can do something great for you.

A Beautiful Perseverance

So we fix our eyes not on what is seen, but on what is unseen,
since what is seen is temporary, but what is unseen is eternal.

—2 CORINTHIANS 4:18

A woman planted a rare rosebush, fussed over it, fertilized it, watered it, and was incredibly disappointed when she saw no reward from her labors.

Then one day she visited her neighbor and discovered that shoots from her rosebush had pushed through the fence and were blooming in splendid beauty next door. She immediately thought of some recent disappointments in her prayer life and realized that faith in God is much like tending to her rosebush. You can't always see the results of what God is doing in your life, but if you have patience and perseverance, you will discover that He was creating something beautiful in you all along.

Are there some spiritual issues in your life where you haven't seen the fruit you had hoped for? Are there some relationships and other needs you have been praying for that haven't worked out yet? A difficult child? Advancement at work? A dream you have harbored for years? Don't give up. Persevere. Keep hoping! Why? God is at work in ways that we can't always see!

God, thank you for giving me so much to look forward to. Please strengthen my spirit and help me persevere.

The Mystery of Life

God has chosen to make known among the Gentiles the glorious riches of this mystery, which is Christ in you, the hope of glory.

—COLOSSIANS 1:27

Mysteries and lost codes have always fascinated humans, going back into antiquity. Prophecies, cryptic clues, secret societies, dangerous archaeological searches, untapped divine power, and buried treasures are the components of many a bestselling and entertaining thriller.

The world Paul preached to was similar. In the city of Philippi, Paul notes: "Once when we were going to the place of prayer, we were met by a female slave who had a spirit by which she predicted the future. She earned a great deal of money for her owners by fortune-telling" (Acts 16:16).

Paul knew there was only one mystery worth staking one's life on. He wasn't a man to keep a powerful secret for just a few select individuals, to be hidden and protected from the masses. Instead he revealed the mystery that had eluded humans for generations: *Christ in you, the hope of glory*. The mystery of true life was solved then and for all generations.

Have you experienced the glory and power of God inside you? You don't even have to search for God. He will find you!

God, I am so grateful that I have discovered the answer for life in Jesus Christ.

Keep Going

*Let us draw near to God with a sincere heart and with
the full assurance that faith brings, having our hearts
sprinkled to cleanse us from a guilty conscience and
having our bodies washed with pure water.*

—HEBREWS 10:22

During a long race, it's easy to get discouraged mile after mile, our feet sore and our lungs gasping for more air. But what distance runners know is that being familiar with the course helps to keep up momentum. When you know what to expect, you're able to pace yourself and not become discouraged.

God doesn't map out the exact course of our lives. But some things we can know without a shadow of a doubt: We know troubles will come. We know that God will never abandon us. We know that He strengthens us when we are weak. We know that an eternal reward awaits.

The knowledge that God is in control of our life is the greatest knowledge we can have! With faith, we are able to persevere when the race gets long.

How far have you run in the marathon of life? Are you just getting started? Are you near the end? God runs with you each step of the race. He will provide you with exactly what you need to keep going and finish strong.

God, give me greater confidence in you so that I might persevere in the race of life.

A Sure Foundation

Those who trust in the Lord are like Mount Zion,
which cannot be shaken but endures forever.

—PSALM 125:1

In the midst of the Great Depression, many people lost hope in the government, their churches, their families, and even God as the downward spiral of economic disaster engulfed everything they owned. With the peaks and valleys of the stock market, the unemployment rate, the consumer confidence index, and other economic factors, every couple of years we return to the desperation surrounding the Great Depression to varying degrees, last exemplified by the Great Recession.

Is it possible that living in a prosperous society tempts us to put our hope in the wrong things? The truth is that no earthly thing deserves our trust; recent economic woes and front-page scandals demonstrate once again that even the most stable institution, person, or system can fail.

When we place our hope in God, we find His protection and renewal in even the deepest valleys of our lives on earth. He alone is a worthy foundation on which to build our lives.

Lord, you are the one who holds my life in your hands. Today I put my trust in you.

Always with Me

Even though I walk through the darkest valley, I will fear no evil,
for you are with me; your rod and your staff, they comfort me.

—PSALM 23:4

A CLASSIC DEVOTION FROM THOMAS MERTON
(TWENTIETH CENTURY)

My Lord God, I have no idea where I am going.

I do not see the road ahead of me.

I cannot know for certain where it will end.

Nor do I really know myself, and the fact that I think I am following your will does not mean that I am actually doing so.

But I believe that the desire to please you does in fact please you.

And I hope I have that desire in all that I am doing.

I hope that I will never do anything apart from that desire.

And I know that, if I do this, you will lead me by the right road, though I may know nothing about it.

Therefore I will trust you always though I may seem to be lost and in the shadow of death. I will not fear, for you are ever with me, and you will never leave me to face my troubles alone.

You are my guide, O God. When I feel lost, help me to turn my eyes to you for direction.

Contagious Hope

Through Him you believe in God, who raised Him from the dead
and glorified Him, and so your faith and hope are in God.

—1 PETER 1:21

Eugene Lang founded a company that held patents on a variety of emerging technologies, from ATM machines to LCD screens and more. He made a fortune, and as his wealth grew, he put a priority on philanthropy. It is estimated he donated more than $150 million in that category.

But something he did just as he was becoming successful may have been his biggest donation. Mr. Lang had been asked to speak to a class of fifty-nine sixth graders. Scrapping his prepared notes, he decided to speak from his heart.

"Stay in school and I'll help pay the college tuition for every one of you." Now that's a speech! And it had an impact for years to come. In a time and place when few students graduated from high school, nearly 90 percent of that class went on to graduate from college!

Hope is powerful in our own lives. When we cultivate hope to the degree that we share it with others, we create a brighter future for them and us. Hope truly is contagious.

Father, help me to give away what has been given to me in abundance: hope.

A Shared Hope

*And let us consider how we may spur one another on toward
love and good deeds not giving up meeting together, as some
are in the habit of doing, but encouraging one another.*

—HEBREWS 10:24-25

C hurch attendance is down in America. Fewer people attend, and those who attend do so less often. Lapsed churchgoers give a number of reasons, including:

- We're so busy, this is the only time we have for relaxation or other activities.
- The church isn't meeting the needs of people today.
- The church tries too hard to be relevant and makes it too easy for people to be casual Christians.
- Church is boring.
- Church members are hypocritical. They live no better than those who don't attend church.

Whether you agree or disagree with any of the reasons given above, one thing is certain: Hebrews says that meeting together is essential for the spiritual vitality of believers, and we need to encourage one another and spur one another on to good deeds.

Do you have a weekly place where you meet with other believers for spiritual growth and encouragement?

**Dear Father, help me to commit myself to the body of Christ
and help others to grow in their faith—while I grow in my
faith too.**

So Many Reasons to Hope

Be joyful in hope, patient in affliction, faithful in prayer.

—ROMANS 12:12

When Paul met Jesus Christ in a blinding light, his life was never the same. Some reasons that Paul says we can live with hope even in the midst of adversity include:

- God forgives us: "Therefore, since we have been justified through faith, we have peace with God through our Lord Jesus Christ" (Romans 5:1). When we are at peace with our Creator, the future is always bright.
- God favors us: "But God demonstrates His own love for us in this: While we were still sinners, Christ died for us" (Romans 5:8). We don't have to crawl to God and beg Him to help us with our problems. He is absolutely crazy about you.
- God turns suffering into hope: "Not only so, but we also glory in our sufferings, because we know that suffering produces perseverance; perseverance, character; and character, hope" (Romans 5:3–4). With God at work in our lives, the very trials that could crush our spirits actually make our hope stronger.

What oxygen is to the lungs, such is hope to the meaning of life.

O Lord, when I am discouraged and my hope wanes, remind me of the hope you have placed inside of me.

The Rescue Boat

Now faith is being sure of what we hope for
and certain of what we do not see.

—**HEBREWS 11:1**

A board a sinking ship, a woman stood with her blind husband as she grasped for the rescue boat. "Women and children only in these boats!" snapped an officer. The wife pleaded with him, explaining that he was blind and that she couldn't go without him. The officer then waved them both onto the rescue boat.

The man's hope was in his wife whom he could not see, but he trusted her in faith because he knew her and knew the love she had for him.

Our culture stresses what can be observed, whether in plain sight or through the lens of a microscope or telescope. The prevailing attitude is "I'll believe it when I see it." People of faith are not anti-observation, but realize that in the spiritual realm, "I'll see it when I believe it."

We cannot physically see God here on earth, but we can hope in what we cannot see because of His faithful love in the past and His promises for our future.

Do you need hope? You'll see it when you believe.

Lord, I can't see you, but I know you're real and at work in my life. Thank you for the reassurance of your presence and love.

Hope Out Loud

But in your hearts revere Christ as Lord. Always be prepared to give an answer to everyone who asks you to give the reason for the hope that you have. But do this with gentleness and respect.

—1 PETER 3:15

"What's wrong with the world today?" is a perennial topic of discussion. It is discussed 24/7 on news programs. Wars, worldwide strife, death and sickness, natural disasters, cultural divides within countries and communities, economic disparities, and other challenges—ours is truly a hurting world.

That's at the heart of the reason Peter instructed his fellow disciples to be ready to explain the hope that they had. Knowing that it's God who saves us and gives us hope for the future is good for our own spiritual life. Sharing that reason for hope with others offers them what they need to hear and is, again, good for our own souls.

When others describe the world with utter disgust and pessimism, can you share a more hopeful perspective? Most importantly, is your heart filled with enough hope that it spills over in your conversations?

The hope that is in us is not passive; it must be active in order to be effective. Nurture it within yourself, and be ready and able to proclaim it to everyone you know.

Lord, give me renewed hope in you and the words to say to share that hope with others.

A Peek at What We Hope For

But God will never forget the needy; the hope
of the afflicted will never perish.

—PSALM 9:18

Joni Eareckson Tada is one who understands the real meaning of hope when everything looks hopeless. At age eighteen, on a swimming trip with her sister and friends, she dove into the Chesapeake Bay, not knowing the water was shallow in that spot. The injury to her spinal column left her paralyzed from the shoulders down and in a wheelchair for life.

Her first years of rehabilitation were filled with anger and despair. Slowly but surely, her faith and hope grew. In her book simply titled *Joni*, her insight on hope offers inspiration to all of us:

"The best we can hope for in this life is a knothole peek at the shining realities ahead. Yet a glimpse is enough. It's enough to convince our hearts that whatever sufferings and sorrows currently assail us aren't worthy of comparison to that which waits over the horizon."

Joni's life and story has inspired millions to look for that "knothole peek" of hope that we, no matter how challenging our circumstances, find in the living Christ. He does not allow suffering without hope.

Lord, thank you for sustaining me even in the most difficult and painful circumstances. Teach me to look to you for hope for the future.

Wait on the Lord

*For the revelation awaits an appointed time; it speaks
of the end and will not prove false. Though it linger, wait
for it; it will certainly come and will not delay.*

—HABAKKUK 2:3

A CLASSIC DEVOTION FROM FREDERICK B. MEYER (NINETEENTH CENTURY)

Sometimes it looks as if we are bound to act. Everyone says we must do something; and, indeed, things seem to have reached so desperate a pitch that we must. Behind are the Egyptians, right and left are inaccessible precipices; before is the sea. It is not easy at such times to stand still and see the salvation of God; but we must.

It is remarkable how God guides us by circumstances. At one moment the way may seem utterly blocked, and then shortly afterward some trivial incident occurs, which might not seem much to others, but which to the keen eye of faith speaks volumes.

The circumstances of our daily life are to us an infallible indication of God's will, when they concur with the inward promptings of the Spirit and with the Word of God. So long as they are stationary, wait. When you must act, they will open, and a way will be made through oceans and rivers, wastes and rocks.

Father God, give me the faith to know that you will come to my aid exactly when I need you most.

He Speaks First

When a Samaritan woman came to draw water, Jesus said to her, "Will you give me a drink?" The Samaritan woman said to Him, "You are a Jew and I am a Samaritan woman. How can you ask me for a drink?"

—JOHN 4:7, 9

We don't know what was on the heart and mind of this Samaritan woman on this day she came to the village well by herself. Did she need some time alone to reflect on her life? Or was it just another day?

The wonderful news is that it didn't matter what brought her to that place; what mattered was that Jesus was there. He wasn't unapproachable. In fact, going against the custom of the day—Jews didn't speak to Samaritans, and men didn't speak to women—He initiated the conversation. He spoke first. His request for a drink of water may have seemed straightforward and simple, but our kind and tender Savior was already reaching out with a message of love to this lonely woman who had shut herself off from the world.

Isn't that just like Jesus? He makes the first move; He speaks the first words to break down barriers of shame and alienation. He did it for "the woman at the well," and He did it for me and for you.

Father, you brought the world into existence with your Words—and you bring salvation to us through your Words today. Help me to hear.

God is for Real

Hope that is seen is no hope at all. Who hopes for
what he already has? But if we hope for what we
do not yet have, we wait for it patiently.

—ROMANS 8:24-25

Is it possible to prove God is real without a shadow of a doubt? Most people believe in the existence of God, but some don't. Is it possible to convince them?

If we can't convince everybody and absolutely prove that God is for real, is this a problem? Is it troubling? Should we get discouraged? Not at all! If God could be seen through a telescope or under a microscope, would He be the Almighty God proclaimed in His Word? He's the Creator and cannot be studied in the same way as His creation.

Paul asks, "Who hopes for what he already has?" He also says, "Hope that is seen is no hope at all." Hope is a deeper spiritual experience that requires the open hearts and eyes of faith.

I believe in the sun even if it isn't shining. I believe in love even when I am alone. I believe in God even when He is silent.

Lord, thank you for revealing yourself to me in my heart and for the faith to see you.

All Spiritual Blessings Are Already Yours

Praise be to the God and Father of our Lord Jesus
Christ, who has blessed us in the Heavenly realms
with every spiritual blessing in Christ.

—EPHESIANS 1:3

I f we have received every spiritual blessing, then why aren't we experiencing those blessings in the same measure as others? Why do others seem more filled with grace?

The issue is not what God has provided. The issue is what we have accepted and appropriated into our lives. God gives all good gifts and everything we need to live a successful Christian life. God's blessings belong to us now. It is our job to recognize, receive, and use what is there for us.

How do we recognize, receive, and use what God has provided for us? Some of us still feel we are missing something. The prayer of faith is what opens our hands to all that God is offering us. Prayer is the hand that takes to ourselves the blessings that God has already provided in His son.

God requires that we ask in prayer. James tells us that "You do not have because you do not ask God" (James 4:2).

What seems to be missing from your spiritual life? Ask and you shall receive!

Lord, thank you for your abundant blessings—including the ones I have yet to experience. Teach me to ask you for what I need.

A Hopeless Hope

Against all hope, Abraham in hope believed and so
became the father of many nations, just as it had
been said to him, "So shall your offspring be."

—ROMANS 4:18

A braham is known as the father of our faith. That title didn't come easily! If you read throughout Genesis, you will discover that Abraham was a great warrior and won many battles.

But the hardest thing in life that Abraham dealt with could not be solved in battle; it was that he and his wife could not have children. No land to call his own; no son to be his heir. How do you become the father of a nation when you have no land and no child?

But Abraham never gave up, which is the reason he is known as the father of faith, and at an old age received his reward. He and Sarah became parents when she was ninety and he was one hundred. They waited that long for the birth of Isaac with what most of us would consider a hopeless hope.

Will your faith persevere when you see no immediate results to encourage your hope?

Lord, thank you for speaking to me and giving me a vision of my future. Keep my faith and sense of hope strong!

A Delayed Hope

These were all commended for their faith, yet none of them received
what had been promised. God had planned something better for
us so that only together with us would they be made perfect.

—HEBREWS 11:39-40

W hen you were a child or teen, did you ever hope for something with seemingly all of your heart—but it never came to pass? A particular toy. A part in the musical. A certain someone to be your boyfriend or girlfriend.

Even when it comes to temporal desires, Solomon says that "Hope deferred makes the heart sick, but a longing fulfilled is a tree of life" (Proverbs 13:12). How are we supposed to handle the grown-up disappointment of having noble and spiritually motivated hopes delayed and deferred?

People of great faith accomplish great things. And some receive what they are promised. But others don't—at least not here on earth. And therein lies the secret. It's the realization that in eternity, all hope is realized. All healing, all wealth, all joy, all love, all everything and anything we could ever hope for.

It takes some of us a lifetime to learn that Christ, our Good Shepherd, knows exactly what He is doing with us. Will you maintain your faith and hope no matter what?

Lord, I affirm a positive sense of expectation that you will do all that you have promised in my life!

Wise Words on Hope

*There is surely a future hope for you, and
your hope will not be cut off.*

—PROVERBS 23:18

Everything that is done in this world is done through hope.

—MARTIN LUTHER

*Many things are possible for the person who has hope. Even
more is possible for the person who has faith. And still more is
possible for the person who knows how to love. But everything
is possible for the person who practices all three virtues.*

—BROTHER LAWRENCE

Hope is passion for what is possible.

—SØREN KIERKEGAARD

I've read the last page of the Bible. It's all going to turn out all right.

—BILLY GRAHAM

*We must accept finite disappointment, but
we must never lose infinite hope.*

—MARTIN LUTHER KING JR.

**Father, thank you for the seeds of hope that you have planted
in my heart. I look forward to them growing to full fruition.**

Pass It On

"Come, follow me," Jesus said, "and I will send you out to fish for people."

—MARK 1:17

A CLASSIC DEVOTION FROM A. B. BRUCE
(NINETEENTH CENTURY)

"Follow Me," said Jesus to the fishermen of Bethsaida, "and I will make you fishers of men." These words...show that the great Founder of the faith desired not only to have disciples, but to have about Him men who would make disciples of others: to cast the net of divine truth into the sea of the world, and to land on the shores of the divine kingdom a great multitude of believing souls.

The humble fishermen of Galilee had much to learn before they could satisfy these high requirements; so much, that the time of their apprenticeship for their apostolic work, even reckoning it from the very commencement of Christ's ministry, seems all too short. They were indeed godly men, showing the sincerity of their piety by forsaking all for their Master's sake. They had much to unlearn of what was bad, as well as much to learn of what was good, and they were slow both to learn and to unlearn. ...Men of good honest heart, the soil of their spiritual nature was fitted to produce an abundant harvest.

God of love, thank you for those who have helped me grow in faith. I pray that I will be a blessing to others.

29

A Glorious Hope

He will wipe every tear from their eyes. There will
be no more death or mourning or crying or pain,
for the old order of things has passed away.

—REVELATION 21:4

Jodie had not left her mother's side for weeks. The doctor had said it was only a matter of days, if not hours. Jodie, now in her midfifties, flew home immediately to cherish every second with the mother she loved so much. For several days, her mom was unresponsive, but Jodie was there, holding her hand. Suddenly, her mom's eyes fluttered open. She looked at Jodie with a faint smile and said, "Honey, I've been talking to Jesus. I'm ready to be with Him. But I know how hard you're holding on. It's time to let go."

Jodie sobbed, but over the next few hours she "let go" of her mom. An hour later, her mother entered glory.

Death is not the end for Christians. Woven into the heartache of loss, there is hope for all who know God. Death is not the final chapter of life, but rather a doorway into an eternity with God.

Heaven is a place of no more tears. No two Christians will ever meet for the last time on earth.

Father, thank you for the gift of eternal life and the promise of being face-to-face with you in heaven.

The Glory of Heaven

My Father's house has many rooms; if that were not so, would I
have told you that I am going there to prepare a place for you?

—JOHN 14:2

Our focus needs to be on serving God and others (Matthew 6:33); but it is also true that we receive encouragement as we think about our future in heaven. Heaven truly is a wonderful place!

- It's a place of restoration: "He will wipe every tear from their eyes. There will be no more death or mourning or crying or pain, for the old order of things has passed away" (Revelation 21:4).
- It's a place of purity: "There will be no more night. They will not need the light of a lamp or the light of the sun, for the Lord God will give them light. And they will reign for ever and ever" (Revelation 22:5). Sin and anything that distorts the true pleasures of humanity will no longer corrupt.
- It's a place of joy: "You have been faithful with a few things; I will put you in charge of many things. Come and share your master's happiness!" (Matthew 25:21). Think of the happiest day you have ever experienced. It will not compare to the joy you will celebrate in heaven.

I live each day, my Heavenly Father, in preparation and anticipation of the indescribable joy of heaven.

MAY

31

A Prayer of Tenacious Hope

But one thing I do: Forgetting what is behind and straining toward what is ahead, I press on toward the goal to win the prize for which God has called me heavenward in Christ Jesus.

—PHILIPPIANS 3:13-14

Dear Lord,

Even if my friends forsake me...I won't give up.

Even if my children go through a period of rebelliousness...I won't give up.

Even if my spouse and I struggle for a season...I won't give up.

Even if my church experiences problems and strife...I won't give up.

Even if my own life doesn't measure up to what you expect from me and what I expect from myself...I won't give up.

You have helped me to plant seeds of faith and grace. And you have promised that if I persist, if I don't give up, there will be a great harvest in the right season.

Lord, great days are ahead. I'm not quitting now!

June
Attitudes

A pessimist sees the difficulty in every opportunity; an optimist sees the opportunity of every difficulty.
—WINSTON CHURCHILL

Do We Really Have a Choice?

*You have taken off your old self with its practices
and have put on the new self, which is being renewed
in knowledge in the image of its Creator.*

—COLOSSIANS 3:9-10

For centuries, people have debated what makes a person who they are—are we born the way we are, or do we become this way through the things that happen to us?

Though our genes and life experiences have a huge impact on us, aren't you glad that there is a miraculous, powerful God who is able to change even the most stubborn, damaged, sinful heart? After a change of heart at the moment of conversion, God isn't finished with us, either. Paul says: "And we all, who with unveiled faces contemplate the Lord's glory, are being transformed into His image with ever-increasing glory, which comes from the Lord, who is the Spirit" (2 Corinthians 3:18).

Through grace, faith, and the help of godly friends, we can say along with Paul: "Forgetting what is behind and straining toward what is ahead, I press on toward the goal to win the prize for which God has called me heavenward in Christ Jesus" (Philippians 3:13–14).

Lord, thank you for working in and through me to make me into the person you want me to be.

Not Mere Words

*What you say can mean life or death. Those
who speak with care will be rewarded.*

—PROVERBS 18:21

John rightfully reminds us that we can't show love to others by words alone, but that we must love with actions (1 John 3:18). However, he is also quick to tell us that words are a powerful force, for both good and bad, in the world.

- Words can reveal, reinforce, and reform the condition of our hearts: "For he is the kind of person who is always thinking about the cost. 'Eat and drink,' he says to you, but His heart is not with you" (Proverbs 23:7). Don't like your thought life? Not satisfied with your heart? Change your words.

- Words provide reconciliation and relationships: "The words of the reckless pierce like swords, but the tongue of the wise brings healing" (Proverbs 12:18). Don't settle for mediocre and broken relationships when your words can magically create new levels of understanding, trust, friendship, and intimacy.

- Words unleash faith: "I can do all this through Him who gives me strength" (Philippians 4:13). Your words can curse or bless your life and the life of others.

Let the words of my mouth be a blessing to others, O Lord, my strength and redeemer.

Joy in a Jail Cell

*May our Lord Jesus Christ Himself and God our
Father, who loved us and by His grace gave us eternal
encouragement and good hope, encourage your hearts
and strengthen you in every good deed and word.*

2 THESSALONIANS 2:16-17

In both his words and his actions, Paul calls for us to rejoice, to be joyful, in spite of suffering (Philippians 1), in the midst of humble service (Philippians 2), and in the face of fear and anxiety (Philippians 4).

But is it practical to think we can rejoice in any situation? In the face of a terminal illness? When we face financial woes? When one of our children is struggling? Is it even healthy to find joy in such times?

Note that Paul does not say rejoice because of hardship; he says rejoice despite and in the midst of pain. And Paul knows what he's talking about. This is the man who was stoned and beaten, shipwrecked, suffered from a painful physical ailment, lived with the guilt of being a persecutor of innocent people in his past, and was imprisoned and sentenced to death for his faith.

Yes, life can be difficult. But even in the midst of suffering we can stand firm—and help others to do the same—as we find our ultimate joy in the Lord.

God of all comfort, I choose joy, even when the circumstances of life are difficult.

Recipes for a Great Attitude

Rather, in humility value others above yourselves, not looking to your own interests but each of you to the interests of the others.

—PHILIPPIANS 2:3-4

Have you ever had a stinky enough attitude that you didn't even want to be around yourself? A negative, critical, harsh attitude is poison to relationships—and to your soul. Here are some surefire cures to get your thoughts and perspective moving in the right direction:

- Smile: "Rejoice in the Lord always. I will say it again: Rejoice!" (Philippians 4:4).
- Say "thank you" often: "Let the peace of Christ rule in your hearts, since as members of one body you were called to peace. And be thankful" (Colossians 3:15).
- Forgive fast: "Do not let the sun go down while you are still angry" (Ephesians 4:26). Unresolved anger and grudges cause us to hurt others—and ourselves.
- Be proactive: "And let us consider how we may spur one another on toward love and good deeds" (Hebrews 10:24). How can you bless someone today?
- Cheer up someone else: "Carry each other's burdens, and in this way you will fulfill the law of Christ" (Galatians 6:2). Helping someone in need will help you too.
- Rejoice: your new attitude begins today!

Lord, help me to find positivity and celebrate in you each day.

Worry

I pray that out of His glorious riches He may strengthen
you with power through His Spirit in your inner being, so
that Christ may dwell in your hearts through faith.

—EPHESIANS 3:16-17

Fear and faith are diametrically opposed. When we live in fear, it erodes our faith in God. When worries creep in and dominate our thinking, we start to feel far from God.

The only way to grow spiritually is to bring more and more of ourselves to our relationship with God. Don't suppress or deny your fears. But don't dwell on them. Don't let them bring sickness to your soul. Instead, treat worry as an opportunity that will lead you closer to God. Take to heart the words of E. Stanley Jones: "I am inwardly fashioned for faith, not for fear. Fear is not my native land; faith is. I am so made that worry and anxiety are sand in the machinery of life; faith is the oil."

What is worrying you today? Remember that God didn't give you a spirit of fear but of faith. Simply name it and rush to God in prayer.

Lord, sometimes I get so anxious. I pray that you would heal me and help me keep my mind on you.

Patience Is a Virtue

Guide me in your truth and teach me, for you are God
my Savior, and my hope is in you all day long.

—PSALM 25:5

W aiting is difficult. Crawling behind a car that is driving below the speed limit, standing in line at the coffee shop as someone scrounges for exact change, looking for the mailman so you can get your hands on that check that was promised weeks ago, and, of course, trying to keep a great attitude in church on the very Sunday that you planned to meet friends for lunch and the pastor is running long. Maybe the toughest waiting is when we ask God for direction on an important life decision.

No, waiting is not easy, but God tells us to wait patiently for Him. Waiting patiently means trusting that God knows what is best for us because we are His children.

A can-do, get-er-done attitude is commendable and shows a willingness to get to work. But don't race down a road if you don't know where you are going. Seek counsel from friends. Think through the issues. Most of all, when in question, wait for your Heavenly Father to guide you in the direction you should go.

Dear God, help me to overcome doubts and the temptation of impatience. Help me to trust you with the choices and decisions of my life because you know what is best for me.

JUNE

7

Supernatural Happiness

Through these He has given us His very great and precious promises,
so that through them you may participate in the divine nature,
having escaped the corruption in the world caused by evil desires.

—2 PETER 1:4

A CLASSIC DEVOTION FROM THOMAS AQUINAS (THIRTEENTH CENTURY)

Now man's happiness is twofold. One is proportionate to human nature, a happiness which man can obtain by means of his natural principles. The other is a happiness surpassing man's nature, and which man can obtain by the power of God alone.

Hence it is necessary for man to receive from God some additional principles, whereby he may be directed to supernatural happiness, even as he is directed to his connatural end, by means of his natural principles, albeit not without divine assistance.

Such like principles are called *theological virtues*: first, because their object is God, inasmuch as they direct us aright to God: secondly, because they are infused in us by God alone: thirdly, because these virtues are not made known to us, save by divine revelation, contained in Holy Writ. These virtues are called divine, not as though God were virtuous by reason of them, but because by them God makes us virtuous, and directs us to Himself.

I thank you for the gift of true happiness, my redeemer God. Help me share it with all I meet.

Peaks and Valleys

Just then there appeared before them Moses and Elijah,
talking with Jesus. Peter said to Jesus, "Lord, it is good
for us to be here. If you wish, I will put up three shelters—
one for you, one for Moses and one for Elijah."

—MATTHEW 17:3-4

What Peter, James, and John experienced when Jesus took them to a mountaintop goes far beyond the beauty and wonder of nature. In a divine moment, Moses and Elijah appeared to Jesus, whose face shone like the sun. Jesus's life, ministry, and divinity were being confirmed. Is it any wonder Peter wanted to build shrines and stay in this place of worship forever?

We will experience mountaintop highs in life—and we will walk through some deep valleys as well. We can't always experience life on top of the world, but the mountaintop moments God grants us—spiritually and through the splendor of His world—will give us reminders of His love when we walk the inevitable valleys that are part of the human journey.

Take time to remember some of those special moments God has brought into your life and be ready to face anything—even the valleys—with optimism, hope, and confidence!

Father, thank you for the moments in my life that bring me joy—and thank you for great memories to help me get through those moments that cause me pain. Help me to lean on you when I'm on top of the world or walking through the valley.

9

Act Now

Let us run with perseverance the race marked out for us.

—HEBREWS 12:1

T he hardest step is often the first step. We struggle to get moving on important issues facing us in all areas of life, including our spiritual life.

What's keeping you from getting started on things that really matter? Why are you wallowing in a self-destructive attitude or habit that deep down you want to be rid of? Is there someone you won't forgive? Is there a temptation you run toward rather than away from? Is there a pattern of negative, destructive communication with a loved one that you allow to continue? Is there a sin from your past that needs to be made right?

What is keeping you from taking the first step? Is it laziness? Is it procrastination? Is it stubborn pride? Is it a fear of failing? Is it that you are too preoccupied with less important things?

Today is your day. Are you ready to act with boldness? Maybe it won't be easy. But you can succeed, with God's help. You must take the first step.

Lord, I've procrastinated too long. Please help me make the move, the first step toward recovery and new life.

Walking with Peter

*Then Peter got down out of the boat, walked
on the water and came toward Jesus.*

—MATTHEW 14:30

OK, he ended up sinking like a rock, but for a moment Peter did something amazing. He walked on water. As amazing as that feat was, perhaps just as remarkable is that he left the boat not in shallow water, not on a beautiful, calm lake day, but in the deepest part of the lake during a storm. Peter was either very brave or very crazy.

Stepping from the boat and into the water took confident faith. For Peter, that belief centered on Jesus. He had seen what He had done and he trusted He would do it again in his life.

Notice, it was only after he took his eyes off Jesus and looked at the swirling waves that Peter sank.

What is courage? It is the ability to be strong in trust, in obedience. To be courageous is to step out in faith—to trust and obey, no matter what.

How is your sense of trust? Are you ready to walk on water when the next storm comes? Will you keep your eyes fixed on Jesus?

Heavenly Father, I do trust you and put myself in your hands. I know you can do amazing things in my life!

Why Me?

He causes His sun to rise on the evil and the good, and
sends rain on the righteous and the unrighteous.

—MATTHEW 5:45

I love God. I serve God. I help out at church. I'm nice to my neighbors. I volunteer in my community. I'm not greedy; I don't ask for much. So why me? Why more problems?

Life doesn't always seem fair. It would seem fair if bad things happened only to bad people and good things happened only to good people. Life is both wonderful and difficult for all of us.

So does it matter that we are loving and serving God? Is there any blessing for doing the right things in life? Absolutely! How we order our days and conduct our business matters now and in eternity. Those who live for God will receive an eternal reward, and those who ignore God will then be ignored by God. How we live today will help us avoid the self-inflicted wounds that scar the lives of so many.

Rain in someone's life is never a sign of God's disapproval. For those of us who love God, the storms of life become wonderful days when we display God's presence within us!

Lord, give me grace under pressure. Thank you for reassurance during difficult days. And thank you that they don't last.

12

Peace with Myself

We have different gifts, according to the grace given to each of us.

—ROMANS 12:6

Some people don't need to fight with anyone to be at war. Their battles are within themselves. Have you seen someone close to you whose emotional life is in constant turmoil? You tell them to let it go, but they don't listen. They rage and storm within themselves.

Maybe it was a traumatic event. Maybe it was a lost opportunity or relationship. Or maybe their battles within are the result of exalted opinions of themselves.

On this earth, few of us will ever be totally at peace within. As we grow older, we should naturally experience that peace to a greater degree. When inner turmoil is strong enough to hinder all other relationships, we need to take a good look inside. Counseling and self-help books are helpful for many. For all who lack peace on the inside, bringing one's self and one's problems to God is the true starting point.

Are you at peace with God? Do you believe He made you the way you are for a purpose? Your answers will lead you to how you need to pray!

God, thank you for making me who I am, with the people you put in my life, and with the plans you have for me.

A Joy No One Can Steal

*Now is your time of grief, but I will see you again and
you will rejoice, and no one will take away your joy.*

—JOHN 16:22

E ven with the most sophisticated security system in the
world, you can never make your home *absolutely* safe. But
there is something valuable in your possession that can't be
stolen from you. What is this treasure? It's your joy in Christ.

Oh, there are some who will try to rob it from you, using hurtful
words or slighting you in some other way. You can decide to let
them take it—but that's your choice, not their cunning.

There are some people who are so committed to killing joy
wherever it is found that we might be wiser just to steer clear of
them. But even in circumstances where there is no escape from
the thief who wants to steal joy so that gloom can take root,
you can still keep your joy by simply putting your eyes on the
author and giver of joy, Jesus Christ.

God made you. He knows how you operate best. He knows
what makes you happy. The happiness He gives doesn't stop
when the party's over. It lasts because it comes from deep within.

**Dear God, your gift of joy makes life wonderful. Help me
experience it and share it, no matter who would try to bring
depression and gloom to my life and world.**

JUNE

14

==== *A Changed Heart* ====

Be merciful, just as your Father is merciful.

—LUKE 6:36

A CLASSIC DEVOTION FROM SAINT FRANCIS OF ASSISI (THIRTEENTH CENTURY)

While I was still in my sins, it seemed to me bitterly unpleasant to see lepers, but the Lord led me among them and gave me pity for them. And when I left them, that which had been bitter to me was turned into sweetness of soul and body.

And afterward, the Lord gave me brothers, and no one showed me what I ought to do, but the Lord Himself revealed to me that I ought to live according to the form of the holy Gospel, and I caused it to be written in a few simple words.

And whoever shall observe them shall be filled in heaven with the blessing of the most high Heavenly Father, and in the earth he shall be filled with the benedictions of His son, with the most holy Spirit, the Paraclete, and with all the virtues of heaven and of all the saints. And I, your poor brother and servant, Franciscus, as far as I can, confirm to you, within and without, that most holy benediction. Amen.

Father, give me eyes to see the world as you do with compassion and love.

15

An Angry Love

Scatter the nations who delight in war.

—PSALM 68:30

When we get angry, it often shows a lack of discipline or is based on self-interest. But God loves the world so much He will rise up and "scatter the nations who delight in war."

Is it because He doesn't love everyone? Of course not. But God cannot tolerate the actions of those who destroy the lives of others. The bloodshed perpetrated by men of evil hearts brings sorrow and anger to God. It is happening all over the world.

Anger can be a negative and destructive force when we allow it to take root in our hearts. But not all anger is sinful. When does anger show love? When it is godly anger that fulfills His plans to redeem the world; when it protects the helpless from persecution; when it stands up against evil people; when it spurs us to act with compassion and truth in the midst of a hurting world.

Righteous God, let me live my life with love and peace. But instill in me a holy anger at the things that make you angry.

The Power of Words

*Those who consider themselves religious and yet
do not keep a tight rein on their tongues deceive
themselves, and their religion is worthless.*

—JAMES 1:26

I n Psalm 64, David calls to God for deliverance from those conspiring against him and speaking ill of him in the political realm. In verse 3 he says, "They sharpen their tongues like swords and aim cruel words like deadly arrows."

One of the reasons words do so much damage is that all of us have the need to belong, to know we are approved of. It is wonderful when we are surrounded by people who affirm us with their kind and encouraging words. But that will not always be the case, even in the midst of loved ones.

But the question is, what about *our* words? Do they build others up, or do we do damage with what we say?

If you have been hurt by damaging words, move on with forgiveness and the knowledge that God's Word about you is what truly matters. If you have spoken words that pierce the hearts of others, ask for forgiveness and repent. Commit yourself to speaking words of life into the people God has brought into your life.

Dear God, you created the world with a word. I pray that my words will always be creative and never destructive.

No Worries

Are not two sparrows sold for a penny? Yet not one of them
will fall to the ground apart from the will of your Father. And
even the very hairs of your head are all numbered. So don't
be afraid; you are worth more than many sparrows.

—MATTHEW 10:29-31

I t is believed by some that worrying is a sin. Do you believe that?

Without attempting to answer that question, all of us can agree that worry is rarely, if ever, helpful—and it is usually detrimental to our quality of life. Worry is bad for our physical and mental health, and it doesn't change anything. It robs us of joy and optimism. It can cloud our thinking and paralyze us from acting. Or, it can trick us into acting rashly and unwisely.

Fundamentally, worry is a lack of faith in God and His protection and provision in our lives. That's why some call it a sin. I would be cautious about labeling it a sin, because the line between healthy, vigilant concern and worry can be very thin.

Are you caught up in worry in your life right now? One bit of sage advice says to do this: Every night, turn all of your worries over to God. You'll sleep better, and He's going to be up all night anyway.

God, you clothe and feed all the birds outside my window, so I know you care for me.

Whatever Is Noble

Finally, brothers, whatever is true, whatever is noble, whatever is
right, whatever is pure, whatever is lovely, whatever is admirable—
if anything is excellent or praiseworthy—think about such things.

—PHILIPPIANS 4:8

To say that our culture has grown coarse and profane is an understatement. The entertainment industry and other forms of media fill popular culture with a constant barrage of words and images that do little or nothing to edify the soul and often bring great damage to it. Paul provides a checklist of virtues we would be wise to dwell on:

- Whatever is noble
- Whatever is true
- Whatever is right
- Whatever is pure
- Whatever is lovely
- Whatever is admirable
- Whatever is excellent or praiseworthy

Is it time for a personal audit of your thought life? Is it perhaps time to take a "fast" from popular entertainment in order to focus on what is ennobling? If we fill our minds with negativity and junk, we shouldn't be surprised if our thoughts and attitudes are negative and unhealthy.

Does your spirit need to be renewed in what is noble and praiseworthy? There's no better place to start than a commitment to reading God's Word.

Lord, thank you for checking my spirit on what I choose to fill my mind with. I turn to thoughts of you and your Word today.

Be Yourself

Just as a body, though one, has many parts, but all its
many parts form one body, so it is with Christ.

—1 CORINTHIANS 12:12

The Church of Corinth was founded by St. Paul. The members were intelligent, but they were imperfect, most notably through a spirit of divisiveness.

Paul begged them to be united in love (1 Corinthians 1:10). He used their spirit of contentiousness as an opportunity to teach them about God's plans for us. He reminded the Corinthians that:

- Each of us has unique gifts (1 Corinthians 12:28).
- Everyone's gifts are needed to complete the Body of Christ (1 Corinthians 12:12).
- We aren't to compare the value of our gifts (1 Corinthians 12:17).
- We aren't united because we are just like each other, but because we love each other (1 Corinthians 12:30–13:1).

The good news is that God has made you unique—just like He has everyone else. Your job is not to be like others, but to discover and fulfill God's gifts for you—and support others in that same quest.

Have you been missing out on God's best for you by trying to please everyone else?

Heavenly Father, help me to use the gifts and talents you have given me to be a blessing in the church and the world.

A Breath of Fresh Air

He brought me out into a spacious place; He
rescued me because He delighted in me.

—PSALM 18:19

When reflecting on the wide-open field where God took David, be reminded of the peace of God that brings a redeeming grace into our lives. We are no longer encumbered by the troubles of this world. What really happens is He brings a spaciousness to our hearts, allowing us to love and live no matter what others around us are doing.

Do you feel trapped by circumstances? Do you feel like you are hiding out in a cave because of troubles in your life? Don't let your heart and attitudes shrink from the pressure of external problems. Don't sour on life and people. Turn to your redeemer. Let His presence fill your heart, soul, and mind to the brim with His thoughts, His care, His comfort, His strength, and His love. Let Him take you to a spiritual "broad place" where you feel a breath of fresh air, savoring the joy of His goodness and His plans for your future.

Gracious Father, when I get comfortable with a cluttered and complicated life, help me to experience the spacious life that your Word promises.

JUNE

21

=== *Never Alone* ===

The Lord Himself goes before you and will be with you; He will never leave you nor forsake you. Do not be afraid; do not be discouraged.

—DEUTERONOMY 31:8

A CLASSIC DEVOTION FROM ALEXANDER MACLAREN (NINETEENTH CENTURY)

Jesus was the loneliest man that ever lived. ...He knew the pain of unappreciated aims, unaccepted love, unbelieved teachings, a heart thrown back upon itself. No man understood Him, no man knew Him, no man thoroughly loved Him or sympathized with Him, and He dwelt apart. He felt the pain of solitude more sharply than sinful men do. Perfect purity is keenly susceptible; a heart fully charged with love is wounded terribly when the love is rejected; with even greater pain the more unselfish it is.

Some of us, no doubt, have to live outwardly solitary lives. We all live alone after fellowship and communion. We die alone, and in the depths of our souls we all live alone. ...So let us be thankful that the Master knows the bitterness of solitude, and has Himself walked that path.

Jesus Christ's union with the Father was deep, close, constant; altogether transcending any experience of ours. But still He sets before us the path of comfort for every lonely heart: "I am not alone, for the Father is with me."

Gracious Father, with you I am never truly alone.

22

It Is Well with My Soul

The Lord gives strength to His people; the
Lord blesses His people with peace.

—PSALM 29:11

I n 1873, Horatio Spafford sent his family ahead of him to Europe by ocean liner, planning to join them later. But the ship carrying his wife and four daughters sank before arrival in the UK. His wife survived, but was devastated at the loss of their children.

Spafford took the next ship available to reach his wife. When his ship passed over the site of the shipwreck, the captain showed him where his daughters had lost their lives. As he stood, weeping, God led him to write the words to the classic hymn, "It Is Well with My Soul." The opening lines still provide comfort today: "When peace like a river attendeth my way, when sorrow like sea billows roll, whatever my lot Thou hast taught me to say, it is well, it is well with my soul."

Grief and heartache are real. But even in the middle of tragedy, when we go to the secret spot in the depth of our hearts in prayer and accept God's loving care, we can experience perfect and indescribable peace.

God, please strengthen my trust in you so that I can rest in your peace during times of tragedy.

I Trust You

But you, God, will bring down the wicked into the pit
of decay; the bloodthirsty and deceitful will not live
out half their days. But as for me, I trust in you.

—PSALM 55:23

Sometimes the seas of life are smooth, and a comforting breeze blows gently across our faces. Sometimes the seas are choppy—not terribly dangerous, but definitely uncomfortable. The temptation is to assume that God is with us in the good times but that we are alone when times are rough. If that wasn't true for the giants of our faith, including David, then why would it be true for us? Remember to embrace the truth that Jesus spoke when He said, "And surely I am with you always, to the very end of the age" (Mathew 28:20).

When David states, "I trust in you," you can sense a new focus in his life. No longer is he preoccupied with his enemies—his problems—but his eyes are on the Lord. No matter what you are going through, only two parties ultimately matter in your spiritual life: God and you. Two is good company, but three is a crowd.

When was the last time you said to God: I trust you? I truly trust in you.

God, whether sunny skies or storm clouds, you are with me—and I trust you.

24

God Wants You to Be Happy

The Lord has done it this very day; let us rejoice today and be glad.

—PSALM 118:24

Amy experienced considerable stress on her job as a nurse. Although she tried to spare her kids from her moods, her son took notice when her nerves would get ragged. One evening, he begged while he hugged her goodbye, "Mom, while you're at work, think happy thoughts."

With a smile, she said, "Thanks, baby, I will." And that night she did just that—for him. That night's shift went so much better than usual that she soon found herself thinking happy thoughts for herself. The wisdom of a child challenged her to make a dramatic life change and become a person of joy, leaving behind the spirit of discontent and complaint that had dominated her thinking.

Seek to cultivate a buoyant, joyous sense of the kindnesses of God in your daily life. Do it for others so you are more pleasant to be around. Then do it for yourself. But ultimately, do it for God, who loves to see His children filled with optimism and joy.

God, today I choose, with your help, to think about the good things in my life. Thank you for helping me to walk in joy.

Different Vantage Points

Whoever dwells in the shelter of the Most High
will rest in the shadow of the Almighty.

—PSALM 91:1

A family was traveling home when they were caught in a terrible storm. However, rather than seek shelter, they were in awe at this ferocious display of nature. They actually wanted to get closer to see the majestic beauty, as lightning seemed to dance across the sky and around the buildings.

From one vantage point, a storm poses danger and warrants fear. From another vantage point, storms provide us a beautiful display of God's creation that entertains and excites the senses.

In the ups and downs of life, is it possible to see anything beautiful in the thunder and lightning that surrounds us? Can we find anything good in pain and suffering?

If we see storms as an opportunity to grow; if we see storms as an opportunity to trust God more; if we see storms as an opportunity to focus on what is most important in life; if we see storms as an opportunity to see the hand of God on our lives... then yes, in all of these ways, a different vantage point allows us to see the beauty.

Father, give me patience and wisdom so that I might see your hand at work in my world, creating something beautiful.

It's Party Time!

"But the father said to his servants, 'Quick! Bring the best robe and put it on him. Put a ring on his finger and sandals on his feet. Bring the fattened calf and kill it. Let's have a feast and celebrate.'"

—LUKE 15:22-23

Our faith is a serious matter. It is not something to take lightly. But some religious people have ignored God's call to joyfully celebrate and are suspicious of any setting that seems frivolous. They try to suck the joy out of walking with God.

That's not what God wants! God loves to throw a party. Jesus Himself was criticized sharply by religious leaders for attending parties.

God has created a rhythm to life. To be healthy and balanced, we need work and worship and rest, yes, but also play. Sure, some people need to rein themselves in and play a little less. Some parties are probably not a good idea to attend. But God has given us reasons to celebrate, and we should devote time to rejoicing as an act of worship.

Go ahead and throw that party sooner than later. It could be just what you—and your family and friends—need to draw closer to God.

Dear Lord, you have given me much to celebrate. Thank you for inviting me to walk joyously.

Too Busy to Worry

Do not let your hearts be troubled. You
believe in God; believe also in me.

—JOHN 14:1

The attitude of hope is so much more enjoyable than the attitude of worrying. And yet, far too often, we find it much easier to mull over our worries than to think about the hope God offers us. What is it about dwelling on the negative that attracts our thinking? There are many negative voices in the world that go so far as to ridicule the person of hope.

An old blessing declares: "Blessed is the person who is too busy to worry in the daytime, and too sleepy to worry at night."

Is your heart troubled? Reading the Psalms, making a list of God's works in our own lives, singing along to a favorite worship song, serving others as a volunteer—there are all kinds of positive ways to spend our time that cultivate faith in God's promises and keep us from brooding over what may or may not happen. Declare your belief in God the Father and God the Son to set your heart in the right direction.

God, thank you for your faithfulness. Help me set my mind on you today.

JUNE

28

=== *The Bitter and the Sweet* ===

Consider the ravens: They do not sow or reap, they
have no storeroom or barn; yet God feeds them. And
how much more valuable you are than birds!

—LUKE 12:24

A CLASSIC DEVOTION FROM BROTHER LAWRENCE (SEVENTEENTH CENTURY)

God knows best what we need, and all that He does is for our good. If we knew how much He loves us, we would always be prepared to receive equally and without preference the sweet or the bitter that comes from His hand; we would be pleased with anything that comes from Him.

Don't entertain yourself with the trifles of life. Do not seek to love God for any of the favors and comforts He brings you—even if those favors are good and noble. Such blessings, great or small, don't bring us close to Him. Only faith can do that. So don't seek Him for what you'll get but seek Him in faith. It is rude and worthy of blame if we ignore God because we are distracted by acquiring the trifles of life. This isn't what pleases God. Beware lest your pursuit of comforts and possessions cost you terribly.

Simply and earnestly be devoted to Him. Get rid of distractions from your heart; let Him possess even your desires.

Dear God, grant me the power and perspective to accept both the ups and downs of life with grace.

29

Your Turnaround

But unless you repent, you too will all perish.

—LUKE 13:3

I s it fair to say we live in a lax, permissive, indulgent age?

Part of this prevailing attitude is due to our desire not to be judgmental. That is a good impulse. But some of the attitude comes from being too comfortable in our relative wealth and easy lifestyle!

We need to heed the words of Jesus in our godless culture: "Enter through the narrow gate. For wide is the gate and broad is the road that leads to destruction, and many enter through it. But small is the gate and narrow the road that leads to life, and only a few find it" (Matthew 7:13–14).

Repentance is turning away from sin and going in an opposite direction. Not all of our choices deal with sin, but nevertheless, the wise person incorporates discipline and even self-denial to grow toward maturity.

In what ways do you need more discipline in your life? In what areas of your life are you on the wrong road, and where do you need to make an immediate U-turn?

Dear God, it is by your grace I am saved, but thank you for giving me the power to make decisions that help me grow and become stronger.

A Prayer for a Renewed Attitude

May He strengthen your hearts so that you will be
blameless and holy in the presence of our God and Father
when our Lord Jesus comes with all His holy ones.

—1 THESSALONIANS 3:13

God of peace,
I do not feel at peace inside my heart and mind right now. I am struggling with an attitude that is muddying how I look at situations. I feel negative because something negative is inside me. I can pretend with some people that everything is OK, but you know my heart. And you know how it got that way.

I need you to give me a new outlook, based on a new heart inside of me. If I have unconfessed sin, a long-held resentment or grudge, a stubborn spirit, a fear, a refusal to forgive others, or some other act of disobedience that is nurturing this attitude, I pray you will help me to receive your grace at the source of the problem. In faith and obedience, I give myself completely to you right now—including all my attitudes.

I pray that you will renew my mind and heart so that I can see the world with fresh eyes, free from the snare of rotten attitudes.

In Jesus's name I pray this. Amen.

July
Strength

Do not pray for easy lives. Pray to be stronger men! Do not pray for tasks equal to your powers. Pray for powers equal to your tasks! Then the doing of your work shall be no miracle, but you shall be the miracle.
—PHILLIPS BROOKS

Daily Dependence

*Trust in the Lord with all your heart and lean not on
your own understanding; in all your ways submit to
Him, and He will make your paths straight.*

—PROVERBS 3:5-6

We rightfully teach our children—and attempt to live our own lives—by the credos of responsibility, self-control, and mature self-reliance. But when our attitude reaches the point where we trust more in ourselves than in God, twin temptations, both of which lead to spiritual shipwreck, suddenly confront us.

One temptation is pride, an unhealthy arrogance that slips into our thinking when things are going great in our lives. We become convinced that we are in control of our own world. The second temptation, despair, works itself into our hearts when we face the inevitable difficulties and setbacks of life that are outside of our control—illness, a difficult relationship, an economic downturn.

A child's humility is one of trust—it pleases God when we trust Him as a child trusts and depends on his father. The good news is that with complete and total trust in Him, He directs our steps in the most fulfilling paths for our lives.

Faithful God, I put my total trust in you to sustain me in all the moments of my life.

A Fresh Start

Praise be to the God and Father of our Lord Jesus Christ! In
His great mercy He has given us new birth into a living hope
through the resurrection of Jesus Christ from the dead.

—1 PETER 1:3

*J*ust about the time I feel I'm really growing in my Christian walk, I stumble and fall flat on my face. I get angry and vent about someone I love. I get envious of others. I put myself in a compromising situation. All of a sudden, I wake up and wonder if I even know God at all.

We note our spiritual weakness and make promises to God to do better, only to leave them by the wayside in the days and weeks ahead. If we want a fresh start, the first step is to accept God's unconditional love for us and put all our hope there. Then we stop trying harder to be the right person and allow Him to work through us.

Ask God first for direction, then for strength to accomplish the tasks He sets before you. Jesus called Himself our Good Shepherd. When we follow Him, we find green pastures and an abundance of joy.

Lord, give me wisdom as I try to live for you. Show me what you would have me accomplish. And thank you for your ever-present love and strength.

A Paradoxical Power

That is why, for Christ's sake, I delight in weaknesses,
in insults, in hardships, in persecutions, in difficulties.
For when I am weak, then I am strong.

—2 CORINTHIANS 12:10

Yes, God's power is a mighty, prevailing force that cannot be withstood by His enemies. But God has most often elected to reveal and exercise His power in the strangest and subtlest of ways:

- God uses "cracked pots" to minister: "But we have this treasure in jars of clay to show that this all-surpassing power is from God and not from us" (2 Corinthians 4:7). God can use people like you and me!
- God sacrifices Himself: "For even the Son of Man did not come to be served, but to serve, and to give His life as a ransom for many" (Mark 10:45).
- God never forsakes us: "Never will I leave you; never will I forsake you" (Hebrews 13:5). Jesus's sacrifice allowed the rest of us to live with the confidence and assurance that He is always present in our lives.

There is no danger, no enemy, no circumstance that can equal God's power in your life.

Father, even when I am weak, thank you for giving me a strength to conquer all problems and challenges.

Obedient Strength

Sovereign Lord, remember me. Please, God, strengthen
me just once more, and let me with one blow get
revenge on the Philistines for my two eyes.

—JUDGES 16:28

His mother had committed Samson to the Lord when he was a baby. He took the vows of a Nazarite, which meant no fermented beverages and no cutting his hair. Generations later, the cousin of Jesus, John the Baptist, took the same vows.

It was only when Samson rejected his vows before God, allowing his hair to be cut, that the Philistines could subdue him, again relying on the charms of Delilah to set the trap. He was chained to a millstone. His eyes were poked out. He was flogged. As a final humiliation, the rulers of the Philistines brought him to the temple to be mocked. However, when God answered Samson's repentance and prayer, in that single moment he accomplished more than he had at any other time in his life. He pushed down the pillars of the Philistine temple and destroyed three thousand men.

Despite his disobedience, God used Samson when he repented. Is it possible that, had Samson always been obedient, God would have worked within him to do even greater things?

Heavenly Father, forgive any sin in my life and help me to trust and obey you each day.

Blessed Obedience

"I am the Lord's servant," Mary answered.
"May your word to me be fulfilled."

—LUKE 1:38

M ary, the mother of Jesus, is perhaps the best known of all the women of the Bible—people across the world know who she was and honor her. It was to Mary that God first revealed His specific plan to "save His people from their sins" through her son (Matthew 1:21).

Mary could have asked a lot of questions—"What will Joseph think?" "What will happen to us?" If Mary was thinking these questions, she didn't say so. She never argued or said, "Let me think this over." She simply said yes to God's plan: "I am the Lord's servant" (Luke 1:38). She placed her reputation, her marriage, and her entire life at risk to be obedient to God—and trusted that His will was perfect.

Because of her trust and obedience, salvation became available to all humanity. Mary's simple faith and readiness to do God's will brought the blessing of God into her life—and that same faith and obedience will bless your life today.

Lord, give me a heart and spirit that is always ready to trust and obey.

JULY

6

Wear the Armor

But since we belong to the day, let us be sober, putting on faith
and love as a breastplate, and the hope of salvation as a helmet.

—1 THESSALONIANS 5:8

None of us would go to battle without the proper weapons. It would be a foolish act of suicide. Soldiers need offensive and defensive weapons. In the battle for our soul, we need weapons too!

God sees us in our need, saves us from our sins, and puts us on the right path.

Rather than live in a cycle of defeat, wouldn't it be better to remember that God is the source of our salvation and strength? Paul tells us to put on the whole armor of God, including the sword of truth, the breastplate of righteousness, and a shield of faith. None of those defenses come from our strength and savvy, but are gifts from God to claim and cling to.

Are you trying to master your life with your own sufficiency and strength? Are you trying to fight spiritual battles without a sword, a breastplate, or a shield? Or are you wearing His armor?

Lord, I acknowledge my need for you. You are my strength and salvation. Help me to walk humbly with you.

Count the Cost

*"Suppose one of you wants to build a tower. Won't
you first sit down and estimate the cost to see if
you have enough money to complete it?"*

—LUKE 14:28

A CLASSIC DEVOTION FROM ROBERT HAWKER
(NINETEENTH CENTURY)

Ponder, my soul, over this very striking image concerning the divine life. The picture of a builder is most aptly chosen; for the Christian builder is building for eternity. And the figure of a warrior, which our Lord also joins to it, is no less so, for the battle is for life, and that life is eternal. Have you counted the cost? Have you entered upon the work? Is the foundation stone, which God hath laid in Zion, the rock on which you are building?

Oh! It is blessed to make Christ the all in all of the spiritual temple; blessed to make Him the first in point of strength, to support and bear the weight of the whole building; blessed to make Him the grand cement, to unite and keep together, in one harmonious proportion and regularity, every part of the building; and blessed to bring forth the capstone of the building, by His strength and glory, crying, "Grace, grace unto it."

**Father, continue to teach and encourage me to keep Christ
as the foundation of my life.**

Supernatural Confidence

Have I not commanded you? Be strong and courageous.
Do not be terrified; do not be discouraged, for the
Lord your God will be with you wherever you go.

—JOSHUA 1:9

Confidence means taking bold steps. But not all of us feel particularly bold. Such was the case for the children of Israel as they were on the cusp of crossing into the Promised Land. For forty years, they had wandered in the desert as punishment for their grumbling spirit. Now they weren't sure they wanted to step out of a parched land and into a land flowing with milk and honey. Why? They were afraid.

I'm just not very brave. I never have been. I'm actually a little bit shy. A lot of things frighten me.

Courage is not the absence of fear. It is about facing your fears and doing the right thing anyway. Courage is not about personality types. It is for everyone, whether we are introverted or extroverted. Each of us can take bold steps, even if we don't feel very confident. Why? Because we can live in the supernatural confidence that comes from knowing God is with us wherever we go.

Lord, help me to do the best job I can for you.

Accomplishing the Impossible

We are hard pressed on every side, but not crushed;
perplexed, but not in despair; persecuted, but not
abandoned; struck down, but not destroyed.

—2 CORINTHIANS 4:8-9

In many ways, Keeley Green is just like any other five-year-old. But in one aspect, Keeley isn't like other kids. Keeley has only half a brain.

At sixteen months, a rare neurological condition that caused uncontrollable seizures, which stopped her breathing, forced Keeley to undergo surgery to remove the left side of her brain. The operation paralyzed her right side and took away most of her verbal skills, as well as the vision in her right eye and the ability to eat normally.

Of course, Keeley's mom and dad were devastated at first. But they've watched their daughter win daily uphill battles in her quest to achieve the improbable and accomplish the impossible. "She has so much to offer this world," her parents say. "Keeley might have only half a brain, but she's still got a beautiful mind."

If you're facing an uphill battle, I hope you'll remember the story of a little girl named Keeley. If you'll be like Keeley and persevere with courage and determination, you can stay the course and overcome the impossible.

Dear Father, give me courage to face the obstacles in front of me, and remind me today of your grace and power to overcome.

Hold On

You intended to harm me, but God intended it for good to accomplish what is now being done, the saving of many lives.

—GENESIS 50:20

God promised to make Abraham the father of a great nation, with descendants as numerous as the stars in the sky (Genesis 15:5). Can you blame him for questioning when this was going to happen when he was still childless at age seventy-five (Genesis 12:4; 15:2-3)?

Why doesn't God just bring about His plans in our lives right now? Could it be that one of the ways God makes us like Jesus is by allowing us to express our faith in Him through waiting?

In Proverbs, Solomon points out the natural truism that "Hope deferred makes the heart sick, but a longing fulfilled is a tree of life" (Proverbs 13:12). But Paul's testimony that "our present sufferings are not worth comparing with the glory that will be revealed in us" (Romans 8:18) is a powerful reminder that God may not be early—but He's always right on time with just what we need.

Is your soul weary with worry? Are you frustrated waiting to know what God wants to do in your life? Hold on. God is on the way right now.

Dear God, my confidence is in you. I know you will deliver me and meet my needs at just the right moment.

Renewal

But those who hope in the Lord will renew their strength.
They will soar on wings like eagles; they will run and
not grow weary, they will walk and not be faint.

—ISAIAH 40:31

I n a world that can wear us down mentally, physically, and spiritually, how do we renew our strength? What do we do in the face of too many projects, too many temptations, too many conflicts, and too many other soul- and energy-sapping dynamics at work in life?

Others might help you. Great. But don't put your hope in them. You might be able to muster some more determination to get the job done. Wonderful. But don't even place your hope in yourself. The only place to turn for a renewed spirit is the One who has given you every good and perfect gift, including any strength or talent you were born with. What a wonderful promise, that we can run without growing weary!

So how is your day? How has your week been going? How does this month look to be shaping up for you? Are you hopeful and inspired? Or are you discouraged? Either way, place your hope in the Lord, and let Him renew your strength, so that you can run and not grow weary.

Heavenly Father, you truly are the source of my hope for today, tomorrow, and all the days ahead of me. Thank you.

Pray Scripture

If you remain in me and my words remain in you, ask
whatever you wish, and it will be done for you.

—JOHN 15:7

James, the brother of Jesus, tells us, "The prayer of a righteous person is powerful and effective" (James 5:16). When we face hard times, prayer can sustain us like nothing else—both the prayers of others and the continual prayers we offer for our own situation.

Perhaps one of the most effective ways to pray powerfully is to pray the words of Scripture. Just as Jesus responded to temptation with Scripture, so we can experience spiritual victory with the Word of God.

Pray God's promises and ask for their fulfillment in your life. Pray that those close to you will follow God's path for them. Pray for His kingdom to come, for His will to be done on earth as it is in heaven. There can be no better words of comfort, strength, healing, love, and hope than the very words and thoughts of God as revealed in His Word.

A final blessing to consider is that when we pray to God with words from Scripture, we can pray with incredible confidence, knowing that we are praying His will.

Father, God, thank you for your Word, which is powerful. I pray that my prayer life will become more powerful and effective. May my prayers move hearts and mountains.

The Power of One Day

Then he said to the crowd, "If any of you wants to be my follower, you must give up your own way, take up your cross daily, and follow me."

—LUKE 9:23

A ttending church once a week probably isn't enough spiritual nourishment to cover the other six days. Most of the important things in life—a marriage, raising a kid, a career, a reputation—require daily attention.

No wonder the power of our daily habits is woven throughout God's Word.

- God's mercies are new every single day (Lamentations 3:23).
- God's strength is provided for us each day to meet the challenges of that particular day (Deuteronomy 33:25).
- Jesus calls us to follow Him daily (Luke 9:23).

If we were to list all the verses that talk about the importance of a single day and our daily activities, that list alone would give us enough to study for an entire year. That's why I'm so certain that spending time each day with God—in His Word, in prayer, in reflection of His love and plans for you—will make a tremendous positive difference in your life and spirit. It will become your source of spiritual power.

Are you spending time with God every day?

Mighty God, forgive me for the times when I have not paid attention to my relationship with you. Thank your for walking with me each day.

Living by Principle

Do everything without grumbling or arguing, so that
you may become blameless and pure, "children of God
without fault in a warped and crooked generation." Then
you will shine among them like stars in the sky.

—PHILIPPIANS 2:14–15

A CLASSIC DEVOTION BY JAMES ALLEN
(NINETEENTH CENTURY)

The man that stands upon a principle is the same calm, daunt-less, self-possessed man under all circumstances. When the hour of trial comes, and he has to decide between his personal comforts and Truth, he gives up his comforts and remains firm. Even the prospect of torture and death cannot alter or deter him.

The man of self regards the loss of his wealth, his comforts, or his life as the greatest calamities which can befall him. The man of principle looks upon these incidents as comparatively insignificant, and not to be weighed with loss of character, or loss of Truth. To desert Truth is, to him, the only happening which can really be called a calamity.

Rather than desert that principle of Divine Love on which he rested, and in which all his trust was placed, Jesus endured the utmost extremity of agony and deprivation; and today the world prostrates itself at his pierced feet in rapt adoration.

Father God, strengthen me inside that I may stand true no matter what the external circumstances.

I Will Uphold You

So do not fear, for I am with you; do not be dismayed,
for I am your God. I will strengthen you and help you;
I will uphold you with my righteous right hand.

—ISAIAH 41:10

Fear is wired into our brains, a part of our physiology. John, Jesus's "beloved disciple," contrasts fear and love in 1 John 4:18—the two are complete opposites. And if God is love, He is the solution to out-of-control fear. Whatever you're afraid of, surrender that fear to a loving relationship with God. If you're afraid of the past, remember that He makes all things new. If you dread the future, meditate on His purpose and plans for you. If you fear the loss of relationships, remember that He will never leave you, and then ask Him to help you nurture love and closeness with those around you. And if you fear dying or losing someone, remember that He has conquered death.

Per John Newton: "If the Lord be with us, we have no cause of fear. His eye is upon us, His arm over us, His ear open to our prayer, His grace sufficient, His promise unchangeable."

Fear can be a formidable foe. But God is truly able to help us expel it from our lives.

Father, I know that you can do anything. I ask for your spirit to fill me with your love so that I might be free from fear.

JULY

16

Desiring God

He gives strength to the weary and increases the power of the weak.

—ISAIAH 40:29

As humans, we are not immune to hardships. For Christians and non-Christians alike, a part of living here on earth is dealing with all the hardships that befall those in a fallen world. However, we as Christians are able to access our faith and know our God, finding strength in the Lord in tough times by turning to Him for help.

When we ask God for aid in such times, what are we really asking for? Are we asking for God to use His strength to solve our problems, or are we asking for personal strength? Most often, God's answer to our prayer can be found in increased capacities to trust His promises, to trust Him and not lose heart. God provides us with strength in good times and in bad. Despite the temptation to perceive moments of hardship as abandonment from God, there is always a message within our suffering.

When you face the inevitable hardships of life, realize this is an opportunity to trust God more and to experience His strength.

Almighty God, thank you for providing the strength I need in all situations in life.

Stay Connected

I am the vine; you are the branches. If you remain in me and I in you, you will bear much fruit; apart from me you can do nothing.

—JOHN 15:5

I'd like to do more. But honestly, I am worn out taking care of myself and my own family. I just don't have anything left in the tank to give to others. I feel guilty, but I'm being realistic.

Movement, growth, work, heavy lifting, serving, life itself—all require energy. The power source for the Christian life is connection to Jesus Christ. Jesus paints a picture of a vineyard. It may spread over acres, but every living branch that bears fruit is connected to the vine.

Maybe we need to first take a step backward and ask ourselves a few simple questions: How connected am I to Jesus Christ? Am I close to Him? Does He have my faith and love? Am I living and serving with a sense of His love for me?

It's amazing how everything falls into place when those questions are answered positively, particularly when it comes to having the power to serve. You just might discover you have hidden streams of life flowing within you. You just might discover you have a lot more energy than you ever dreamed of.

Are you bearing fruit? Are you serving others joyfully? Are you connected to the vine?

Heavenly Father, I love you and want nothing more than to be close to you. Fill me with your power from within.

A Faithful Heart

The worries of this life, the deceitfulness of wealth and the desires
for other things come in and choke the word, making it unfruitful.

—MARK 4:19

Would you consider someone likely to be highly success-ful who was conceived out of wedlock? Who was born into a poor family? Who lost his father at an early age? Who was looked down on because of his race? Who was a simple manual laborer? Who was from a small town that was barely a dot on the map? Who depended on the gifts of others for food and shelter? Who was scorned by the religious and political leaders of his day? Who was arrested and imprisoned? Who was executed as a criminal?

Jesus, from an obscure country and city at the edge of the greatest kingdom in the world of its day, was all those things—and yet He changed the world. Jesus set aside all the trappings of worldly success in order to bring glory to His Heavenly Father (John 10:17).

There's nothing wrong with experiencing the kind of success that the world recognizes. But if the choice before you is the applause of the world or the applause of heaven, only one reward is worth pursuing.

Faithful Savior, keep me faithful for all the days of my life.

The Right Place at the Right Time

"For if you remain silent at this time, relief and
deliverance for the Jews will arise from another place,
but you and your father's family will perish."

—ESTHER 4:14

Esther was a beautiful young Jewish woman living in Persia who was raised by her cousin Mordecai as a daughter. Esther was taken to the house of Xerxes, King of Persia, to become one of his many wives. Her beauty and character were remarkable, and Xerxes appointed her as his queen.

Haman, an advisor to the king, hatched a plot of revenge. The evil man planned to exterminate every Jew living in the city of Sousa.

Mordecai appealed Esther to speak to the king on behalf of her people. This was dangerous because anyone who came into the king's presence without being summoned could be put to death. Esther fasted for three days, then went to the king. He welcomed her. Her faith won the king's favor, saving her people.

God's deliverance does not always show up in the form of a miracle. In this case, His providence put Esther in the right place at the right time. Deliverance came through the courageous faithfulness of His servant.

Has God put you in a particular place to make a difference?

Dear God, give me to courage to stand up for what is right. Thank you for putting me in the right place at the right time.

Just as He Promised

He has helped his servant Israel, remembering
to be merciful to Abraham and his descendants
forever, just as He promised our ancestors.

—LUKE 1:54–55

O ne of the amazing things about people of great faith is that they not only celebrate God's faithfulness to His promises after they have become reality in their lives, but people of great faith recognize His promises as something complete and finished even before they have come to pass. Mary had an awesome and simple faith that God had already fulfilled His promise to her even before the birth of Jesus.

When Mary went to visit her cousin Elizabeth, Elizabeth was filled with the Holy Spirit and prophesied over her: "Blessed are you among women, and blessed is the child you will bear! But why am I so favored, that the mother of my Lord should come to me? …Blessed is she who has believed that the Lord would fulfill His promises to her!" (Luke 1:42–43, 45).

To receive such affirmation from a loved one made Mary feel like she was hearing words directly from God.

When you feel doubts, when people question your faith, are you able to declare all will come to pass just as He promises?

Heavenly Father, you have always been true to me. I praise you and thank you for your favor and your promises in my life. I am truly blessed.

The Habits of Strength

Like newborn babies, crave pure spiritual milk, so that by it you may grow up in your salvation, now that you have tasted that the Lord is good.

—1 PETER 2:2-3

A CLASSIC DEVOTION FROM JOHN OF THE CROSS (SIXTEENTH CENTURY)

It must be known that the soul, after it has surrendered to the service of God, is nurtured and loved by Him, even as the newborn child is nurtured by its loving mother, who keeps it warm and cared for in her arms.

...Yet these new souls, even though taking part with great efficacy, persistence, and care, often find themselves, spiritually speaking, very weak and imperfect. For since they are moved to these things by the consolation and pleasure that they find in them, and since they have not been prepared for them through the practice of discipline, they have many faults and imperfections.

After all, any man's actions correspond to the habit of perfection attained by him. And, as these individuals have not had the opportunity to acquire these habits of strength, it will be clearly seen how like children they are in all they do. And it will also be seen how many blessings the dark night brings with it, since it cleanses the soul and purifies it from all these imperfections.

God of strength, I pray that I attain the strength to make a difference for you in my world.

Strong Words and a Strong Walk

*But to the wicked person, God says: "What right have you
to recite my laws or take my covenant on your lips? You
hate my instruction and cast my words behind you."*

— PSALM 50:16-17

W hat does God think of people who speak the Word
with their lips but live an entirely different life with
their actions? When He says, "I will tear you to pieces" (Psalm
50:22), the answer to that question is perhaps too emphatic to
keep us comfortable.

Today is not so different from biblical days. So many live a
life where their seen and unseen actions do not remotely match
up with the words they claim. People walk in sin and wonder
why God doesn't seem to be at work in their lives.

God's heart for us is to not only proclaim truth, but walk in
the power of truth, not living as we please, but living to please
God. To live in victory, acknowledge any besetting sin in your
life, confess it, and ask the Lord to continue to strengthen you
in your pursuit of truth, that your words and actions may be as
one. The joy, peace, and freedom that reign on the other side of
obedience are incomparable.

**Father, may my thoughts, my words, and my actions all
proclaim your truth.**

JULY

23

First Thing in the Morning

In the morning, Lord, you hear my voice; in the morning
I lay my requests before you and wait expectantly.

—PSALM 5:3

Does an athlete wake up a few minutes before an important competition, throw on a uniform, bounce into the parking lot minutes before the meet or match, and then secure a victory? Well, the successful ones don't. Watching swimmers and runners and other great athletes in the Olympics, I am reminded of their commitment to training and a lifestyle of constant preparation. Some of their warm-ups would be more than a workout for many of us!

How about our spiritual lives? Do we share this same commitment to preparation?

To be aware of God's favor and presence in every moment of your day is one of the greatest treasures you'll ever discover. That discovery happens when you "look up" in the morning and throughout the day, getting your attitude and expectations attuned to hearing God's voice.

Prepare for life every morning. Open your eyes, take a breath, and then thank God for the new day. Look to heaven and ask God for wisdom, direction, and courage, that your life may be a blessing to everyone you encounter.

In the morning I will look up to you for guidance and strength, to express my love and gratitude to you, my Lord.

Climb God's Mountain

As for me, I call to God, and the Lord saves me.

—PSALM 55:16

W e have an enemy that would discourage and destroy us. He attacks as a lion and as an angel, but he also tries to sap our strength through other people.

In Psalm 55, David describes the fear and pain of broken trust at the hands of people he thought loved and supported him. His first response is that he just wants to run away. We have felt the same way. It is so easy to start to build walls of protection around our hearts so we don't get hurt again. But this is not the way forward.

Have you been betrayed by a loved one? Follow in the footsteps of David. Confidently climb the mountain of the Lord. He will save you and restore your strength. No person, no power, no circumstance can rob you of the joy of walking with the Lord.

If others have wounded and weakened you, don't run. Don't surrender what God has given you. Nothing can separate you from God's love and presence. Now is the time to climb God's mountain in prayer.

God of heaven, I call upon you now. I don't have the strength to handle my problems by myself. I turn to you!

Helping Hands

*Only Luke is with me. Get Mark and bring him with
you, because he is helpful to me in my ministry.*

—2 TIMOTHY 4:11

Herman Ostry's barn floor was under 29 inches of water after a flood. He needed a miracle—and fast—to salvage his barn and be ready for winter. He needed to move his entire 17,000 pound barn to a new foundation 143 feet away.

After one practice lift, 344 volunteers slowly walked the barn up a slight incline, each supporting less than 50 pounds. In just three minutes, the barn was on its new foundation. And Herman had his miracle.

If you're holding out for a miracle today, don't be surprised if the one God sends you comes at the hands of your friends and neighbors. We can always count on Him to come through, but He very often uses those nearest to us to see us through a difficult time.

There are some things in life that only we can do. We are strongest when we work as a team. Ask God to connect you with a group of fellow believers who will help you lift the heavy loads in life. You just might experience a miracle.

Father, send people into my life that I can bless, that can bless me, and that we can bless you and your work together.

JULY

26

The Prayer of Jabez

*Jabez cried out to the God of Israel, "Oh, that you would
bless me and enlarge my territory! Let your hand be with me,
and keep me from harm so that I will be free from pain."*

—1 CHRONICLES 4:10

B ruce Wilkinson's bestselling book, *The Prayer of Jabez*, introduced to millions of people a little-known character from the Bible. He is mentioned in only two verses. His prayer is printed above. The heart of Jabez's prayer is that he wanted more land, which would mean more wealth and influence.

Isn't that selfish? Isn't that self-centered prayer?

Wilkinson points out that the prayer is not just about material blessing, but is even more so about spiritual blessing: "But when, in faith, you start to pray for more ministry, amazing things occur. As your opportunities expand, your ability and resources supernaturally increase too."

Jabez's prayer is ultimately about receiving greater strength to do greater things.

Yes, we need to be happy where we are and with what we have. But God has a plan and a purpose for our life. That often means stretching our spiritual muscles and asking Him for more so we can do more.

Are you ready to expand your territory?

Father, keep my heart open and ready to grow into new opportunities, most of all in my service to you.

217

Roll Up Your Sleeves

Therefore, with minds that are alert and fully sober, set your hope on the grace to be brought to you when Jesus Christ is revealed at His coming. As obedient children, do not conform to the evil desires you had when you lived in ignorance.

—1 PETER 1:13-14

"Idleness is the devil's workshop" is not a quote from the Bible, but it has its roots in Scripture. Paul writes further about the danger of idleness in one of his letters: "They get into the habit of being idle and going about from house to house. And not only do they become idlers, but also busybodies who talk nonsense, saying things they ought not to" (1 Timothy 5:13).

Idleness is not the same as rest. The Bible commands us to rest (the Sabbath), and taking breaks from work is good. Being lazy means we are doing nothing when we should be doing something.

We live in a sinful world. A person who doesn't have something particular to do will invariably be more tempted to fall into sin. Satan is very eager to supply us with things to do when we are idle.

Do you need to roll up your sleeves, beginning today?

Thank you, Heavenly Father, that you are a God of love and mercy. Thank you also that you expect my best—and that you provide the strength and grace I need to please you with my life.

JULY

28

A Quiet Confidence

Do any of the worthless idols of the nations bring rain? Do the
skies themselves send down showers? No, it is you, Lord our God.
Therefore our hope is in you, for you are the One who does all this.

—JEREMIAH 14:22

A CLASSIC DEVOTION FROM MATTHEW HENRY (SEVENTEENTH CENTURY)

Those who deal with God will find it is not in vain to trust in Him; for, one, He is good to those who do so. He is good to all; His tender mercies are over all His works; all His creatures taste of His goodness. But He is in a particular manner good to those who wait for Him, to the soul that seeks Him.

Two, those who do so will find it good for them; it is good (it is our duty, and will be our unspeakable comfort and satisfaction) to hope and quietly wait for the salvation of the Lord; to hope that it will come, though the difficulties that lie in the way of it seem insupportable, to wait till it does come, though it be long delayed; and while we wait, to be quiet and silent, not quarreling with God, nor making ourselves uneasy, but acquiescing in the divine disposals; *Father, thy will be done.* If we call this to mind, we may have hope that all will end well at last.

Father, I want your will for my life, knowing that is when I serve you and others with strength and confidence.

I Can Do All This

I can do all this through Him who gives me strength.

—PHILIPPIANS 4:13

But isn't saying "I can do all this" the same as bragging?
It would be were it not for the rest of the verse: "through Him who gives me strength."

The main reason Paul was so careful to clarify what he boasted in, only the Cross, was that he didn't want anyone to think that human intelligence, ability, and effort could compare to the grace of God.

It is clear Paul's confidence and hope are built in the power of Christ alone. And that is exactly what makes his pronouncement that "I can do all this" so authentic and bold. If he was wishy-washy in his beliefs and took some credit for his deeds, past and present, no way could he have made such a strong statement.

Where is your hope and confidence? If it is in Him who gives you strength, you too can do all things.

Mighty God, thank you for the power that is mine through complete trust in you.

Words of Strength

*The Lord is my strength and defense; He has become
my salvation. He is my God, and I will praise Him,
my father's God, and I will exalt Him.*

—EXODUS 15:2

*"Anxiety does not empty tomorrow of its sorrows,
but only empties today of its strength."*

—CHARLES H. SPURGEON

*"If we desire our faith to be strengthened, we should not
shrink from opportunities where our faith may be tried,
and therefore, through trial, be strengthened."*

—GEORGE MUELLER

*"We can be tired, weary, and emotionally distraught,
but after spending time alone with God, we find that He
injects into our bodies energy, power, and strength."*

—CHARLES STANLEY

"He who stands upon his own strength will never stand."

—THOMAS BROOKS

You, O mighty God, are my strength, my hope, my joy,
my redeemer!

A Prayer for Strength

The bolts of your gates will be iron and bronze,
and your strength will equal your days.

—DEUTERONOMY 33:25

God of strength,
I am not handling all that I am facing very well at the moment. I feel like an excessive burden is always on my shoulders. There is so much to be done that I'm not accomplishing much of anything.

First of all, I pray that you help me look at my life realistically. Help me to simplify appropriately. Second, I pray that you give me a spirit that is willing to accept challenges. If my work ethic is not where it should be, I ask for my determination and resolve. If I get in trouble because I procrastinate, help me to get busy now. Third, I pray you will bring people into my life who will help me shoulder the load. Fourth, I pray you will strengthen me in every area of my life, so that the tasks before me don't feel so heavy and simply aren't as hard.

But most of all I pray that you will be my helper. Help me understand that you will not allow more to come into my life than I can handle.

I pray this in the strong name of Jesus. Amen.

August
Forgiveness

We are not nearly as vigorous in appropriating God's forgiveness as He is in extending it. Consequently, instead of living in the sunshine of God's forgiveness through Christ, we tend to live under an overcast sky of guilt most of the time.

—JERRY BRIDGES

Forgiving Others

Get rid of all bitterness, rage and anger, brawling and slander,
along with every form of malice. Be kind and compassionate to one
another, forgiving each other, just as in Christ God forgave you.

—EPHESIANS 4:31–32

F orgiveness is one of the most profound, pervasive, and powerful teachings within the Bible—but also one of the most difficult! Are we required to forgive someone who abuses us? The clear and simple message of Jesus is that we are to forgive anyone and always.

But not everyone deserves to be forgiven!

This is very true. In fact, none of us deserve to be forgiven. This is what makes God's forgiveness of us so incredible and unexpected.

Does this mean that the sin against me doesn't really matter?

God never requires or asks us to minimize the pain and trauma of sin. God doesn't want us to be in denial as to what happened to us. And even after we forgive someone, it doesn't mean that all the earthly penalty is absolved. If someone has committed a crime, the legal system will still do its work.

What if I can't forgive?

Present your situation and sorrow to God and trust that He is working in your life right now, even if the feelings aren't there.

God of mercy, I confess there are people in my life whom I don't want to forgive. Grant me a heart like yours.

2

A Spiritual Roller Coaster

The law of the Lord is perfect, refreshing the soul. The statutes of the Lord are trustworthy, making wise the simple.

—PSALM 19:7

Talk about the thrill of victory and the agony of defeat in one person's spiritual life! Peter's journey with Jesus Christ was quite a roller-coaster ride. But Peter didn't stay on the spiritual roller coaster. It was he who boldly preached to the crowds in Jerusalem even when authorities warned him not to (Acts 2:14); it was he who convinced the early church that the Gospel was for all people (Acts 10:34–45); and it was he who followed his Lord in death by crucifixion at the hands of the Romans.

Every relationship—including our relationship with God—will have emotional highs and lows. And though emotions are important, what matters most is faith—knowing and believing that God loves us and that we belong to Him.

If you are at a low ebb in your walk with Jesus, ask yourself to deal with whatever issues are unresolved by seeking forgiveness, then rest in the assurance of His love for you.

Savior God, thank you for your patience with me as I grow closer to you.

The Joy of Forgiveness

Have mercy on me, O God, according to your unfailing love;
according to your great compassion blot out my transgressions.
Wash away all my iniquity and cleanse me from my sin.

—PSALM 51:1-2

A granddaughter timidly approached her grandmother to tell her of something she had done wrong. The two hugged and cried and prayed together. The granddaughter asked for forgiveness and repented. After asking for forgiveness, she promised her grandmother she would never act that way again. Ever.

Her grandmother forgave her and told her how much she appreciated her heart and her intentions. But then she added that she might not be able to keep her promise, because as long as we live on earth we will struggle with sin. Then she told her the story of King David and how he had to repent from sin numerous times—even though he was known as a man after God's heart.

Jesus saves us from our sins. He wants us not to sin. But if we do, we are to confess, repent, and ask for forgiveness, and He says that He is faithful to forgive us. God's love is a forgiving love and a nurturing love. He delights in seeing His children get it right even after we have gotten it wrong.

Father, thank you for your love that always welcomes me back home and helps me find the right path. May my life be pleasing to you today.

A Deep, Deep Love

And I pray that you, being rooted and established in love,
may have power, together with all the saints, to grasp how
wide and long and high and deep is the love of Christ.

—EPHESIANS 3:17–19

When everything around us crumbles, we will always have the love of God. No matter how bad we mess up, no matter how unloved—or unlovable—we've been, His love endures forever. His love is so deep that it's incomprehensible. Sometimes the lack of love we give and receive makes it hard for us to accept and understand that God truly loves us. But He does, and His grace can help us understand and live out the loving affection our Father has for us.

When was the last time you considered the height and depth of God's love for you? There are depths of the ocean that remain unexplored—we don't have the scientific and technical capability of going that deep. In the spiritual realm, we may never grasp the vastness of God's love. But start where you are and accept what you do understand. You'll find a haven of sweet rest.

Father, I know that you love me, but sometimes that reality is hard to accept. Help me live in your love today, and help me share it with others.

A New Heart

I will give you a new heart and put a new spirit in you; I will remove
from you your heart of stone and give you a heart of flesh.

—EZEKIEL 36:26

Suffering from congestive heart failure, the man was near death at much too young an age. He was near the top of the transplant list, but it was a race for time and he was losing. Then word came that a new heart was available from a young organ donor who lost his life. The man suffering from heart failure was rushed into surgery.

With the new heart came a new life. The recovery was slow, but steadily he was restored.

His comment in a church testimony was poignant: "I am so sorry for the young man who died for me and the family members he left behind. As a Christian, this tragic and joyous experience has made me more fully understand that God gave His only begotten son so that I could have new life, not just here on earth but for eternity. I am grateful to God for the gift of life and the sacrifice."

God gives us a new heart with new beginnings. His very best gift of life is one we will experience throughout eternity.

Father, thank you for the new life you have given me in Christ.

The Second Birth

Therefore, if anyone is in Christ, he is a new creation; the old has gone, the new has come! All this is from God, who reconciled us to Himself through Christ and gave us the ministry of reconciliation.

— **2 CORINTHIANS 5:17–18**

Think about it: you can be made new! It doesn't matter where you've been or what you've done. Even if you have failed in business. Even if you have experienced broken relationships. Even if you have been a bad parent. Even if you have been to jail. Even if you have turned your back on God and done exactly what you wanted to do—and known that everything you were doing was wrong.

With this new status as children of God, we receive a new purpose, a new mission in life. We become ambassadors for Christ's message of new life, sharing this message of hope with a world that desperately needs hope.

It doesn't matter where you've been or what you've done. What matters is where you are going through the gift of new life provided by Jesus Christ.

Are you looking backward or forward?

Lord, thank you for saving me and for giving me the precious opportunity of sharing the love you have given to me with others.

7

Renew Our Land

If my people, who are called by my name, will humble themselves and pray and seek my face and turn from their wicked ways, then I will hear from heaven, and I will forgive their sin and will heal their land.

—2 CHRONICLES 7:14

A CLASSIC DEVOTION FROM ROBERT MURRAY M'CHEYNE (NINETEENTH CENTURY)

The Lord Jesus has been making Himself known and the Holy Spirit has been quickening whom He will. Still in most parts of our land, it is to be feared that God is a stranger. How few conversions are there in the midst of us?

In times of reviving, when God is present with power in any land, not only are unconverted persons awakened to Christ, but those who were in Christ before receive new measures of the Spirit; they are brought into the palace of the King, and say, "let Him kiss me with the kisses of His mouth, for Thy love is better than wine." How little of this feeling is there among us! How plain that God is a stranger in the land!

How great is the boldness of sinners in sin. When God is present with power, then open sinners, though they may remain unconverted, are often much restrained. There is an awe of God upon their spirits.

Should we not solemnly ask ourselves, "Why is God such a stranger in this land?"

Loving Heavenly Father, bring revival and renewal to our land.

All My Sins

Look upon my affliction and my distress and take away all my sins.

—PSALM 25:18

The enemy has always had a great way of trying to keep each of us tied to past sin, weighing us down with the sorrow of pain and regret. Feeling heavy under the weight of knowing you made stupid mistakes, will, if you allow it, cripple you for life. We have all fallen short of God's best for our lives. There is no one on earth who has not made mistakes and fallen into the trap of sin.

But walking in the miracle of forgiveness gives God much glory. The ability to live life without the snares and chains of the past is one of the most glorious surprises you discover after asking the Lord for forgiveness. Do you remember feeling almost light when you were first saved? It's the literal removal of the weightiness of sin.

Take a moment to look backward, asking for forgiveness if you need to. But then step forward to face whatever task God has laid before you, knowing you are whole and free.

Heavenly Father, saturate us in the love and forgiveness of your son. Help us discover who we truly are and be ready to serve you like we never have before.

Precious Blood

For you know that it was not with perishable things such as
silver or gold that you were redeemed from the empty way
of life handed down to you from your ancestors, but with the
precious blood of Christ, a lamb without blemish or defect.

—1 PETER 1:18-20

In most cases from biblical times, redeeming a person from the grievous sin of slavery was accomplished by the exchange of money for a human life. The Apostle Peter wrote his letters to scattered Christians throughout the Roman Empire. Slavery was almost universally accepted and practiced. In describing the cost of redeeming them from a life of sin, Peter makes sure Christians know it did not happen with silver or gold, the two most valuable metals of his day. No, redemption was bought with something much more valuable: the precious blood of Jesus.

Jesus lived a perfect life, which meant He was the perfect sacrifice. By His death on the Cross, He did for us what we could not do ourselves, both in salvation and in godly living.

When was the last time you stopped to ponder the cost of your salvation? You were not bought with coins, but with the precious blood of the Lamb of God.

Father, thank you for the ultimate sacrifice of your son Jesus Christ.

The Old You, the New You

*If we have been united with Him like this in His death, we will
certainly also be united with Him in His resurrection.*

—ROMANS 6:5

Life is filled with experiences where two things, one positive
and one negative, happen at the same time.

- We move to a new location and leave friends and the familiar behind.
- A couple exchanges wedding vows to become one, leaving behind their primary family relationships.
- A graduate makes new friends at college but says goodbye to high school classmates.

Some of these experiences are bittersweet. But there is one
experience that, while it includes a loss, is only positive: salvation. When we receive new life in Christ, something else, our
"old man," that part of us that rebelled against God, is destroyed.

Does this mean we lose all desire to sin? No, sin will continue
to hold a certain allure. What dies is our slavery to sin that comes
from being an enemy of God. Now that we have received forgiveness and salvation into our lives, our desire is to live for Him and
please Him. Just as Christ's crucifixion was painful and prolonged,
our battle with sin will take time and will cause us pain.

**Father, thank you for your redemption and restoration, for
making my heart brand-new.**

The God of the Living

He is not the God of the dead, but of the
living, for to Him all are alive.

—LUKE 20:38

From the very start of His public ministry, Jesus had enemies, particularly among the religious leaders. Critics and skeptics hounded Jesus with questions and objections to His teachings and ministry. A Sadducee, a teacher who didn't believe in the afterlife, tried to make Jesus look foolish by asking who a woman would be married to in heaven if her first husband died and she had taken a second husband (see Luke 20:27–39).

As He often did, Jesus simply hijacked the question and made the bold proclamation that all that really matters is whether you—the Sadducee, the other listeners, and each of us reading His words today—have been made new and have personally experienced the power of the resurrection.

Being made new doesn't happen through being religious or being a good person. It's a miracle we must ask for and receive as a gift from God. What is it based on? Jesus's resurrection.

Have you been made alive?

Father, I pray that you will make me alive through the power of Christ's resurrection.

Changing Names

Then Saul, who was also called Paul, filled with the Holy Spirit.

—ACTS 13:9

He was educated at the highest levels in both law and theology. He was an international traveler, aware and sophisticated in the ways of the world. A young leader with all the right connections, he was climbing the career ladder at a rapid pace. Devout. Respected. Even feared. But he was a man at war with himself. He was Saul.

On his way to Damascus, a trip where he planned to strike a violent blow against this new branch of the Jewish faith that was spreading like wildfire, he encountered the risen Christ. He was struck blind, and Jesus spoke to him in an audible voice: "Saul! Saul! Why do you persecute me?" (Acts 22:7).

From that moment, the persecutor became a preacher; the man who was roiling inside with turmoil came to inner peace. Saul was renamed by God Himself and became Paul. Meeting the risen Lord changes everything!

Thank you for giving me a new life and new heart when I met you, God.

Forgive to Live

Therefore, as God's chosen people, holy and dearly loved, clothe yourselves with compassion, kindness, humility, gentleness and patience. Bear with each other and forgive whatever grievances you may have against one another. Forgive as the Lord forgave you.

COLOSSIANS 3:12-13

Grudges and grievances. We feel them; we welcome them; we ponder them; they grow; they make themselves at home in our lives. But eventually, grudges rob us of joy and spirituality through Christ. What we think is going to protect and boost our precious self is the thing that gnaws at it and diminishes it.

The antidote to holding onto grudges is simple. Not easy, but simple. Forgiveness. Not holding someone's wrongs against them. Considering their slights and any injury they have caused as for naught, as if what they had done never happened to us.

Will they accept our forgiveness? Did they even ask for it? Those questions are on their heart. They have to resolve that for themselves.

Take care of your heart. That's what you are responsible for. Go ahead and say it. *I forgive you.* A simple phrase. A difficult task. But a task commanded, empowered, and rewarded by God!

Lord, I forgive others as you have forgiven me.

A Pursuing Love

What do you think? If a man owns a hundred sheep, and one
of them wanders away, will he not leave the ninety-nine on
the hills and go to look for the one that wandered off?

—MATTHEW 18:12

A CLASSIC DEVOTION FROM DONALD BARNHOUSE (TWENTIETH CENTURY)

The pursuing love of God is the greatest wonder of the spiritual universe. We leave God in the heat of our own self-desire and run from His will because we want so much to have our own way. We get to a crossroads and look back in pride, thinking that we have outdistanced Him. Just as we are about to congratulate ourselves on our achievement of self-enthronement, we feel a touch on our arm and turn in that direction to find Him there.

"My child," He says in great tenderness, "I love you; and when I saw you running away from all that is good, I pursued you through a shortcut that love knows well, and awaited you here at the crossroads."

He will always say, "My child, my name and nature are Love, and I must act according to that which I am. So it is that I have pursued you, to tell you that when you are tired of your running and your wandering, I will be there to draw you to myself once more."

Gracious and loving God, thank you for pursuing me when I had turned my back on you.

15

Clean Hands

*I have been blameless before Him and have kept myself from
sin. The Lord has rewarded me according to my righteousness,
according to the cleanness of my hands in His sight.*

—PSALM 18:23-24

It is not by works that we are saved, and our own righteous acts are as filthy rags before Him, so what then is David talking about? If you read this text in the spirit it was written, you will see that the man after God's own heart, having been slandered, takes a stand, voicing his integrity and vigorously defending his character.

Charles Spurgeon points out: "There is no self-righteousness in an honest man knowing he is honest, nor even in believing that God rewards him because of his honesty, for such is often a most evident matter of fact; but it would be self-righteousness indeed if we transferred such thoughts...into the rule of the spiritual kingdom, for there grace reigns not only supreme but sole in the distribution of divine favors."

A life lived under the light of truth will bring rewards—just as God intended—but we must always remember where our help comes from and give the Lord all the glory due to His wonderful name.

Father, you have called for me to live a life of purity, which enables me to serve you with power. Cleanse me from anything that is not pleasing to you.

Restore the Joy of My Salvation

Restore to me the joy of your salvation and
grant me a willing spirit, to sustain me.

—PSALM 51:12

How can you mess up worse than David did? The poet-warrior king was known as a man who had God's heart inside him. He did many great things and withstood many bad in his love for God. But in a season of weakness, he looked at another man's wife in lust, which started a series of escalating events that culminated in David having the husband killed in order to cover up his sin. It doesn't get much worse than that.

David doesn't just want forgiveness, he wants to be made new: "Create in me a pure heart, O God, and renew a steadfast spirit within me. Do not cast me from your presence or take your Holy Spirit from me. Restore to me the joy of your salvation and grant me a willing spirit, to sustain me" (Psalm 51:10–12).

Have you lost the joy of your salvation? Have you lost a sense of God's presence in your life? Are you trapped in a pattern of sin? Go to Him for cleansing and to be given a new heart.

God of forgiveness, plant a new heart inside of me that I might not sin against you.

A Living Sacrifice

Therefore, I urge you, brothers and sisters, in view of God's
mercy, to offer your bodies as a living sacrifice, holy and
pleasing to God—this is your true and proper worship.

—ROMANS 12:1

You cannot tie apples to a telephone pole and call it an apple tree. Even if the apples look delicious, they will soon wither. They are not connected to a life force.

Paul spends the first eleven chapters of Romans establishing that salvation is a gift from God; there is no justification before Him on the basis of our works.

But in chapter 12 of Romans, Paul makes a major transition, using the word "therefore." Based on everything God has done for you, in view of His mercy, there is something you need to do. You need to offer yourself as a living sacrifice. With that statement, Paul shows that good works, obedience, sacrifice, commitment, discipline, and lifestyle are a huge part of what it means to be a Christian. Because of God's mercy—His gift of new life through the blood of Jesus—Paul urges us to offer ourselves as living sacrifices.

Worship is our response to the overtures of love from the heart of the Father. Have you given yourself completely to God as your spiritual worship?

Heavenly Father, thank you for your mercy that gave me new life. I give that life to you.

Get Rid of the Extra Weight

*Let us throw off everything that hinders and
the sin that so easily entangles.*

—HEBREWS 12:1

Paul often used images from athletic competition to make a spiritual point. He said to Timothy: "Train yourself to be godly. For physical training is of some value, but godliness has value for all things, holding promise for both the present life and the life to come" (1 Timothy 4:7–8).

When we ask for forgiveness, we throw off the sin that so easily entangles us. But God wants us to rid our lives of other things that, while they may not be sinful, certainly don't encourage and often hinder our Christian journey.

Have you made some compromises that foster sin in your life? Do you have interests and habits that are a spiritual hindrance and entanglement? Don't mess around. Don't try to float by. Get rid of—throw off—anything that keeps you from walking in God's grace fully. It is game time.

Thank you for the gift of salvation, God. Help me to be wise to rid my life of anything that hinders my walk with you.

19

The Riches of His Grace

Let us then approach God's throne of grace with confidence, so that we may receive mercy and find grace to help us in our time of need.

—HEBREWS 4:16

D o you know how much God loves you? Not because you have lots of talents; not because you do many good deeds—though these characteristics may be abundant in your life! No, God favors you out of His deep, abiding love for you, a love that is not contingent upon any effort you put forth. Consider these dynamics of grace:

- Grace means God loved you and knew you before you were even born: "Before I formed you in the womb I knew you, before you were born I set you apart; I appointed you as a prophet to the nations" (Jeremiah 1:5).
- Grace provides the gift of salvation, a gift that can't be earned: "For it is by grace you have been saved, through faith—and this is not from yourselves, it is the gift of God—not by works, so that no one can boast" (Ephesians 2:8–9).

Whatever need you have in your life today, be assured, God is on your side. He is ready and able to help you as you respond to Him with faith.

Thank you for providing me everything I need, O Lord.

20

======= *One Solitary Life* =======

*On coming to the house, they saw the child with His
mother Mary, and they bowed down and worshiped
Him. Then they opened their treasures and presented
Him with gifts of gold, frankincense and myrrh.*

—MATTHEW 2:11

A CLASSIC DEVOTION FROM JAMES ALLEN FRANCIS (NINETEENTH CENTURY)

Here is a man who was born in an obscure village, the child of a peasant woman. He worked in a carpenter shop until He was thirty, and then for three brief years He was an itinerant preacher. While still a young man, the tide of popular feeling turned against Him. His friends ran away. One of them denied Him. He was turned over to His enemies. He went through the mockery of a trial. He was nailed to a cross between two thieves. When He was dead He was taken down and laid in a borrowed grave through the pity of a friend.

Nineteen wide centuries have come and gone and today He is the centerpiece of the human race and the leader of the column of progress. All the armies that ever marched, all the navies that ever were built, and all the parliaments that ever sat, all the kings that ever reigned, put together have not affected the life of man upon this earth as powerfully as has that One Solitary Life.

Father God, I am in awe of the one solitary life who changed my life forever.

Receive the Gift

It is we who extol the Lord, both now and forevermore. Praise the Lord.

—PSALM 115:18

A CLASSIC DEVOTION FROM THOMAS BOSTON (EIGHTEENTH CENTURY)

O the love of God to poor sinners of mankind! ...The greatest work that God ever did was for their salvation. He made the world for man and gave it to Him, and the visible heavens, too. How many have never spent a few minutes in the consideration and admiration of Him? Have you not gazed upon and wondered at some trifle more than at this greatest of the works of God? Have you not been more deeply in love with some person or thing for its shadowy excellencies than with this miraculous person?

...Be exhorted, then, to give this wonderful One your heart.

...Let your souls solemnly consent to the Gospel offer.

Part with all for Him, as the wise merchant who sold all that he had and bought the one pearl of great price.

Dwell in the contemplation of His matchless excellencies. Let it be the substance of your religion to love Him, to admire Him, to be swallowed up in His love.

Redeemer God, as I contemplate your matchless gift of salvation, I renew my love and commitment to you today.

Hidden Sin

*Whoever conceals their sins does not prosper, but the
one who confesses and renounces them finds mercy.*

—PROVERBS 28:13

One legend of Sparta tells of a boy who stole a fox. When he was confronted, he quickly hid it underneath his cloak, held tightly to his stomach. When asked if he stole, the boy refused to admit it. Without a sound or even a grimace, he held the fox close, though it gnawed out his entrails.

That gruesome image is a powerful portrayal of what happens to us when we refuse to confess our sins and instead hide them. They gnaw at us until our spiritual life slips away.

One of the most hope-filled and powerful passages in the Bible is found in 1 John 1:8–9: "If we claim to be without sin, we deceive ourselves and the truth is not in us. If we confess our sins, he is faithful and just and will forgive us our sins and purify us from all unrighteousness."

God doesn't want us to sin. But if and when we do, He promises forgiveness and purification—if we only confess.

Asking forgiveness is asking Jesus to remember us in His kingdom.

Father, may I not sin, but if I do, please forgive and purify me.

23

Pursuing Peace with Others

*Let us therefore make every effort to do what
leads to peace and to mutual edification.*

—ROMANS 14:19

God made peace with us through the atoning work of Jesus Christ. In the work of the Cross, He planted peace inside of us and called for us to be peacemakers.

Dr. Martin Luther King Jr. said of the peacemaker: "One day we must come to see that peace is not merely a distant goal we seek, but that it is a means by which we arrive at that goal. We must pursue peaceful ends through peaceful means."

Here are just a few of the attributes and qualities for an effective peacemaker:

- Not self-absorbed and insistent on one's own way;
- Generous and happy to share;
- Not envious of others' success and blessings;
- Not harshly critical;
- More focused on solutions than problems;
- Self-confident, not getting feelings hurt easily;
- Able to see the big picture of life, not getting lost in petty quarrels.

When others see you—and when you look in the mirror—do you see a peacemaker?

Lord, help me to bring peace into all my relationships and all areas of my own life.

His Perfect Joy

And let us run with perseverance the race marked out for us,
fixing our eyes on Jesus, the pioneer and perfecter of faith.
For the joy set before Him He endured the Cross, scorning its
shame, and sat down at the right hand of the throne of God.

—HEBREWS 12:1–2

What was Jesus's most joyful moment that we read of in Scripture? Was it when He turned the water into wine at a wedding feast to save the celebration? Was it when He fed five thousand people with only a few loaves of bread and fish to work from? Was it when He helped Zacchaeus climb down from a tree and headed to his home for a celebration of salvation? Was it when thousands sat on a hillside and hung on His every word?

Jesus was intense and serious, but He also told jokes and loved a good party. He hugged children and brought joy everywhere He went. In His final instructions, He was teaching those He loved how to have the same joy He had through closeness to God the Father. It was on the Cross that He paid the price that made this joy possible.

Next time you struggle with a sense of joy, fix your eyes on Jesus. Remember the joy He experienced even as He approached the Cross. Remember His desire that you live in joy.

Lord, thank you for the Cross that saves me and brings me to you. Thank you for the joy of knowing you. I love you.

In the Fiery Furnace

When you walk through the fire, you will not be burned; the flames will not set you ablaze.

—ISAIAH 43:2

In the biblical story of Shadrach, Meshach, and Abednego—three young men abducted from Jerusalem into Babylonia during King Nebuchadnezzar's reign—we literally see grace under fire. The three young men refused to serve any god other than the god of their fathers. When the king decreed that anyone who would not bow to an idol would be thrown into a fiery furnace, they stayed true to their principles. The king had them bound and dragged into the furnace. Amazingly, the three emerged from the flames not only unscathed, but without even the smell of smoke on them.

They believed that God would rescue them. Just as importantly, they determined, even if He did not, they would not bow down to an idol. They had faith in God and faithfulness to Him. One tends to feed the other.

Maybe you aren't facing a fiery furnace today, but you probably have your own tests of faith. If you cultivate faithfulness like Shadrach, Meshach, and Abednego's, your faith will grow. And you just might witness the impossible.

Lord, please give me the faith and confidence in you so that I will always exhibit faith under fire.

The Right Motivation

But God demonstrates His own love for us in this:
While we were still sinners, Christ died for us.

—ROMANS 5:8

M arie was overweight and suffering from hypertension and the first stages of diabetes. Following her doctor's advice, she and her husband purchased a treadmill to combat her conditions. For several days, she trudged along on it faithfully. Before long, however, she quit with a list of excuses.

"It's boring" was the first. Her husband mounted a television on the wall above the treadmill.

"It's too hot." Her husband purchased a fan.

"My feet are hurting," she moaned. Together, they went shopping and bought her a pair of walking shoes.

Marie eventually understood her husband's deep concern for her—he only wanted her to be healthy. She decided to walk faithfully and quit making excuses.

Somehow it's easier to persevere when we're doing so for someone we love. Whatever God has asked you to do, remember that He loves you. Get yourself into the presence of the loving Father. Just place yourself before Him, and think of His love—His wonderful, tender love. Reflecting on His abundant love will make the task at hand lighter and easier.

Lord, I know that you love me. Help me to see your love in each circumstance of my life.

27

My Heart Was Strangely Warmed

Let us draw near to God with a sincere heart in full assurance of faith, having our hearts sprinkled to cleanse us from a guilty conscience and having our bodies washed with pure water.

—HEBREWS 10:22

You can do everything right and still not feel at peace in your heart about your relationship with God. Eighteenth-century John Wesley came to America as a young man serving as a missionary. Despite all efforts, he still felt insecure and unsure of his salvation.

If Wesley had a troubled heart, what hope is there for us?

What he discovered was that peace of heart, assurance of our relationship with God, can only come from God Himself. While someone was reading from Luther's Preface to the Epistle to Romans at a prayer meeting on Aldersgate Road, he had an experience that changed his life forever:

"While he was describing the change which God works in the heart through faith in Christ, I felt my heart strangely warmed. I felt I did trust in Christ, Christ alone for salvation; and an assurance was given me that He had taken away my sins, even mine, and saved me from the law of sin and death."

If you're lacking assurance, turn to Christ alone, and your heart, too, can be "strangely warmed."

Lord, I need peace and assurance of your presence. Help me to trust in you and not my own efforts.

28

Repentance

Repent, then, and turn to God, so that your sins may be wiped
out, that times of refreshing may come from the Lord.

—ACTS 3:19

A CLASSIC DEVOTION FROM HARRY IRONSIDE (TWENTIETH CENTURY)

When the Lord Jesus, in the days of His earthly ministry, sent forth the twelve apostles to go throughout the land of Israel heralding His Word, He evidently commanded them to emphasize the same message that John the Baptist preached and which He Himself proclaimed; for we are told in Mark 6:12 that "they went out and preached that people should repent."

True, forgiveness is by faith, but there can be no faith without repentance, and no repentance without faith.

Scripture clearly teaches that God is sovereign. It just as plainly shows us that man is a responsible creature, who has the power of choice and is called upon by the Lord to exercise that power and to turn to himself: "Turn! Turn from your evil ways! Why will you die?" "Choose for yourselves this day whom you will serve." "Let the one who wishes take the free gift of the water of life."

Lord, out of love and devotion for you, I turn my heart toward you today.

Keep in Step

Since we live by the Spirit, let us keep in step with the Spirit.

—GALATIANS 5:25

What goes into living the Christian life? Many traditions of the faith have answered that question with certain emphases and nuances, but three common traits have always been part of the Christian walk:

- Faith: "Now faith is confidence in what we hope for and assurance about what we do not see" (Hebrews 11:1).
- Trust: "Though He slay me, yet will I hope in Him" (Job 13:15).
- Obedience: "But if we walk in the light, as He is in the light, we have fellowship with one another, and the blood of Jesus, His Son, purifies us from all sin" (1 John 1:7).

We don't need forgiveness only on the first day we accept Jesus Christ into our hearts. We need forgiveness and cleansing to restore us when we stumble in our walk with God. But forgiveness spurs us to obedience, and obedience in turn spurs us to our need for continued cleansing.

Walk in the light as the blood of Jesus purifies you from all sin.

Lord, I want to keep in step with the Spirit. Give me the faith and trust to obey your commands and will in all my steps.

Beautiful Words on Forgiveness

*"Don't be alarmed," he said. "You are looking for Jesus
the Nazarene, who was crucified. He has risen! He is
not here. See the place where they laid Him."*

—MARK 16:6

*All of heaven is interested in the Cross of Christ, hell afraid
of it, while men are the only ones to ignore its meaning.*

—OSWALD CHAMBERS

The entire plan for the future has its key in the resurrection.

—BILLY GRAHAM

*Christ died. He left a will in which He gave His soul to His Father,
His body to Joseph of Arimathea, His clothes to the soldiers, and
His mother to John. But to His disciples, who had left all to follow
Him, He left not silver or gold, but something far better—His peace!*

—MATTHEW HENRY

*The stone was rolled away from the door, not to permit
Christ to come out, but to enable the disciples to go in.*

—PETER MARSHALL

Loving God, I am forever grateful for the gift of your son,
Jesus Christ, who brought new life into my being.

A Prayer for Forgiveness

*As far as the east is from the west, so far has He
removed our transgressions from us.*

—PSALM 103:12

Dear God of forgiveness,

When I was lost and without you, you called me by name and spoke to me with words of mercy, forgiveness, and healing. You offered me new life and forgiveness, not the spiritual death and guilt I was living in. I will never forget the moment that I truly recognized for the first time how empty my life was without you.

I can't shake feelings of guilt over my past sins. I know there is a good conviction that leads to repentance. But I also know that, when I confess my sins, you are faithful to forgive me of all unrighteousness. I don't know why you are so loving and gracious, but I know that is your promise to me.

If there is some ongoing sin that has entangled me, I ask for forgiveness and freedom now. I receive your spiritual provision in faith.

I know in my heart that I am united with Jesus Christ—and I pray that I will experience that in my heart and emotions as well.

In Jesus's merciful name. Amen.

September

Wisdom and Knowledge

Nothing makes a man so virtuous as belief of the truth.
A lying doctrine will soon beget a lying practice. A man
cannot have an erroneous belief without by-and-by
having an erroneous life. I believe the one
thing naturally begets the other.
—CHARLES SPURGEON

The Benefits of God's Word

For the Word of God is alive and active. Sharper
than any double-edged sword.

—HEBREWS 4:12

N o other book has had a greater impact on world history than the Bible. Why is this book still so important?

- God's Word sustains spiritual life: "It is written: 'Man shall not live on bread alone, but on every word that comes from the mouth of God'" (Matthew 4:4). The writer of Hebrews tells us that it is spiritual sustenance (5:12–14); Paul says it is refreshing water (Ephesians 5:26); Solomon says it is medicine for our soul (Proverbs 4:22); for Job, it was his daily bread (23:12).

- God's Word keeps us from sin: "How can a young person stay on the path of purity? By living according to your word" (Psalm 119:9). If more Christians in the world read, studied, and memorized God's Word, fewer would fall into the trap of temptation.

- God's Word makes us wise: "The law of the Lord is perfect, refreshing the soul. The statutes of the Lord are trustworthy, making wise the simple" (Psalm 19:7).

God's Word is enduring and will keep us on the path to eternal life.

All-knowing God, I do want to walk in your wisdom. I turn my heart and mind to better knowing your Word.

Get Away from the Noise

And pray in the Spirit on all occasions with all kinds of
prayers and requests. With this in mind, be alert and
always keep on praying for all the Lord's people.

—EPHESIANS 6:18

At the beginning of His ministry, despite having so much to do in such a short amount of time, Jesus pulled away from everyone to spend forty days in the wilderness to pray and fast. While alone, Jesus was tested three times by Satan, but each time answered the challenge with Scripture and a profound sense of His purpose (Matthew 4:1–11).

At the end of His earthly life, Jesus pulled away from the crowds to pray alone in the garden of Gethsemane (Mark 14:35–36). It was there, with the agony of the Cross just before Him, that He reaffirmed His most earnest desire: "Not my will, but yours be done" (Luke 22:42).

If Jesus Christ sought solitude and quiet, how much more important is it for us? We can come to the end of the day—or the week or even the month—and discover that we made no time at all to be alone with God. Your soul will thrive as you pull away from the noise to hear the voice of your Father.

Thank you for inviting me to spend time with just you, O God, the One who knows me best and loves me most.

First Things First

*"Few things are needed—or indeed only one. Mary has chosen
what is better, and it will not be taken away from her."*

—LUKE 10:42

I n Luke 10, we discover that Martha holds deep resentment toward a younger sibling. Mary, her younger sister, is not immoral, but she certainly doesn't have Martha's sense of responsibility. She leaves the dishes and chores to her sister so that she can sit at Jesus's feet.

Wouldn't you feel a little resentful too? Jesus's answer to Martha's demand that He tell Mary to get busy is: "'Martha, Martha,' the Lord answered, 'you are worried and upset about many things, but few things are needed—or indeed only one. Mary has chosen what is better, and it will not be taken away from her'" (Luke 10:41–42).

Is Jesus's point that we not care for our responsibilities? Of course not. But He does remind us that the heart of our faith, our reason for living, is to love and worship God. Nothing else comes first!

Lord, you come first in my life, before any other relationship or responsibility.

Wait for God's Best

The Lord bestows favor and honor; no good thing does
He withhold from those whose walk is blameless.

—PSALM 84:11

Children can be impulsive and often want everything "now!" It is the wise parent who does not give in to every demand, but rather keeps some things on hold until the time is right.

God deals with us the same way. He makes every good thing available to His children—but only in the right time. As our Father, He loves to prepare us for all that He has for us to know and enjoy. But out of fatherly wisdom, He trains us to trust Him—even when we want something right now—so that we will become mature, Christlike adults, who are better able to appreciate and enjoy His blessings.

Do you remember a time when you made a big decision or purchase when you really weren't ready for it? Most of us have. This is where we need to grow in trust. There is a right season for everything.

To try and move ahead of God's perfect plan for us is to deny Him the privilege of teaching us and watching us grow to be like Him.

Father, how grateful I am for the good things you have brought into my life, but even more so, for the blessing of your hand of guidance. Help me to wait for you.

Abide in Me

Remain in me, as I also remain in you. No branch can bear fruit by itself; it must remain in the vine. Neither can you bear fruit unless you remain in me.

—JOHN 15:4

If someone told you that they really loved you, but never wanted to spend any time with you, would you believe them? Not for a second! But that's how many of us treat God. We tell Him we love Him, but never find time for Him. Jesus, shortly before His death and resurrection, tells His disciples, "Remain in me, as I also remain in you" (John 15:4). In other words, stay close to me, and I'll stay close to you. What happens when we abide in Jesus?

- He makes us fruitful (John 15:4). That means we can be more effective and successful in life than we can through any efforts separate from Him. Jesus and you together make a winning team.

- He answers our prayers (John 14:13). Can someone who isn't close to God call out to Him for help? Absolutely. God is kind and gracious to everyone. But when we are close to Jesus, we start to think the way He does, and we pray for the same things He wants done. No wonder our prayers get answered.

My Savior and my friend, thank you for the invitation to spend time together in order that I may know you and serve you more fully.

Live Smart

*We are consumed by your anger and terrified by your
indignation. You have set our iniquities before you,
our secret sins in the light of your presence.*

—PSALM 90:7-8

S ome troubles come though we have done nothing to deserve them. An illness. An accident. A betrayal. An act of evil.

But other troubles come our way because we call for them through carelessness, questionable decisions, and sin. In Psalm 90, David catalogs how hard life can be and what may befall us for our own sins. He particularly warns us that our secret sins will find us out. He experienced troubles that were not of his own making, but he also experienced heartache and woe that he brought on himself, particularly in stealing the wife of another man. No wonder he told us to live, order, and walk our days rightly (Psalm 90:12). We are wise to heed the words of one who knows.

Your life will include hardships. It rains on both the righteous and the wicked. But the key question for you is, are you the source of some of the woes that visit you? Are there thoughts and deeds in your life that are inviting trouble? Listen to David. Smarten up!

**O God, help me to walk with wisdom and righteousness
every day of my life.**

Seek God

But we do see Jesus, who was made lower than the angels for a little while, now crowned with glory and honor because He suffered death, so that by the grace of God He might taste death for everyone.

—HEBREWS 2:9

A CLASSIC DEVOTION FROM SAINT ANSELM OF CANTERBURY (ELEVENTH CENTURY)

I have never seen thee, O Lord, my God; I do not know thy form. What shall this man do, an exile far from thee? It is thou that hast made me, and hast made me anew, and hast bestowed upon me all the blessing I enjoy; and not yet do I know thee. I was created to see thee, and not yet have I done that for which I was made.

...Be it mine to look up to thy light, even from afar, even from the depths. Teach me to seek thee, and reveal thyself to me, when I seek thee, for I cannot seek thee, except thou teach me, nor find thee, except thou reveal thyself. Lord, I acknowledge and I thank thee that thou hast created me in thine image, in order that I may be mindful of thee, may conceive of thee, and love thee; but that image has been so consumed and wasted away by vices, and obscured by the smoke of wrongdoing, that it cannot achieve that for which it was made, except thou renew it, and create it anew.

Renew my spirit as I seek your face, O Lord!

God's Way or Your Way?

"But my people would not listen to me; Israel would
not submit to me. So I gave them over to their
stubborn hearts to follow their own devices."

—PSALM 81:11-12

If you've ever wondered about the wisdom of doing things God's way, of the power and joy found in obedience, then read Psalm 81 over and over until it settles in your heart.

The lessons on the blessings of obedience, love, and service are rich. We learn of the magnificent protective hand of our God. His heart toward us is indescribable. But in the end, He does not force us to do what we steadfastly reject.

What is it about God's beloved children that they demand to do things their own way? Why do we fight the hand that created us?

Even though our sinful nature fights us, if we choose to serve God and do things as He has set out for us, then His covenant protects us not only from our enemies, but from ourselves. Then we experience His plans and purpose for our lives fully.

God, sometimes obedience is hard, but not my will, but yours be done in my life.

God Still Speaks Today

In your distress you called and I rescued you, I
answered you out of a thundercloud.

—PSALM 81:7

P salm 81 begins with the command that we are to sing joyfully and shout happily to the Lord. The psalmist doesn't stop with us just using our voices. He is a musician and worship leader. He tells us to sound the tambourine and drums in our song, to add some sweet-sounding strings, and then to blow the horn boldly. None of this is to be timid. We are to make a joyful noise in praise of the Almighty God.

To take the gift of music and use it for the reason God gave it to us is nothing short of miraculous, no matter how simple or how elaborate the offering is. As long as it proclaims truth and comes from a heart of praise, our singing delights the heart of God.

But what is truly amazing is that when we sing to the Lord, He speaks back to us.

Don't let that truth slip by you. Savor the thought that the Maker of heaven and earth cares enough to bow down and speak with us.

In my praise and worship, I will listen for your voice, O God.

People of the Word

Consequently, faith comes from hearing the message, and
the message is heard through the word about Christ.

—ROMANS 10:17

Jesus was not born into the wealthiest or most powerful or most technologically advanced of nations. Israel was a small country at the crossroads of great empires that overshadowed the small tract of land. But the small kingdom projected a much bigger influence on the world than its small size. The children of God were known throughout the world as the "People of the Word."

Our culture has changed. No longer do the majority of people attend church to hear the preaching of God's Word. Family devotions, Sunday school, and other settings for instruction in God's Word have faded to the point where they are the exception and not the rule. No longer are we are a nation that is considered biblically literate. It is no surprise to see the pervasive breakdown of virtues and values.

What can be done to return to biblical values and being a modern-day people of the Word? There's one place you can start: your own life. Open God's Word and watch your faith grow!

Almighty God, thank you for the gift of your Word to bring truth and renewal into my life.

=== *The Search for Truth* ===

For the time will come when people will not put up with
sound doctrine. Instead, to suit their own desires, they
will gather around them a great number of teachers to say
what their itching ears want to hear. They will turn their
ears away from the truth and turn aside to myths.

−2 TIMOTHY 4:3-4

One of the prevailing temptations and sins of our pluralistic, highly educated culture is to view truth as relative. Nothing is absolute. Right and wrong, the attributes of God, the need and nature of salvation: essential beliefs and practices are not considered absolute, but merely suggestive. After all, there are many paths to God, right? That is the prevailing attitude of our day.

Throughout Scripture, we are told that some issues are a matter of personal conscience, so there is plenty of room for debate and personal conviction. We don't have to agree on everything, but there are essentials.

How do we know what is absolute and what involves personal conviction? There is only one sure source of revelation: God's Word. Listen to good preachers and teachers, but never let them take the place of getting to know God's Word for yourself.

Where do you seek truth?

Father in heaven, thank you for speaking directly to me through your Word.

Make a Plan

All His laws are before me; I have not turned away from His decrees.

—PSALM 18:22

Great individuals of faith have always been mighty in God's Word. Martin Luther made this note in his journal: "For some years now I have read through the Bible twice every year. If you picture the Bible to be a mighty tree and every word a little branch, I have shaken every one of these branches because I wanted to know what it was and what it meant."

How many branches have you been shaking?

Your Bible may have a reading plan near the front that will direct you to finish the whole Bible in one year. If not, there are plenty of other ways to read a wider range of Scripture than you ever have before. Do an Internet search for reading plans; some sites offer plans you can even check off as you go along. Select an unfamiliar book of the Bible each month to read.

Whatever method or plan you use, ask God to help you grow in love for His Word. It's time to start shaking some branches!

God, thank you for speaking to me through the Bible. Help me to grow more and more familiar with it.

Wisely and Well

Be very careful, then, how you live—not as unwise but as wise,
making the most of every opportunity, because the days are evil.

—EPHESIANS 5:15–16

A woman named Jessica needed an operation to remove a life-threatening tumor. The operation, however, would leave her deaf. She had no alternative but to agree to the surgery, one month later.

During that month, Jessica prepared for the transition from a sound-filled world to silence. She got a video camera in the hope that one day the images would remind her of what she had lost. She taught herself sign language. She listened to music and attended concerts.

The night before her surgery was spent laughing with family and friends. The next morning, she heard the last words she would ever hear—her mother saying, "I love you."

What would you do if you knew you would soon lose one of your senses?

Don't wait until the basic pleasures of life are gone before realizing the blessings you have. Instead, I hope you do as Jessica did and as Scripture teaches us. Live every day to the fullest—wisely and well.

Dear God, teach me to do your will every day and to savor every moment.

Live by the Word

For the word of God is alive and active. Sharper than any double-edged sword, it penetrates even to dividing soul and spirit, joints and marrow; it judges the thoughts and attitudes of the heart.

—HEBREWS 4:12

A CLASSIC DEVOTION FROM BILLY GRAHAM (TWENTIETH CENTURY)

When Jesus was upon the earth, He held His crowds spellbound. He talked to the leaders of His day, He spoke as one having authority, and He absolutely shook them by the great authority with which He spoke, because it was the authority of God the Father.

The great prophets of the past also spoke with authority. Their secret is traceable to the fact that they believed their message, and they would say time after time, "Thus saith the Lord."

Today, if you want to be used of God, if you want people to turn from false messiahs and listen to you, if you want to turn people from darkness unto light and from the power of Satan unto God, you and I must speak, we must work, and we must live with that authority that our Lord Himself had. The world longs for authority and certainty; it is weary of theological floundering and uncertainty; nothing is gained psychologically or spiritually by casting aspersions on the light.

Heavenly Father, I will walk in the light and wisdom of your Word.

The Hard-hearted Fool

Why does the wicked man revile God? Why does he
say to himself, "He won't call me to account"?

—PSALM 10:13

The fool despises God's instruction. Why? He thinks he is smarter. The wicked reviles God. Why? He doesn't believe God has power over him—"he won't call me to account." He has no fear of God's power and judgment.

That people reject God and bow to the idol of self should not catch us by surprise. God's most beautiful creature, His star of heaven, was Lucifer. Out of an arrogant pride that demanded equality with God, Lucifer was cast from heaven, becoming the enemy of God and man.

There are many people who reveal the same spirit of pride, denigrating God and His attributes and His works. Most don't go so far, but many of us are careless in our use of God's name and show little fear of Him in the way we live and think. His love and mercy are enduring, it is true. But He is ever righteous and will ultimately judge each and every one of us.

Do you fear and revere the Lord in how you speak of Him and how you walk with Him?

Father, I honor you; I praise you; I worship you; I love you. May I never fall into the sin of pride where I consider myself before you.

The Wisdom of Integrity

You must have accurate and honest weights and measures, so that you may live long in the land the Lord your God is giving you.

—DEUTERONOMY 25:15

All around us, integrity is crumbling. Examples of dishonesty and corruption abound in modern life—and our nation and world are not the better for it. It is impossible to ignore the importance of integrity as one of the most important dynamics in your life, making you wise or foolish. So what does the Bible have to say about integrity?

- Integrity means treating people fairly and honestly: "Honest scales and balances belong to the Lord" (Proverbs 16:11). Any gain from cheating or fudging the truth is sure to be temporary. The long-term impact is always a breach of trust.

- Integrity is giving your word and keeping it: "Do not testify against your neighbor without cause" (Proverbs 24:28). Many of us want to please the people in our lives and say what they want to hear—only to have to backtrack and apologize later. Be direct and honest up front—your reputation for follow-through is at stake. (See Exodus 8:28–32.)

O God, may I walk worthy of your calling. Make me an example of integrity and honesty.

True Competence

Not that we are competent in ourselves to claim anything
for ourselves, but our competence comes from God.

—2 CORINTHIANS 3:5

D o right. Live wisely. Take care of business. Don't cultivate habits of incompetence.

But never claim that your ultimate competence is something you can create and maintain. All blessings are from God. Acknowledge that He is the one source of all good gifts and success and the only safe refuge when life is difficult. Then you will steer clear from the dangers of pride and despair.

Creating a life centered in Christ allows for us as His children to find true happiness as we honor the Lord. By living a life that produces purpose, we produce joy. As the world continues to shift and grow, there is more and more pressure on all of us to sacrifice convenience for competence and lower the standards of our expectations.

The good news is that with complete and total trust in Him, He directs our steps in the most fulfilling paths for our lives. The real question now is if we as God's children are willing to listen to those steps, despite any difficulty we may perceive.

God, I know that you alone are in control of all things, including my life. Help me trust in you day by day, moment by moment.

Blessed Is the One Who Reads

Blessed is the one who reads aloud the words of this prophecy, and blessed are those who hear it and take to heart what is written in it, because the time is near.

— REVELATION 1:3

A CLASSIC DEVOTION FROM BILLY GRAHAM (TWENTIETH CENTURY)

Peter and John were with Jesus shortly before His return to His Father's right side. In a poignant conversation, Jesus foretold Peter's violent death as a martyr and John's long life. (See John 21:18–24.) All the other apostles died at the hands of those who persecuted the Christian faith, but John died of old age as an exile on the island of Patmos. It was there that he received a vision that came directly from God, which is known as the book of Revelation, the final entry in the New Testament.

This is not just a book of prophecy, but a hard look at how believers—now and then—live in the present.

Down through the centuries, in times of trouble and trial, God has brought courage to the hearts of those who love Him. The Bible is filled with assurances of God's help and comfort in every kind of trouble that might cause fears to arise in the human heart. You can look ahead with promise, hope, and joy.

Lord, thank you for the blessings that follow when I read your Word. Today I choose to make reading Scripture a priority in my life.

Friendship and Fear

The Lord confides in those who fear Him; He
makes His covenant known to them.

—PSALM 25:14

F riendship and fear don't naturally go together. You're probably not too afraid of the people you call friends, nor do they fear you. And yet our relationship with God is characterized by both familiarity and formality, closeness and reverence, comfort and awe, trust and fear. But biblical fear of God is much different than being afraid; rather, it means a deep respect.

Friendship with God is a miraculous gift. In the Old Testament, only a few were said to enjoy friendship with God. But in the New Testament, Jesus tells His disciples, "I have called you friends" (John 15:15).

When we fear God—hold Him in reverence and respect—we get to enjoy His company and guidance through prayer and His Word. That is truly a friendship to celebrate.

Do you have a reverence for God? Does it show up in your words and actions? God is gracious and kind, but to be in a right relationship with Him, we must bow before Him in worship.

Dear God, thank you for reaching out to me. Please cultivate in my heart a healthy fear of you and help me to walk in your ways.

The Wisdom of Nations

*I urge, then, first of all, that petitions, prayers, intercession
and thanksgiving be made for all people.*

—1 TIMOTHY 2:1

When Queen Victoria was asked the secret of England's greatness, she took down a copy of the Scriptures, and pointing to the Bible, she said, "That book explains the power of Great Britain."

Wisdom comes from many different sources and in many different forms. But the wisdom of the Bible teaches us not only how to order our earthly lives for maximum success, but how to align our hearts and spirit with the Almighty God.

When Paul wrote a letter of encouragement to his spiritual son, Timothy, he reminded him and others who would read his words to pray for wise rulers and to pray for good, stable government. Your political affiliation is irrelevant. You are still called to pray for the one in leadership.

Many Americans hold a strong belief that the country has drifted dangerously far from its moral foundations. So don't limit your prayers to leaders and government, but pray for everyone, all people, that revival will spread across the land.

The words of God are a firm foundation for nations. And for our lives.

Thank you, God, for the solid foundation of your Word. Help me to know it and to build my life upon it.

Going beyond Yourself

But seek His kingdom, and these things will be given to you as well.

—LUKE 12:31

A CLASSIC DEVOTION FROM KARL BARTH
(TWENTIETH CENTURY)

Within the Bible there is a strange new world, the world of God. This answer is the same that came to the first martyr, Stephen: "Behold, I see the heavens opened and the Son of Man standing on the right hand of God." Neither by the earnestness of our belief nor by the depth and richness of our experience have we deserved the right to this answer. But if we wish to come to grips with the contents of the Bible, we must dare to reach far beyond ourselves.

It is the Bible itself that drives us out beyond ourselves and invites us, without regard to our worthiness or unworthiness, to reach for the last highest answer. And that answer is: A new world, the world of God. This daring is faith; and we read the Bible rightly when we read it in faith. The Bible unfolds to us as we are met, guided, drawn on, and made to grow by the grace of God.

Dear God, help me to keep following you and to grow in your grace as I become all you intend me to be.

A Wise Ruler

"Give me wisdom and knowledge, that I may lead this people,
for who is able to govern this great people of yours?"

—2 CHRONICLES 1:10

Solomon is known as the wisest man who ever lived. But when he began to make moral and spiritual compromises, his judgment suffered. As a result, he left behind an unstable kingdom that split in two upon his death.

What might the kingdom of Israel have looked like if it were not torn apart from inside? Could that have been avoided if Solomon had kept his heart focused on his prayer for wisdom and knowledge to lead God's people?

Solomon's life trajectory is a poignant reminder that it's not just how we start the walk of faith, but it's how we are living it at the moment we enter into eternity.

Two reminders that you can take to prayer are first, watch your own heart and mind. Are you staying attuned to God's will and ways? Second, as Paul and Peter told us in their letters, we should pray for our rulers to be wise. Solomon is a vivid reminder of the temptation to turn to one's own thoughts rather than God's thoughts.

Father, may I always acknowledge my need for your wisdom and power.

Humility and Wisdom

When pride comes, then comes disgrace,
but with humility comes wisdom.

—PROVERBS 11:2

The wise person is wise because of a godly humility. The person of pride is foolish because he does not fear the Lord, and is limited to knowing only what the human mind can conceive. Even if the person who fears the Lord has a lower IQ than the person of pride, his capacity for wisdom is not constrained by the limits of human comprehension. But even in the human realm, humility is superior to pride in attaining wisdom. The humble are teachable and open to change and growth. The proud do not like to admit errors and the need for growth.

Jesus echoed this thought when He said, "Everyone who hears these words of mine and puts them into practice is like a wise man who built his house on the rock" (Matthew 7:24).

What is your basis for wisdom? Is it how smart or clever you are? It's great to be smart and clever. But wisdom is knowing how to live the way we were created to live by God, and that begins in humility.

Father, I come before you with humility, asking you to guide my thoughts, attitudes, and actions today.

Joyful Wisdom

Blessed is the one who does not walk in step with the wicked, or stand in the way that sinners take, or sit in the company of mockers.

—PSALM 1:1

The very first verse of the Psalms is one of blessing. We can experience a supreme happiness, a joy that resides deep inside our heart. This joy is vibrant and life-giving, leading to wisdom and success in all our endeavors.

The condition for this blessing is really quite simple. Don't follow the advice of the wicked or hang around with mockers. But being simple doesn't make the condition easy. We are surrounded on every side by bankrupt ideas and disillusioned people who make cynical mockery a full-time job.

The people we admire and trust in life will have a tremendous influence on our attitudes and behaviors. If we don't like the fruit of our heart and mind, if we aren't satisfied that our efforts are prospering, if we don't feel God's life force surging through us, we need to look at our closest relationships. The wise person guards their heart and mind from those who are wicked and negative.

Seek godly counsel and fellowship, and be blessed!

Loving Father, bring the right people into my life to help me grow closer to you and experience your joy.

Soaking in the Word

I reach out for your commands, which I love,
that I may meditate on your decrees.

—PSALM 119:48

M editation is the activity of calling to mind, thinking over, dwelling on, and applying to oneself the various things that one knows about the works and ways and purposes and promises of God. That means we need to withdraw from the distractions of life for this time of serious pondering.

Are you worried, angry, tempted, distracted, resentful? Why not bathe in God's Word right now? It's good to read through the full range of writings from the Bible, but for this activity, pick a short passage from the Psalms or New Testament. Read it slowly a couple of times. Ask God to speak to you while you read each time. Memorize a key phrase or two. Repeat those phrases throughout your day. Truly bask and soak in the heart of God as you savor His Words to you.

God, today I choose to ignore all distractions and focus my mind on truths from your Word. Let your Words sink deep into my spirit.

No Pearls for Pigs

Do not give dogs what is sacred; do not throw your
pearls to pigs. If you do, they may trample them under
their feet, and turn and tear you to pieces.

— MATTHEW 7:6

The meaning of these word pictures is obvious. Don't waste time sharing the Gospel, dispensing truth, or debating with people who have rejected God. Yes, we are to witness and evangelize, but when people show a stubborn defiance, it's time to back off. When sending His disciples out to share the Gospel, Jesus instructed them, "If anyone will not welcome you or listen to your words, leave that home or town and shake the dust off your feet" (Matthew 10:14).

Some people have an incredible gift of sharing the Gospel and arguing for truth in even the most hostile of settings. They are called and equipped to do what most of us aren't able to do.

If someone you know and love has rejected the Gospel, by all means watch for signs of a softening heart. But don't push them even further from the love of Christ by hectoring them when they are clearly not open to truth.

Father God, give me a discerning heart to know when to impart wisdom or share the Gospel with the lost.

Carry Your Sword

Take the helmet of salvation and the sword of
the Spirit, which is the word of God.

—EPHESIANS 6:17

The fantastic and legendary tale of King Arthur and Camelot includes a famous sword: Excalibur. When young Arthur pulls the shimmering blade from the stone, the people immediately recognize that Arthur is the man to lead them and become the high king of England.

What sword do you carry in battle? Per Charles Spurgeon:

> We have to deal with fierce foes, who are only to be met with keen weapons. ...You may be of a very quiet spirit, but your adversaries are not so. If you attempt to play at Christian warfare, they will not. ...They mean mischief. Nothing but your eternal damnation will satisfy the fiendish hearts of Satan and his crew. You must take...a sword to use, and a specially sharp sword too.

God has given us the sword of Spirit through which we need to live for Him. We must be equipped with His spiritual blessings and resources. Now is the time to take up a mighty sword that is forged from the fires of God's Word.

Lord, may I ever be ready for battle by learning your Word.

Light of the World

In the same way, let your light shine before others, that they
may see your good deeds and glorify your Father in heaven.

—MATTHEW 5:16

A CLASSIC DEVOTION FROM MALCOLM MUGGERIDGE (TWENTIETH CENTURY)

How I should love to be able to speak with even a thousandth part of the certainty and luminosity of St. Paul, when he and his companions were, in the most literal sense, turning the world upside down by insisting, contrary to Caesar's decrees, *that there [was] another king, one Jesus*. Golden words; a bright and shining light indeed. Now something had happened to him, as it had to Christ's disciples, transforming them from rather inarticulate, cowardly men who ran away for cover when their leader was arrested, into the most lion hearted, eloquent, quick-witted, and even [joyful] evangelists the world has ever known. Well, what had happened to them? They were reborn. They were new men with a new allegiance, not to any form of earthly authority but to this other king, this Jesus. Ever since their time, with all the ups and downs, this notion has persisted, of being reborn, of dying in order to live.

Father, make me a light in a dark world. Kindle the flame of knowing Jesus in my heart.

Words of Wisdom from Proverbs

*Trust in the Lord with all your heart and lean
not on your own understanding.*

—3:5

Above all else, guard your heart, for everything you do flows from it.

—4:23

As iron sharpens iron, so one person sharpens another.

—27:17

*The fear of the Lord is the beginning of wisdom, and
knowledge of the Holy One is understanding.*

—9:10

*A cheerful heart is good medicine, but a
crushed spirit dries up the bones.*

—17:22

A gentle answer turns away wrath, but a harsh word stirs up anger.

—15:1

God of wisdom, make me wise through my love for you. Help
me to always seek your ways.

A Prayer for Spiritual Wisdom

Watch out for false prophets. They come to you in sheep's clothing, but inwardly they are ferocious wolves.

—MATTHEW 7:15

Dear God,

We live in a day of spiritual confusion. There are thousands of voices who claim to know truth and the way to peace, happiness, and eternal life. Many of these teachers do not know or acknowledge that you are the One True God, who is alone worthy to be praised.

In times of crisis, false teachers will prey on those who are not strong in their faith, who are not familiar with your Word. I pray that you will raise up men and women who will boldly proclaim the truth of Jesus Christ. I pray that you will protect the innocent and gullible from wolves in sheep's clothing.

God, I pray that I will always be able to give a reason for the hope that lies within me. I pray that I will not be tossed back and forth by waves of false teaching. I pray that I will continue to grow in wisdom and faith; that I will be mature and complete, lacking in nothing of spiritual value.

In Jesus's matchless name. Amen.

October
Encouragement

If I could hear Christ praying for me in the next room,
I would not fear a million enemies. Yet distance
makes no difference. He is praying for me.
—ROBERT MURRAY M'CHEYNE

OCTOBER

1

When Afraid

*"Come," He said. Then Peter got down out of the boat,
walked on the water and came toward Jesus.*

—MATTHEW 14:29

Nothing can rob you of joy, confidence, optimism, and opportunities more quickly than a spirit of fear. Behavioral scientists have long debated whether the first emotion a baby experiences is love or fear. Because of the "startle reflex," many researchers believe it is the latter. When faced with danger, the two foundational responses that appear to be hardwired into the human psyche are fight and flight. So are you a fight or a flight person?

There are many sources of fear. Some are unreasonable (to everyone else but the persons experiencing them!), and are considered unhealthy phobias. But whatever the source—a sense of the unknown, the future, physical danger, spiritual warfare, financial crises, or reputation issues—fear is real and must be faced honestly. One of the greatest promises of God is that we don't have to face our fears alone. He is always with us; never will He forsake us (Hebrews 13:5).

Are you ready to walk boldly, with a new sense of confidence today? Take a few steps, even if they're baby steps.

Mighty God, you are greater than any fear I experience; deliver me from my fears I pray.

2

Just as You Are

Moses said to the Lord, "Pardon your servant, Lord. I have never been eloquent, neither in the past nor since you have spoken to your servant. I am slow of speech and tongue."

—EXODUS 4:10

We live in a dog-eat-dog world. Many of us question our abilities and are fearful about testing our wings and attempting all that God has called us to do. If you ever struggle with healthy self-confidence, note that one of the greatest leaders in all of history, Moses, had the same hang-up. When God called him to lead the children of Israel out of Egyptian bondage, Moses was full of excuses. *They won't listen to me. I stutter. Send my brother.*

God was patient and didn't demand change from Moses. When Moses trusted God and stepped out on faith to confront the Pharaoh and help forge a free nation, he took to heart God's promise: "I will help you speak and will teach you what to say" (Exodus 4:12).

Yes, we should continually improve ourselves. It's good to strive for excellence in our lives. But we shouldn't forget that God often gives us things to accomplish that are beyond our abilities. Be assured that God can use you just as you are.

I know, dear God, that I can accomplish whatever you ask me to do because you are with me each step of the way.

Tender Mercies

Your father knows what you need before you ask Him.

—MATTHEW 6:8

When we get to the end of our own strength, realizing that we need God to make it in life and keep our soul tender and true, it's good to remember:

- God sent a rainbow to Noah as a symbol that His love for man would never waver (Genesis 9:14–15).
- God spoke to Moses in a burning bush (Exodus 3:2–6) and parted the waters of the sea with His breath to provide deliverance (Exodus 14:21).
- God allowed a young shepherd boy to conquer a mighty warrior with only a slingshot and a single stone (1 Samuel 17:49).
- Jesus healed a blind man (Mark 8:22–25), a person with leprosy (Matthew 8:2–3), a man who had never walked (Matthew 9:2–7), and even raised a young girl from death to life (Luke 8:51–55).

God is at work in our world—and in your life. Sometimes all we need is to open our eyes to see His tender mercies in our lives.

Lord, open my eyes so that I can see the merciful works you are doing in my life.

New Beginnings

*Forget the former things; do not dwell on the past. See, I am
doing a new thing! Now it springs up; do you not perceive it? I am
making a way in the wilderness and streams in the wasteland.*

—ISAIAH 43:18-19

I am stuck in neutral. I am not moving forward or backward.
I've gotten caught up in the business of life and stopped
dreaming; stopped growing; stopped striving to do more.

God promises that He will transform us when we become
part of His family. He will do a new thing in us, and He will
continue to bring forth change that will be for our good and
His highest.

If we want to experience all that He has for us, we must
begin with the simple belief that He loves us and wants to do
something special in us—no matter what has transpired up to
this very moment. One of the ways you show that belief is by
seeking His will for your life, trusting Him for His wisdom to
make right choices and go in the right direction.

Ready for a fresh start? A new start? Turn to God. He is faithful to guide you to a brand-new beginning!

**Thank you, God, for your love that draws me back to you
when I've made a mess of my life, and for showing me your
power to produce flowing rivers in the desert of life.**

Be Your Best You Ever

Whatever you do, do it all for the glory of God.

—1 CORINTHIANS 10:31

All good things we have are gifts from God. Even the faith with which we respond to God's grace is a gift from Him. All talents and strengths are from Him.

Yet God calls us to use what He has given us. He calls for us to work, acquire, learn, plan, and dream. Some of us aren't comfortable with the thought that God just might be calling us to be ambitious. That doesn't sound godly!

Kindness, love, and service all come first. But what is God telling you to get started, to work on in your life now? Or asked another way: what are you going to do with what you've got?

Are you moving forward—or sitting back and relaxing? Are you using the talents God has given you to bless Him, your family, your community, your business, yourself? When God looks at your efforts, will He say, "Well done, good and faithful servant"?

Lord, help me walk forward in all that you have for me to do. Thank you for a bright future!

Slow Down

The Lord your God is with you, the Mighty Warrior who
saves. He will take great delight in you; in His love He will no
longer rebuke you, but will rejoice over you with singing.

—ZEPHANIAH 3:17

We live in a fast-paced, busy, media-saturated, noisy world. Is it any wonder that we really do need a quiet time every day? A time for prayer and God's Word? Because it's too easy to let the noise and activity of modern life cloud and obscure the reality that God is present and in our midst.

Do you have time each day when you turn off the TV and radio? When you stop looking down at your phone to see if you have a new text or email? Do you have a quiet zone that is free from noise and other distractions? Do you slow down long enough to sense God's nearness to you?

The God of Abraham, Isaac, and Jacob is a God of love and comfort, a God who fills the soul and heart of those whom He possesses, a God who makes them conscious of their inward need for Him and His infinite mercy. But before that transformation happens, His people must slow down and acknowledge Him.

Lord, thank you for being there for me, for being present in all the moments of my life. Forgive me when I get too busy to acknowledge you.

True Happiness

We also glory in our sufferings, because we know that
suffering produces perseverance; perseverance, character;
and character, hope. And hope does not put us to shame.

—ROMANS 5:3-5

A CLASSIC DEVOTION FROM JOHN CALVIN (SIXTEENTH CENTURY)

Many are pressed down by distress, and yet continue to swell inwardly with pride and cruelty. But Christ pronounces those to be happy who, chastened and subdued by afflictions, submit themselves wholly to God, and, with inward humility, turn to Him for protection.

The ordinary belief is that calamities render a man unhappy. This arises from the thought that they constantly bring along with them mourning and grief. Now, nothing is supposed to be more inconsistent with happiness than mourning. But Christ does not merely affirm that mourners are not unhappy. He shows that their very mourning contributes to a happy life, by preparing them to receive eternal joy, and by furnishing them with motives to seek true comfort in God alone.

...As we must believe that Christ alone is the guardian of our life, all that remains for us is to "hide [ourselves] under the shadow of [His] wings" (Psalm 17:8).

Dear God, I find true happiness by trusting you completely, in good times and bad.

OCTOBER

8

Adversity

When you walk through the fire, you will not be burned;
the flames will not set you ablaze. For I am the Lord
your God, the Holy One of Israel, your Savior.

—ISAIAH 43:2-3

No matter what our address, most of us live in a relatively healthy, secure, affluent society. Such conditions make it easy to feel a sense of privilege, a sense that we deserve only good things in our lives—a peaceful and comfortable existence.

Innocent, godly men and women all over the world know no such comfort. In fact, at the beginning of the third millennium since Christ's birth, there are more Christians martyred each year than in any previous decade of Christian history. James, the brother of Jesus and the leader of the early church in Jerusalem, witnessed firsthand the horrors of persecution and hardship.

Yet he calls for his fellow believers to face all trials and tests with joy, faith, and optimism. He never asks for us to wish for hard times, but he does remind us that, combined with faith, hard times are opportunities for becoming a mature, spiritual person.

If you are facing adversity in your life right now, take heart, and know that God is doing something wonderful and new in your heart and life.

Knowing that you are with me each step of my journey, especially when the path is dangerous, I will let praise and thanksgiving flow from my mouth.

All My Songs Are Wonderful

I praise you because I am fearfully and wonderfully made;
your works are wonderful, I know that full well.

—PSALM 139:14

Irving Berlin was one of America's best-loved composers, with more than one thousand songs in his catalog. In addition to the familiar favorite, "God Bless America," he wrote "White Christmas," the world's all-time bestselling musical score.

In his nineties, Berlin was asked, "Is there any question that you've never been asked, but that you would like to be asked?"

"Well, yes, there is one," he replied. "'What do you think of the many songs you've written that didn't become hits?' My reply would be that I still think they are wonderful."

God too has an unshakable delight in the things—and people—He has made. Whether or not they're a "hit" in the eyes of others, He thinks each of His children is wonderful! The good news is that you are cherished by God as someone special and wonderfully made. From all eternity, you have been in the mind of God. God's love for you is utterly reliable and has no conditions whatsoever.

How might your life be different if you began to see yourself as a delight to God?

Lord, it boggles my mind that you made me and delight in me. I pray that this knowledge will sink deep into my heart.

Trust God to Do His Work

The Lord is my strength and my shield; my
heart trusts in Him, and He helps me.

—PSALM 28:7

In January of 2009, Captain Chesley Sullenberger had just taken off when his plane struck a flock of birds and both engines lost power. Sully, as he is affectionately known, had to make a snap decision—to try to fly back to the airport, or to land in the icy water of the Hudson River.

And so, in a cool, professional tone, Sully told air traffic controllers, "We're going into the Hudson," and very calmly told his passengers, "Prepare for impact." Sully then guided the plane to a picture-perfect splashdown. All 155 passengers and crew were safely rescued.

This miracle occurred, in part, because the captain and his crew were well-trained. But ultimately, this miracle occurred because God is in control. God made sure that the right people were in the right place at the right time.

The next time you face an emergency situation, I hope you'll remember God's plans and also Flight 1549. Just as Captain Sullenberger and his crew did, I hope you'll prepare yourself for tough times, then trust God to do His work.

Dear God, you give wisdom and help in all situations—thank you for your presence with us.

This Is My Song

He restores my soul. He guides me in paths of
righteousness for His name's sake.

—PSALM 23:3

F anny Crosby was blinded at six weeks old. As she moved through her childhood, she never believed that God was punishing her, and she believed that if she kept her heart open to Him, He would lead her.

At her school for the blind, she learned to play music and sing. She went on to spend her whole life serving the Lord through her poetry and music, writing such beloved hymns as "Blessed Assurance" and "Jesus Is Tenderly Calling You Home."

When asked how she coped with being blind, her grace-filled response was: "It seemed intended by the blessed providence of God that I should be blind all my life, and I thank Him for the dispensation. If perfect earthly sight were offered me tomorrow I would not accept it. I might not have sung hymns to the praise of God if I had been distracted by the beautiful and interesting things about me."

When we find ourselves hindered by circumstances or handicaps, if we keep trusting God, He can use us where we are and with what we have.

God, I trust that you can use me, and I pray that you will make me ready to serve you.

I Love a Rainy Day

*I have set my rainbow in the clouds, and it will be the
sign of the covenant between me and the earth.*

—GENESIS 9:13

W hen you have an outdoor wedding or a big family-
reunion picnic or a round of golf or a lake trip planned,
a rainy day feels like a disaster. *Why did it have to rain on
the weekend when I'm off work?!* But don't get too negative
about a rainy day. Most of the time, there are lots of reasons
to celebrate them!

Rainy days can be wonderful! Kids still know how to make
the best of them as they head outside to splash in puddles and
make mud pies. Rainy days may or may not be your favorite.
But like all other days, they offer something positive. And since
all days are God's days, a blessing can always be found in a
storm cloud!

The next time the heavens open over your head, go outside
and take in the experience. Let each raindrop remind you to lift
your head in praise.

**Father, thank you for both rain and sunshine in my life. I
know that I need both experiences. And thank you that your
presence and blessings are found no matter the weather.**

Game Day

*For physical training is of some value, but godliness has value for all
things, holding promise for both the present life and the life to come.*

—1 TIMOTHY 4:8

Athletes love to compete. Nothing beats game day: a brisk
fall evening of football, a hot summer day of baseball, a
basketball or volleyball game in a packed field house where the
winds of winter are forgotten, or a doubles tennis match with a
group of good friends. Game days are what you work for, what
you live for as an athlete.

Now, practice is a different matter for many of these same
athletes. *Practice? Ugh.*

Life is filled with challenges. Some are the training ground
in life to build our strength and character so we can face the
big battles that come our way. Other challenges are more like
hurricanes: they are the game days of life. They represent the
moments when all our training and knowledge is put to the test.

Don't underestimate the fortitude required to stay in training and win the small victories. Dwight L. Moody reminds us:
"True willpower and courage are not on the battlefield, but in
everyday conquests over our inertia, laziness, and boredom."

Are you ready for game day?

**Dear God, thank you for all the challenges of life that help
me grow stronger in spirit and faith. I pray that I will always
be ready for whatever life throws my way.**

A Safe Harbor

The Son is the image of the invisible God, the firstborn over all
creation. For in Him all things were created: things in heaven and
on earth, visible and invisible, whether thrones or powers or rulers
or authorities; all things have been created through Him and for
Him. He is before all things, and in Him all things hold together.

—COLOSSIANS 1:15–17

A CLASSIC DEVOTION FROM HILARY OF POITIERS (FOURTH CENTURY)

At length, with the Holy Ghost speeding our way, we are approaching the safe, calm harbor of a firm faith. We are in the position of men, long tossed about by sea and wind, to whom it very often happens, that while great waves delay them for a time around the coasts near the ports, at last that very surge of the vast and dreadful billows drives them on into a trusty, well-known anchorage.

But we have by our side the unfailing Spirit of faith, abiding with us by the gift of the Only-begotten God, and leading us to smooth waters in an unwavering course. For we recognize the Lord Christ as no creature, for indeed He is none such; nor as something that has been made, since He is Himself the Lord of all things that are made; but we know Him to be God, God the true generation of God the Father.

Eternal God, I trust in you alone for the certainty of my faith.

OCTOBER

15

The Great Race

*Commit to the Lord whatever you do, and
He will establish your plans.*

—PROVERBS 16:3

Life has often been compared to a race, and succeeding in either endeavor is usually thought of as a test of our will, our endurance, and our resilience. Determination is a good thing and is a gift from God.

What's the secret of making it to the finish line spiritually? Is it determination? Is it trying harder? Is it mustering every ounce of courage we can find? Is it asking admirable people to help us?

The Christian life has always been and will always be about trusting God and relying on His power and help, not just to bring us salvation, but also to help us take each step of our life journey. That victorious finish will not come by trying harder— but by trusting Him more!

God has a great race for you to run. Under His care, you'll go where you've never been and serve in ways you've never dreamed. But you have to keep your eyes on Him and lean on His power.

Dear God, I know I can't win the race of life on my own. I need your help and guidance every step of the way. Thank you for being there for me!

The Rumble of Thunder

In peace I will lie down and sleep, for you
alone, Lord, make me dwell in safety.

—PSALM 4:8

E ven though we tell our children that they are safe under the roof of our house and that thunder will not hurt them, once they see a streak of lightning turn night to day with the rumble of thunder right behind, you better believe they are racing to jump in bed with mom and dad. Even the fearless watchdog howls in fright and turns in your direction.

Our Heavenly Father finds the same joy in comforting us. He loves it when we acknowledge we need Him. He wants to reassure us that He will always provide for us and protect us. And He delights to hear our prayers.

Has a bolt of lightning hit uncomfortably close to your house? Is the crash of thunder shaking the windows? Are you frightened? Run to your loving Heavenly Father. He will comfort you in the storm.

Lord, thank you for being such a perfect, loving parent. Thank you for your love and comfort in the midst of storms.

God Hears Our Prayers

But God has surely listened and has heard my prayer. Praise be to God, who has not rejected my prayer or withheld His love from me!

—PSALM 66:19–20

A farmer who lived near London during World War II wrote to the Scripture Gift Mission requesting prayer that no bombs would fall on his small farm. He enclosed a five-shilling offering. He explained that he didn't have enough money to bring in water for his parched crops. He could not afford another setback without losing his farm.

The secretary of the mission wrote back and said he could not ask that his farm be spared but instead would pray that God's will would be done.

Soon afterward the German arsenal hit the man's farm. The impact was so immense that it unearthed an underground spring of water. The spring not only amply watered the farmer's fields, but also enabled him to share water with his neighbors. He enjoyed an abundant harvest.

Have you ever prayed for one thing and received something better in its place?

Don't be surprised when God answers your prayers in ways that are much more for your good. Thank God for unexpected blessings.

Lord, thank you for your power to work for my good even in the worst of events. I trust you fully to take care of me.

We Need Others

*God chose the lowly things of this world and the despised things—
and the things that are not—to nullify the things that are.*

—1 CORINTHIANS 1:28

Very few men have made a bigger splash in their chosen profession than Michael Jordan. He entered in the NBA in 1984 and averaged 28.4 points as a rookie. He led the league in scoring four of his first six seasons—but lacked what he wanted most, a championship. Interestingly, when he began scoring fewer points and depending more on others, he finally got what he coveted.

In life, we want to be masters of our destiny, but then we discover the reality that not all of life is under our control. The good news is that we can turn to God and others.

God has blessed you with gifts and talents to make a difference in your world. But He's also created you with the need to depend on Him and others consistently. Sometimes the greatest challenge in our lives is not to try harder but to trust more.

Dear God, may I always trust in you. Bring people into my life who will bless me and to whom I can be a blessing.

He Heals the Brokenhearted

He heals the brokenhearted and binds up their wounds.

—PSALM 147:3

Dong Yoon immigrated to America from Korea in 1989. He became a citizen, got a job, and lived in San Diego with his wife, two daughters, and mother-in-law. Life was good.

However, one December day, a military pilot was flying to the Marine Corps air station Miramar. Less than two miles from the runway, the plane became disabled. The pilot was forced to eject as the plane spun out of control. It crashed into Dong's house, where all four of his loved ones died in the fire.

Dong was devastated. Even so, his first thoughts were about the pilot who had survived. "Please pray for him not to suffer from this accident," Dong said. "I don't blame him." And then as the extent of the tragedy overwhelmed him, Dong concluded, "There are many people who have experienced more terrible things than I have. But please tell me how to get through it. I don't know what to do."

Fortunately, the answer is you don't get through this alone. You must let God carry you when you're too weak to stand. Using human effort alone, we will never find true joy again after a tragedy. But with divine intervention, we can and will make it through. That's the best way, the only way.

Dear Lord, I know that you love us perfectly, even when disaster strikes. Please hear my cries and heal my heart.

When a Storm Isn't Really a Storm

Praise the Lord, my soul, and forget not all His benefits.

—PSALM 103:2

Not all the things that we view as problems are really problems. Some of the situations we moan over really aren't a big deal. We just need to toughen up a little and gain perspective. Of course, this doesn't apply to everything you or anyone else is going through. However, in many instances, problems that feel as though they are the end of the world quite simply are not.

We live in a prosperous time, when even the "poor" are often wealthier than those who are considered wealthy in another culture. We've become so accustomed to having so much that what once felt like a special blessing now feels like a necessity. Many of us need to do a reality check on what we think we need to be happy.

How about you? Are you more demanding than giving? Have you turned blessings into necessities? Maybe the trouble is not God's goodness, but our ability to receive the gifts He gives us.

Dear God, help me to cry for justice and fairness on the same things that burden your heart. And help me to take in stride the petty annoyances of life!

Call His Name

Like your name, O God, your praise reaches to the ends of
the earth; your right hand is filled with righteousness.

—PSALM 48:10

A CLASSIC DEVOTION FROM RALPH ERSKINE (NINETEENTH CENTURY)

Do you need peace, external, internal, or eternal? His name is the Prince of peace; seek, for His name's sake. Do you need healing? O sirs, His name is Jehovah-Rophi, the Lord the healer and physician; seek, for His name's sake, that He may heal all your diseases. Do you need pardon? His name is Jehovah-Tsidkenu, the Lord our righteousness; seek, for His name's sake, that He may be merciful to your unrighteousness. Do you need defense and protection? His name is Jehovah-Nissi, the Lord your banner; seek for His name's sake, that His banner of love and grace may be spread over you. Do you need provision in extreme want? His name is Jehovah-Jireh, in the mount of the Lord it shall be seen, the Lord will provide. Do you need His presence? His name is Jehovah-Shammah, the Lord is there: Immanuel, God with us. Do you need strength? His name is the Strength of Israel. Do you need comfort? His name is the Consolation of Israel. Do you need shelter? His name is the City of Refuge. Have you nothing and need all? His name is All in All.

Wonderful God, I thank you that when I call your name, you always hear and answer me.

Faithfulness in the Pit

*But while Joseph was there in the prison, the Lord was with him; He
showed him kindness and granted him favor in the eyes of the prison
warden. So the warden put Joseph in charge of all those held in the
prison, and he was made responsible for all that was done there. The
warden paid no attention to anything under Joseph's care, because
the Lord was with Joseph and gave him success in whatever he did.*

—GENESIS 39:20–23

One of the most fascinating characters in all the Bible is
Joseph. This handsome, proud, brilliant, favorite son—he
had everything going for him—lost everything he held dear in
an instant: his privilege, the love of his family, his freedom.

But because Joseph was a man who loved the Lord faithfully,
God blessed him even in the pit of prison, and Joseph was soon
put in charge of all the other prisoners. Many years and events
later, Joseph was made ruler over Egypt, second in command
only to the pharaoh.

If there ever was a person who had reason to rage against
life's unfairness, it was Joseph. But he was a man with so much
faith in God that he conducted himself with a sense of peace
and purpose even while living in the pit of despair.

**Heavenly Father, you are with me and provide everything I
need—even in the pits of life.**

Peace in the Storm

*I said, "Oh, that I had the wings of a dove! I would
fly away and be at rest...I would hurry to my place
of shelter, far from the tempest and storm."*

—PSALM 55:6-8

Jack Dawson painted *Peace in the Midst of the Storm* to
portray what that calm looks like for Christians. The paint-
ing shows a raging storm that is lashing sheets of water from
sky and sea against an outcropping of jagged mountainous
rocks. You have to look closely to find it, but nestled in one of
the rocks is a bird resting peacefully, seemingly unaware of the
storm's salvos from the tossing sea or the wind that are causing
the water to spray high above.

God wants to give us a supernatural peace that is hard for the
world to understand. When the storms of life assail us, we are
able to calmly watch as the crashing waters break and the wind
blows spray all around us. He wants us to experience a perfect
peace—His peace—trusting that the storm will move on by and
that we will be safe in the arms of Jesus.

**Dear Lord, I want to experience perfect peace in the middle
of life's storms. Be my shelter and refuge, Father.**

God Will Never Let You Go

*Trust in the Lord and do good; dwell in the land and
enjoy safe pasture. Take delight in the Lord, and
He will give you the desires of your heart.*

—PSALM 37:3-4

E rnie was a highly paid television anchorman for thirty-six years. But all of that changed when Ernie became a victim of the economic downturn. Suddenly, his six-figure salary came to an end.

So what did Ernie do? For starters, he never stopped believing that when one door closes, another door opens. He enrolled at a nearby community college and became a veterinary technician. He had to adjust and downsize to a simpler lifestyle. "It's hard," he said, "but my worth as a person hasn't taken a hit. What I'm going to do now is priceless. Nobody can take that away from me."

Jesus addressed this in Matthew 6: "Do not store up for yourselves treasures on earth. ...But store up for yourselves treasures in heaven, where moths and vermin do not destroy, and where thieves do not break in and steal. ...But seek first His kingdom and His righteousness, and all these things will be given to you as well" (Matthew 6:19–20, 33).

May these words encourage you to rely on the only one who will never let you go.

Dear Father, thank you for your faithfulness! Help me look to you for provision today.

All Things!

*And we know that in all things God works for the good of those
who love Him, who have been called according to His purpose.*

—ROMANS 8:28

Our culture craves comfort, the avoidance of pain, easy projects, uninterrupted success, lots of leisure time, instant entertainment, fun hobbies, high quality with cheap prices, great taste with few calories, and anything else that can fit under the umbrella of "smooth sailing."

When things don't go right—a slip on the ice, conflict with a loved one, a demanding and troublesome boss, a leaky roof, car trouble, a financial setback, a fender bender, an unexpected illness—there is a prevailing attitude of surprised anger and resentment, a strong sense that life is unfair and cruel.

Accept that not everything that happens in life is pleasant or welcome. Accept that you cannot live in a constant state of smooth sailing. Ask God to help you to receive the blessings only He can provide in the midst of the difficulties you encounter. You might feel pain for a moment, but the long-term rewards will be great.

Do you love God? Have you been called according to His purpose? Then be assured that *all things* will work for your good.

**Heavenly Father, I don't understand why bad things happen
and especially don't understand how you can use them for
good in my life, but you do. Thank you!**

Shipwrecked

Three times I was beaten with rods, once I was
pelted with stones, three times I was shipwrecked,
I spent a night and a day in the open sea.

—2 CORINTHIANS 11:25

Paul knew something about storms. If you read through 2 Corinthians 11, you will discover an extensive list of sufferings he experienced. A man of the world, accustomed to international travel before and after his conversion, he experienced plenty of rough waters. Luke, one of Paul's traveling companions, tells of one particular occasion when he was shipwrecked. (See Acts 27:13–44.)

When the waters we are sailing on grow turbulent, it's easy to take our eyes off what matters and try some desperate moves. In financial storms, some have stolen and swindled; in relationship storms, some have left and filed for divorce; in storms at work, some have falsified reports and cheated on margins; in parenting storms, some have given up on their children.

Paul did what he always did: he trusted and obeyed God with a calm confidence. The only sure way to get safely to shore is through simple obedience to God's will for our lives.

Lord, give me even greater resolve to do what is right when storms rage around me.

Worst-Case Scenario

He replied, "You of little faith, why are you so
afraid?" Then he got up and rebuked the winds
and the waves, and it was completely calm.

—MATTHEW 8:26

Many of Jesus's disciples were fisherman, and they knew from experience that the Sea of Galilee was notorious for its sudden and violent storms. The squall recorded in Matthew 8:23–27 was especially furious. As the high winds whipped up the sea into vicious waves, the disciples grew frightened and frantic. They were certain the boat would capsize and all of them would drown.

Incredibly, while all this was happening, Jesus was sleeping calmly in the back of the boat. The disciples finally had to wake Him because they were certain they were about to drown! Jesus woke up and told the storm to be still. And it obeyed Him. He then looked at His disciples and asked why they had such little faith! They were awestruck and speechless.

Hardships and problems in this world are real. It is natural to be terrified when waves are crashing and wind blows violently. Jesus certainly takes none of that lightly. But there is an eternal confidence that puts the ups and downs of life in perspective.

Lord, I pray that the knowledge of your eternal love and protection will so pervade my heart that I can walk through life's storms with confidence in you.

Prayer Changes Things

Therefore confess your sins to each other and pray
for each other so that you may be healed. The prayer
of a righteous person is powerful and effective.

—JAMES 5:16

A CLASSIC DEVOTION FROM DWIGHT L. MOODY (NINETEENTH CENTURY)

Those who have left the deepest impression on this sin-cursed earth have been men and women of prayer. You will find that prayer has been the mighty power that has moved not only God, but man. Abraham was a man of prayer, and angels came down from heaven to converse with him. Jacob's prayer was answered in the wonderful interview at Peniel that resulted in his having such a mighty blessing, and in softening the heart of his brother Esau. The child Samuel was given in answer to Hannah's prayer. Elijah's prayer closed up the heavens for three years and six months, and he prayed again and the heavens gave rain.

The Apostle James tells us that the prophet Elijah was a man "subject to like passions as we are." I am thankful that those men and women who were so mighty in prayer were just like ourselves. To be sure they lived in a much darker age, but they were of like passions with ourselves.

My Lord and Savior, teach me to pray with the faith of those who have gone before me.

A Whale of a Storm

*Now the Lord provided a huge fish to swallow Jonah, and Jonah
was in the belly of the fish three days and three nights.*

—JONAH 1:17

Amazingly, Jonah's preaching saved a wicked people from destruction. The Ninevites, enemies to God's people, heard Jonah preach, and his words spoke to them such that they repented. It is too bad that Jonah's preaching didn't do the same for him. His words of salvation never did instill love in his own heart. He continued to grouse about reaching out to enemies. Perhaps if he too had repented, God's work would have been established in that city for centuries.

The next time you find yourself in the belly of a fish—a time when God is setting you in a new direction—don't just obey, but do so with repentance and a joyful heart. What you least want to do may be an opportunity for you to do something bold for God on behalf of others. When enthusiasm replaces reluctance, you might experience your most powerful moment in God's service.

**Father, help me to be obedient to your calling on my life,
and give me eyes of mercy toward others.**

Wonderful Words of Encouragement

*Therefore encourage one another and build each
other up, just as in fact you are doing.*

—1 THESSALONIANS 5:11

*I would go to the deeps a hundred times to cheer a downcast
spirit. It is good for me to have been afflicted, that I might
know how to speak a word in season to one that is weary.*

—CHARLES H. SPURGEON

*If I can put one touch of rosy sunset into the life of any man
or woman, I shall feel that I have worked with God.*

—G. K. CHESTERTON

*Once I knew only darkness and stillness—my life was
without past or future—but a little word from the fingers
of another fell into my hand that clutched at emptiness,
and my heart leaped to the rapture of living.*

—HELEN KELLER

*When we lose one blessing, another is often
most unexpectedly given in its place.*

—C. S. LEWIS

**Father, please keep my heart focused on your mercy and
encouragement, even in times when I feel lost.**

A Prayer for Courage

Be strong and courageous. Do not be afraid or terrified
because of them, for the Lord your God goes with
you; He will never leave you nor forsake you.

—DEUTERONOMY 31:6

Dear God,
Right now, I feel defeated by fear. I am not doing what I am supposed to in life because I am afraid of what will happen to me. I am struggling to trust you to protect and empower me. My eyes are focused on what I perceive to be threats all around me rather than focused on you. Even before I speak it, you know the specific fear that is most plaguing my life right now.

God, I ask that you would do a work in my heart and mind that I cannot do myself. Please remove the fear that is robbing me of joy, purpose, and success. Help me to trust you as the one true source of courage. I don't claim courage through my own strength, but I do receive the courage I need for the challenges and tasks facing me from loving and trusting you.

I affirm your promise that you never leave me nor forsake me. Thank you for the courage that comes from that trust. Amen.

November

Gratitude and Grace

To be grateful is to recognize the love of God in everything He has given us—and He has given us everything. Every breath we draw is a gift of His love, every moment of existence is a grace, for it brings with it immense graces from Him.

—THOMAS MERTON

WIIFM?

"Those who sacrifice thank offerings honor me, and
to the blameless I will show my salvation."

—PSALM 50:23

When the Hebrew children were freed from slavery in Egypt, it took them forty more years to reach the Promised Land—a trip of 250 miles that should have taken less than a year. What happened? One comedian has suggested that since Moses, a man, was leading the party, he refused to stop and ask for directions.

But the real reason is revealed in Exodus, where Moses declares, "You are not grumbling against us, but against the Lord" (16:8). The people began to complain almost the instant they were free—and never stopped the entire journey. Sounds like the day in which we live. The prevailing attitude is WIIFM— "What's in it for me?" When we don't get exactly what we want, we grumble. We blame. We feel a spirit of grievance. We are unhappy with our lot in life.

The antidote, the way God wants us to live, is expressing a spirit of gratitude. That begins with thanksgiving to God for His loving-kindness (Psalm 138:2); His mighty works (Psalm 150:2); His gift of Jesus (2 Corinthians 9:15).

Father, I thank you for your faithfulness, for your love, for your provision, and for the gift of salvation.

2

=== *Not Just a Miracle* ===

Because of the Lord's great love we are not consumed,
for His compassions never fail. They are new
every morning; great is your faithfulness.

—LAMENTATIONS 3:22–23

RJ was mowing his yard when suddenly a large-caliber bullet slammed into his chest. He immediately pulled his cell phone from his shirt pocket to call 911, but as he did so, the phone fell apart in his hands. That's when he realized that the bullet had struck the phone. In an interesting twist, he usually kept the phone in his pants pocket, but for some reason on that particular day, RJ had placed it in a pocket directly over his heart. Doctors told him, "If your cell phone hadn't been there, the bullet would have hit you straight on, and you would be dead."

A miracle like this would certainly increase your faith too. But don't forget that it shouldn't take a miracle to increase our belief in God. Every day is a blessing and a gift from Him; our faith should always be increasing, no matter what happens. As Scripture declares: "Because of the Lord's great love we are not consumed, for His compassions never fail. They are new every morning; great is your faithfulness" (Lamentations 3:22–23).

Dear Lord, thank you for the gift of each day.

A Beautiful Home

God sets the lonely in families.

—PSALM 68:6

S he was a single mother with a ton of bills. Just to stay afloat, she rented a musty, cramped camper at a local RV park. She cringed one day as she overheard someone ask her little boy if he wished he and his mother had a real home. But her grimace was replaced with a tear and a smile of gratitude when she heard him give this reply: "We do have a real home; we don't have a house to put it in."

Maybe you're not happy about where you are in life: your job, your home, your car, your bills. No matter how bad things look today, don't become so focused on where you want to be that you miss the joys you have right now.

God has a wonderful plan for your future—but He has also sprinkled gifts and blessings in the life you have now. Cherish the love and friendships that make life beautiful, no matter how big or small your house is.

Dear Father, thank you for bringing me into your family, and thank you for those intangible blessings that make life wonderful.

His Victory is Ours

If God is for us, who can be against us?

—ROMANS 8:31

In Psalm 68:19, the psalmist declares: "Praise be to the Lord, to God our Savior, who daily bears our burdens."

What a tremendous cry of praise. But these words are also a reminder that God is our Savior and our strength. It is not by our might and cunning that we are saved; victory is a gift from God. His presence literally imparts power and strength to His people.

After any victory in your life, great or small, always take time to express thanksgiving. Don't just move on as if it is business as usual, lest you lose the blessing of learning to trust Him more and more, better able to face bigger and greater things with grace and faith.

It would also be well to remember that God has undoubtedly rescued us countless times that we weren't even aware of!

In your time of prayer today, take time to celebrate the unfathomable power and the simple kindnesses of God in your life.

I praise you as my Savior and thank you for delivering me again and again, O God!

Enthusiastic Worship

But may all who seek you rejoice and be glad in you; may those
who long for your saving help always say, "The Lord is great!"

—PSALM 70:4

Take time today to read Psalm 100 and you will discover a short and beautiful poem that King David wrote for the people of Israel as part of their songbook. Not only are the words lovely to the ear, but they also teach us powerful truths about worship.

- Worship should be enthusiastic. David says: "Shout for joy to the Lord" (100:1). That doesn't mean that every church and every believer must practice or appreciate the same worship style, but all must engage hearts in expressing our love to God.
- Worship should be joyful. David tells his people: "Worship the Lord with gladness; come before Him with joyful songs" (100:2).
- Worship recognizes that God is the Creator. David affirms that: "It is He who made us, and we are His; we are His people, the sheep of His pasture" (100:3).
- Worship expresses gratitude to God for His goodness. David declares: "For the Lord is good and His love endures forever. His faithfulness continues through all generations" (100:5).

Creator God, I worship and adore you with all of my soul, mind, and body.

I Thank God for You

I thank my God every time I remember you.

—PHILIPPIANS 1:3

Who has helped you grow closer to God and grow in your Christian walk? Who has blessed your life with love and encouragement? Who are you most thankful for? Now might be the time to express sincere gratitude to them—and to express gratitude for them to God.

Wouldn't you love to hear someone say to you, "Every time I think of you, I give thanks to my God?" What a fabulous word of encouragement. What a beautiful expression of love. And we know with Paul it was not just a casual and polite remark; he meant it. His life was not focused on himself, but on his Lord Jesus Christ and those whom he reached with the Gospel.

Gratitude is a habit that keeps us from self-centeredness. It is a powerful encouragement to those to whom we express it. We are told to be lavish in our love. Let's be lavish in our gratitude as well.

Thank you, Heavenly Father, for all those who have encouraged me. I bring my friends before you today, thanking you that you have given me an opportunity to be part of their lives.

Untiring Thanksgiving

Surely God is my salvation; I will trust and not be
afraid. The Lord, the Lord Himself, is my strength
and my defense, He has become my salvation.

—ISAIAH 12:2

A CLASSIC DEVOTION FROM SAINT PATRICK
(FIFTH CENTURY)

I, Patrick, a sinner, was taken captive at about sixteen years of
age. I did not know the true God; and I was taken into captivity
in Ireland with many thousands of people, for we did not keep
His precepts, nor were we obedient to our priests who used to
remind us of our salvation.

There the Lord made me aware of my unbelief, that I might
remember my transgressions and turn with all my heart to the
Lord my God. He watched over me before I knew Him, before
I learned sense or even distinguished between good and evil,
and He protected me, consoling me as a father would his son.

Therefore, I cannot keep silent, so many favors and graces
has the Lord bestowed on me in the land of my captivity.

Whatever befalls me, be it good or bad, I should accept it
equally, and give thanks always to God who revealed to me that
I might trust in Him, implicitly and forever.

Dear God, I give my thanks and my trust today and forever.

Always Grateful

Who can proclaim the mighty acts of the
Lord or fully declare His praise?

—PSALM 106:2

Watching the news reports of the devastation of Hurricane Katrina, viewers sadly shook their heads or just looked on in horror at images of the New Orleans streets underwater, waterlogged homes, and stranded survivors. It was an unforgettable natural disaster. But even amid the shock and horror of personally experiencing the destruction, many interviewees looked straight into the camera and our hearts to give testimony of God's protection and provision during the storm. They praised Him with gratitude for the whole world to hear. How can anyone, even a believer, express gratitude in the face of such calamity?

We express gratitude and praise to God because it is the right thing to do. It does wonders within our hearts. But another reason we are to rejoice in God is so that others will know of His goodness. Yes, it's good for our own soul, but it also blesses others.

Our testimony of God's joy—even in the midst of difficulties—can be a life-changing witness to those around us. And in the process, we stir and reinforce our own faith.

Lord, help me to shout for joy as I seek to share your goodness with others.

Remember to Remember

*I will remember the deeds of the Lord; yes, I will
remember your miracles of long ago.*

—PSALM 77:11

The concept of remembering is an important biblical
theme. The command to not forget is given more than
four hundred times. We are to remember:

- The wonders of God's creation and works of His hands:
"Ask now about the former days, long before your time,
from the day God created human beings on the earth; ask
from one end of the heavens to the other. Has anything so
great as this ever happened, or has anything like it ever
been heard of?" (Deuteronomy 4:32).

- That the world belongs to God: "For every animal of the
forest is mine, and the cattle on a thousand hills" (Psalm
50:10).

- The sacrificial gift of Jesus Christ on the Cross: "In the
same way, after supper He took the cup, saying, 'This cup is
the new covenant in my blood; do this, whenever you drink
it, in remembrance of me'" (1 Corinthians 11:25).

Memory keeps gratitude fresh, and gratitude keeps faith
fruitful. Today, have you remembered to remember?

**God, you have done so much for me. Today I choose to
reflect on your goodness in my past with hope for the
present and future.**

Repay Good with Good

Make sure that nobody pays back wrong for wrong, but always
strive to do what is good for each other and for everyone else.

—1 THESSALONIANS 5:15

In one of Aesop's Fables, an ant went to the bank of a river to get a drink. He fell into the stream and found himself on the brink of drowning. A dove sitting on a tree overhanging the water saw what was happening and dropped a leaf into the stream. The ant climbed onto the leaf and floated in safety back to the bank.

Shortly afterward, a bird catcher came and stood under the tree. He began laying a trap for the dove. The ant, seeing his intent, seized the opportunity to repay a good deed. He stung the bird catcher on his foot. The man gave a shout of pain and hopped around on his good foot. The noise alerted the dove to fly away.

It is wonderful to be blessed by random acts of kindness. It's just as wonderful when we can return the favor and do good to someone. That is the nature of kindness and love, particularly when they are stirred to life by gratitude.

Lord, thank you for the people who have helped me in life. Show me how I can be a blessing to others today.

NOVEMBER

11

===== *Greed Quashes Gratitude* =====

I will extol the Lord at all times; His praise will always be on my lips.

—PSALM 34:1

A lawyer successfully handled a difficult case for a wealthy friend. Following the happy outcome of the case, the friend went to the lawyer's office, expressed his appreciation of his work, and handed him a handsome Moroccan leather wallet. The lawyer looked at the wallet in astonishment and handed it back with a sharp rebuke that a wallet could not possibly compensate him for his services. "My fee for that work," snapped the attorney, with acid dripping in his tone, "is $500."

Slowly, the client opened the wallet, removed a check for $1,000, replaced it with $500, and handed back the wallet to his lawyer friend with a smile.

We are tempted to carelessly, pridefully, and way too quickly assess what life "pays" us and demand more. We might be missing out on a greater reward.

Greed quashes gratitude. But an attitude of contentment turns everything into a gift.

God, help me to see the best in others and in what you give me.

He Spoke to Me

*And what does the Lord require of you? To act justly and
to love mercy and to walk humbly with your God.*

—MICAH 6:8

A group of women met weekly for a Bible study. Jill, one young mother of three, tearfully told of her husband leaving her for another woman. Her friends were deeply concerned and took this young woman under their wing.

After a few weeks, there was a change in her spirit. Her despair had turned into courage. She even prayed differently.

The children grew up. Years later, Jill and Gigi ran into each other. As the two caught up, Gigi said to Jill, "I remember the change that came over you during that rough time. What made the difference?"

A smile came to her face as she answered, "In my despair and sorrow, the Lord spoke to me. I know that sounds crazy, but He did. God spoke to me, such an imperfect person, just an average woman with no grand accomplishments and no special talents. I was and still am humbled that Almighty God felt me worthy to speak to my heart and change my life. I still live in gratitude and awe of who He is."

Lord, we come to you because we know who you are and what you can do. I will live in gratitude of your love and grace forever.

I Packed Your Parachute

And whatever you do, whether in word or deed, do it all in the name of the Lord Jesus, giving thanks to God the Father through Him.

—COLOSSIANS 3:17

C harles Plumb was a U.S. Navy jet pilot in Vietnam. After seventy-five combat missions, his plane was shot down, and Plumb parachuted into enemy territory, becoming a POW. He survived his ordeal, however, and eventually returned home. While eating in a restaurant one day, he was approached by a man who said, "You're Plumb! You flew jet fighters in Vietnam and were shot down!"

"How did you know that?" asked Plumb.

"I packed your parachute," the man replied. "I guess it worked!"

Plumb couldn't sleep that night, thinking about the unknown man who'd saved his life. From that day on, he determined to always take notice of—and say thank you to—those who "packed his parachute" each day.

Make the most of each day by thanking those who "pack your parachute." And when it is you who are packing the parachute, make sure you do your assignment to the best of your ability.

Father, I know that you can use even the smallest gestures and efforts. Thank you for all the little things people do for me, and help me to be an encouragement to someone else today.

14

Thankful for This Day

May my prayer be set before you like incense; may the
lifting up of my hands be like the evening sacrifice.

—PSALM 141:2

A CLASSIC DEVOTION BY ROBERT LOUIS STEVENSON (NINETEENTH CENTURY)

We come before Thee, O Lord, in the end of Thy day with thanksgiving. ...Our beloved in the far parts of the earth, those who are now beginning the labors of the day at what time we end them, and those with whom the sun now stands at the point of noon, bless, help, console, and prosper them.

Our guard is relieved, the service of the day is over, and the hour has come to rest. We resign into Thy hands our sleeping bodies, our cold hearths and open doors. Give us to awake with smiles, give us to labor smiling. As the sun returns in the east, so let our patience be renewed with dawn; as the sun lightens the world, so let our loving-kindness make bright this house of our habitation.

Lord, receive our supplications for this house, family, and country. Protect the innocent, restrain the greedy and the treacherous, lead us out of our tribulation into a quiet land.

For His sake, in whose words we now conclude.

Thank you, Heavenly Father, for your presence in my life today and every day.

Man's True Best Friend

*"Call on me in the day of trouble; and I will
deliver you, and you will honor me."*

—PSALM 50:15

When Buddy was a puppy, Joe adopted him from an organization that trains dogs to assist people with special needs. Joe suffers from seizures, and Buddy had been trained to assist when a seizure occurs.

Recently, when Joe went into a seizure, Buddy ran to the phone, lifted the receiver, and pressed the necessary buttons. The 911 system traced the call to Joe's address, and the operator dispatched emergency help. Buddy stayed on the line until paramedics arrived—and then rode in the ambulance with Joe to the hospital.

This story about "man's best friend" reminds us who is truly man's best friend. Buddy's name is spelled with three letters: D-O-G. And man's true best friend is spelled with those same three letters: G-O-D.

We might only rarely encounter situations in which we need emergency help, but all of us find ourselves in need of spiritual help. All we need to do is follow what Scripture says: offer up a sincere prayer to God and rely on man's true best friend.

Dear Lord, thank you for being such a faithful friend. Help me walk closely with you today.

Before You Were Born

*Before I was born, God chose me and called
me by His marvelous grace.*

—GALATIANS 1:15

D id you know that God has been at work in your life even since before you were born?

Some of us did not have a perfect childhood. We didn't experience a warm, nurturing home, filled with love and affirmation. We think back to our earliest memories and feel sadness rather than joy. Would your life be different, would you feel more confidence, if you understood how deeply you were loved all along? Like Jeremiah, ask God to take you back even further in time. Even if your human parents' love was inadequate, someone was loving and affirming you before you were born. God's grace has been active in your life, even before the day you were conceived.

God chose you and called you. He has something special for you to do, something only you can do. Be assured, if you are willing, you are able. Why? Like Paul and Jeremiah, God has been preparing you for this opportunity through the power of His grace.

Loving Father, thank you for putting your hand on my life before I was even aware that your grace was working in and through me.

Thanksgiving in Tough Times

*Though there are no sheep in the pen and no cattle in
the stalls, yet I will rejoice in the Lord, I will be joyful in
God my Savior. The Sovereign Lord is my strength.*

—HABAKKUK 3:17–19

Habakkuk 3 describes an economic nightmare: the vines are not bearing fruit, the fields are not producing food, the livestock are sickly, and many cattle have died. When the right (or wrong) conditions conspire today, perhaps we won't be facing starvation, but we still find ourselves scrambling to get by, staving off a spirit of desperation and dreading the future.

Yet even in the midst of crisis, Habakkuk exults in God. He declares joy. He honors God for his strength. Why? Because he knows that God will save and restore his people. He knows that God has gifted him and the people with a strength to overcome even unbeatable odds.

Gratitude is a discipline that involves a conscious choice. You can choose to be grateful even when your emotions are steeped in hurt, resentment, and fear.

Stop for a minute, take a deep breath, and consciously express praise and thanks to God. He is at work, even if you can't see Him or feel His presence. Express gratitude and then affirm His strength. Your deliverance is closer than you think.

God, even when I'm scared and frustrated, I want to praise you. Strengthen my heart and give me joy in you.

— *Overcome Grumbling with Gratitude* —

The Lord said to Moses, "How long will these people treat me
with contempt? How long will they refuse to believe in me,
in spite of all the signs I have performed among them?"

—NUMBERS 14:11

"**T**hat's not fair!" seems to be written into our DNA, because almost every child has loudly lodged a protest or two with the proper authorities, usually Mom or Dad. What's not fair? A sibling got a larger brownie. A friend got a new bike. Other kids' parents let them watch a movie forbidden to them. But it's not just children who cry, "Unfair!" Teens can do so with style and adults with subtlety.

After being delivered safely from captivity and given free food each morning on their journey, the Hebrew children began a pattern of grumbling, to the point that some said slavery was better than eating manna every day (Numbers 11:4–6). Apparently, few things bother God as much as ungrateful grumblers. And had it not been for Moses's intercession, He would have been done with them.

There is a huge price tag on grumbling, for you and for everyone around you. The antidote to grumbling is always gratitude.

Have you been grumbling lately? Let gratitude overcome your complaints and watch as you draw nearer to God.

Lord, I know that you provide so richly for me. Help me to never take your goodness for granted.

The Older Son

*"Look! All these years I've been slaving for you and never
disobeyed your orders. Yet you never gave me even a
young goat so I could celebrate with my friends."*

—LUKE 15:29

Most discussion of the parable of the prodigal son focuses
on the love of the Father and the wayward son. But there's
another son in the parable, the resentful and grumpy older
brother, who was actually a very responsible son and probably
a nice guy most of the time. He sulked that even though he had
never asked his father for anything, he now had to watch him
lavish gifts on his irresponsible brother.

Let's be honest. Have you wondered why God chose to bless
someone else, someone who didn't appear to deserve it? If so,
the father's words to his eldest son will be meaningful for you
as well: "you are always with me, and everything I have is yours.
But we had to celebrate and be glad, because this brother of
yours was dead and is alive again; he was lost and is found"
(Luke 15:31–32).

God richly blesses us every day. When He throws a party for
someone else, we should celebrate too, knowing what a good
God we have.

**Thank you, God, for the blessing of being your child. I
choose today to be happy for the blessings I see happen in
the lives of others.**

The Wrong Soil for Problems

Let the message of Christ dwell among you richly as you teach and admonish one another with all wisdom through psalms, hymns, and songs from the Spirit, singing to God with gratitude in your hearts.

—COLOSSIANS 3:6

A colloquial story tells of a man who found the barn where Satan stores the seeds he sows in the human heart: envy, greed, anger, hatred, lust, and so on. The man noticed that Satan had more seeds of discouragement than any other kind, and he was told that those seeds were hardy and fruitful and could be made to grow almost anywhere.

But when the man questioned Satan if there was any soil that wouldn't support the seeds of disappointment, Satan reluctantly admitted that there was one place in which he could not get even his best seeds to grow. "Where is that?" asked the man. Satan replied, "In the heart of a thankful man."

When we choose a thankful attitude, our spirits resist the cynicism, discouragement, and pessimism that weigh life down for millions upon millions. We have created the soil where God's love blooms. When God is present, it is no surprise or wonder that Satan cannot gain a foothold in our lives.

God, I pray for a thankful heart. Please nurture in me a spirit of gratitude.

NOVEMBER
21

A Spirit of Grace

*As the rain and the snow come down from heaven, and do not return
to it without watering the earth and making it bud and flourish, so
that it yields seed for the sower and bread for the eater, so is my word
that goes out from my mouth: It will not return to me empty, but will
accomplish what I desire and achieve the purpose for which I sent it.*

—ISAIAH 55:10–11

A CLASSIC DEVOTION FROM MARTIN LUTHER (SIXTEENTH CENTURY)

The Holy Ghost has two offices. First, He is a Spirit of grace that makes God gracious unto us, and receives us as his acceptable children, for Christ's sake. Secondly, He is a Spirit of prayer, that prays for us, and for the whole world, to the end that all evil may be turned from us, and that all good may happen to us. The Spirit of grace teaches people; the Spirit of prayer prays.

We do not separate the Holy Ghost from faith; neither do we teach that He is against faith; for He is the certainty itself in the world, that makes us sure and certain of the Word; so that, without all wavering or doubting, we certainly believe that it is even so and not otherwise than as God's Word says and is delivered unto us. But the Holy Ghost is given to none without the Word.

Thank you, Heavenly Father, for the gift of the Holy Spirit who fills my life with grace.

Don't Miss the Blessing

Let them give thanks to the Lord for His unfailing love
and His wonderful deeds for men, for He satisfies the
thirsty and fills the hungry with good things.

—PSALM 107:8-9

How many times do we miss God's blessings because they are not packaged as we expected?

A poverty-stricken elderly woman in Europe complained that her wealthy son in America was cruel and ungrateful. "Does he never send you any money?" a friend asked.

"Never a penny," she replied. "He sends me pictures quite often, but I do not need pictures; I need money."

The friend said, "Do you have any of these pictures?"

"Oh, yes, I have them all. They are here in the old Bible." When she pulled them out, her friend gasped. The "pictures" were fresh, crisp fifty- and hundred-dollar bills, a huge and generous gift at the turn of the nineteenth century.

To enjoy our blessings, we first have to realize what we have been given. We might be sulking in squalor while we are surrounded by abundance. Are you missing any blessings in your life? Have you allowed misplaced values to rob you of the blessings God has given you?

Lord, open my eyes to see the gifts you have given me.

The Secret of True Wealth

But may the righteous be glad and rejoice before
God; may they be happy and joyful.

—PSALM 68:3

A man lives in a mansion in a zip code known for wealth. His garage is filled with expensive automobiles. And yet he lives in poverty, for he is miserable. The man is never satisfied; nothing seems to make him happy.

Contrast him with the man who works hard every day—including half days on Saturday for the overtime pay—and barely makes ends meet, despite living in a small, tidy home in a neighborhood that has seen better days. But he is wealthy. Life is good. He has a roof over his head, and his family is fed and happy.

How can the man with so much be poor and the man with so little be rich? The difference is simple. One man is grateful for nothing. The other sees blessings everywhere. What is the secret to true wealth? It is having a wealth that can never be taken away by the ups and downs of the stock market or the business cycle. It is found only in the God-given attitude of gratitude.

Lord, help me to see the wealth around me. Help me find my satisfaction in your love and provision, not in earthly wealth.

Saying Grace

*Since my youth, God, you have taught me, and to
this day I declare your marvelous deeds.*

—PSALM 71:17

How many ways have you been blessed by God? Relationally? Materially? Spiritually? Physically? His blessings are all around us, but we too easily get distracted.

One family tradition that has faded away for most is the bowing of heads and saying of grace before mealtimes, even when out in public at a restaurant. Of course, many families barely get together at meals in these busy times, so there are fewer opportunities to say grace together! What if you revived the saying of grace before every meal, whether alone or with others, as a reminder to thank God more often?

Reading through the Psalms, you will quickly notice that it wasn't good enough for David to *feel* gratitude in his heart. He had to say it out loud. Many times, he had to shout it to the mountains.

Whatever God has done for you, stop to acknowledge His blessings and speak a word of thanks. Express out loud what is in your heart.

Lord, when I look back, I can see that you have been with me all my life. Thank you for your goodness to me.

The Ten Percent Club

One of them, when he saw he was healed, came back,
praising God in a loud voice. He threw himself at Jesus's
feet and thanked Him—and he was a Samaritan.

—LUKE 17:15-16

Ten were healed. Only one returned to say thank you to the miracle worker. Does that percentage, only 10 percent, represent those in everyday life who stop to notice and express thanks for the miracles and ordinary blessings bestowed on them by God? Maybe. But this Scripture passage (Luke 17:11–19) is not about percentages. It's not about numbers, but rather one number. A singular number that relates to you and me. It is, of course, the number one. The one Samaritan leper who ran back to thank Jesus gives us a joyful reminder to be one who doesn't take God's blessings for granted and to be the one who always says out loud, "Thank you, Heavenly Father!"

Are you numbered with the ten percent? Are you a kindred spirit with the one who gave thanks? Are you a person who sees miracles and blessings, or one who wonders why things never go your way? Join an elite—though nonexclusive—group: the ten percent club, the ones who savor God's goodness and shout out praise as a result.

God, I never want to neglect to praise you for the ways you bless me. Open my eyes to your miracles today.

26

The Pathway to Worship

Worship the Lord with gladness; Come before Him with joyful songs.

—PSALM 100:2

Have you ever taken a long family trip where everyone broke out into song? A number of the Psalms are known as "Travelers' Psalms" because they were written for pilgrims as they made the journey to Jerusalem at one of the religious feast times. The songs were rarely solos. Everyone sang together as their paths met on the pathway to Jerusalem.

When we recognize all that God has done for us and given us—not least of which is the gift of salvation and promise of His presence—the right response is to worship. Psalm 100, one of the most beloved Travelers' Psalms, offers us a powerful primer for true worship. Imagine people singing the words of the psalm together. What a great way to prepare for worship!

Now might be a good time to read slowly through all of Psalm 100 as a reminder of how to worship and why God deserves our praise. One of the joys of knowing God is the privilege of entering "his gates with thanksgiving and His courts with praise" (100:4).

God, you are so good. Teach me to express praise and worship to you.

Happy Thanksgiving Miracle

*And do not forget to do good and to share with
others, for with such sacrifices God is pleased.*

—HEBREWS 13:16

"When you go grocery shopping, will you pick up some extra food for a needy family?" Martin asked. "There is a family of eight who needs food for Thanksgiving."

Jean sighed and gave a little laugh. Typical Martin. They were struggling financially and he was thinking of someone else.

With her coupons, several buy-one-get-one-free specials, and God's help, Jean bought two carts filled with groceries, a fat, plump turkey in each cart. Jean and Martin drove over to the home of the family that was not certain of enjoying a traditional Thanksgiving Day feast. They knocked on the door and told their friends what they had for them in the car. Six gleeful children paraded the feast from the car to their kitchen.

Even when we're struggling ourselves, with a little creativity, we can often do more than we think we can for someone else. One of the best ways to show our gratitude to God is to help Him help those around us. Some of God's sweetest miracles come from the hands of His faithful and loving children.

**God, I know that you care about the needs around me. Show
me how I can serve you with gratitude by serving others.**

28

Kindling the Fire of Grace

I pray that out of His glorious riches He may strengthen
you with power through His Spirit in your inner being.

—EPHESIANS 3:16

**A CLASSIC DEVOTION FROM JAN VAN RUYSBROECK
(FOURTEENTH CENTURY)**

For like as the sun, by its splendor and its heat, enlightens and gladdens and makes fruitful the whole world, so God does to us through His grace: He enlightens and gladdens and makes fruitful all men who desire to obey Him.

If, however, we would feel God within us, and have the fire of His love ever more burning within us, we must, of our own free will, help to kindle it in four ways: We must abide within ourselves, united with the fire through inwardness. And we must ascend above ourselves with the flame of this fire, through devotion, and thanksgiving, and praise, and fervent prayer, and must ever cleave to God with an upright intention and with sensible love.

And thereby God continues to dwell in us with His grace; for in these four ways is comprehended every exercise which we can do with the reason, and in some wise, but without this exercise no one can please God. He who is most perfect in this exercise, is nearest to God.

Father God, it is by grace I have been saved; help me to always cherish and nourish this gift.

Wise and Grateful Words

Give thanks to the Lord, for He is good. His love endures forever.
—PSALM 136:1

*As we express our gratitude, we must never forget that the
highest appreciation is not to utter words, but to live by them.*
—JOHN F. KENNEDY

*Gratitude can transform common days into
thanksgivings, turn routine jobs into joy, and change
ordinary opportunities into blessings.*
—WILLIAM ARTHUR WARD

*Gratitude unlocks the fullness of life. It turns what we have
into enough, and more. It turns denial into acceptance,
chaos to order, confusion to clarity. It can turn a meal into
a feast, a house into a home, a stranger into a friend.*
—MELODY BEATTIE

*Happiness cannot be traveled to, owned, earned, worn,
or consumed. Happiness is the spiritual experience of
living every minute with love, grace, and gratitude.*
—DENIS WAITLEY

**Thank you for the wonderful blessings that fill my heart and
life, O God.**

A Prayer of Thanksgiving

Enter His gates with thanksgiving and His courts with praise; give thanks to Him and praise His name. For the Lord is good and His love endures forever; His faithfulness continues through all generations.

—PSALM 100:4–5

Dear provider God,

I confess that I have not always been grateful. I have spent more time thinking about what I don't have than what I do have. I haven't appreciated the many gifts you have put into my life. I have taken friends and family members for granted. I don't want to live life negatively, with a sense of poverty—when you have made me rich with blessings.

Even as I say thank you right now for all the things you have done for me and given to me, I pray that you enlarge my sense of gratitude and wonder. Make me the kind of person who blesses others because I recognize what they mean to me and tell them so.

Don't let me waste any more time with feelings of greed and jealousy. I want to experience each day as a gift to be savored and cherished.

Even if I have failed to say it at times, I am grateful to you, my God, who provides for my every need.

In the blessed name of Jesus I pray. Amen.

December

Peace during Christmas

*Christmas, my child, is love in action. Every time
we love, every time we give, it's Christmas.*
—DALE EVANS

Peace

Glory to God in the highest heaven, and on earth
peace to those on whom His favor rests.

—LUKE 2:14

A cross all five hundred miles of World War I's infamous Western Front (a jagged, ever-changing line separating British and German forces), a miracle occurred. A German soldier began singing *"Stille Nacht,"* and his solo soon became a chorus as he was joined by English voices singing "Silent Night." Men from both armies laid down their weapons and crept cautiously and then quickly into No Man's Land to share food, cigars, drinks—and even to play a game of soccer together.

Christmas has always been a time when people of all ages, races, and creeds come together to break bread peacefully.

Angels sang to shepherds, "Peace on Earth, good will to all men," and they announced the simple yet profound truth that enemies can be reconciled, that strangers can become friends, and that those who think and believe differently can still be neighbors.

God of peace, I pray that peace will reign over all the earth. May it begin with me.

DECEMBER

2

Family Time

*And over all these virtues put on love, which
binds them all together in perfect unity.*

—COLOSSIANS 3:14

Families that sweat together, stick together. OK, that may not be a pleasant thought, but the point is crystal clear. Healthy family interaction enriches each family member's emotional and spiritual health. The holiday season is a time for family interaction.

If spending time together is how your family already interacts during the holidays, thank God for the blessing of the bonds of love. If you are living on your own and away from family right now, create holiday traditions with a group of friends—or become an "adopted" member of a family at your church or in your neighborhood.

The blessing of an earthly family gives only a hazy picture of the blessing in God's heavenly family. Don't wait another year—or month or day—in pulling your family together closer than ever before.

Ask God to make this a season of togetherness for you and those you love. Then do what He nudges you in your heart to do.

God, thank you for the people in my life. Be close to us this Christmas and draw us near to you and near to each other.

Make Room

She wrapped Him in cloths and placed Him in a manger,
because there was no guest room available for them.

—LUKE 2:7

In the same manner in which we clean and prepare our homes in the anticipation of welcomed guests and family members this Christmas season, let us also prepare our hearts in anticipation of the Lord's coming. Let's make room for Jesus.

How many blessings and miracles have we missed because we didn't have room in our hearts and homes to receive them? Too often, we fill our lives to the brim with activities and entertainment—much of it good, but much of it unimportant and distracting—so that we can't hear God's voice even if He spoke audibly to us.

Out of room in your life? No more time, money, energy, and other resources to make a difference? No space in your schedule to welcome Jesus? Look around your home. Search your heart. Is there a warm, dry space for Jesus to visit you?

Gracious God, thank you for sending Christ to my home and my heart. I welcome Him now.

Prepare Your Heart

And there were shepherds living out in the fields nearby,
keeping watch over their flocks at night. An angel of
the Lord appeared to them, and the glory of the Lord
shone around them, and they were terrified.

—LUKE 2:8-9

C an you think of anything more boring than watching sheep eat and sleep? Well, it might be pleasant on a vacation in Scotland, but that will only last so long. It wouldn't be interesting hour after hour, day after day, night after night, and week after week. Oh, undoubtedly there were moments of excitement for a shepherd when keeping a wolf or lion away from his flock, but the job was filled with drudgery.

Do you ever wake up knowing that this day will be the same as all others? Isn't that probably what the shepherds felt that first Christmas Eve more than two thousand years ago? Do you ever feel as though nothing ever changes? As though even Christmas and the holidays are the same every year? Maybe we've all gotten into a rut and feel that way. But what if this year a new star shines in the night sky, and the evening is filled with angels?

It happened to shepherds. It could happen to you. Is your heart ready for the Christmas season?

Lord, keep my sense of wonder alive. Help me to see what great thing you are doing in my world and life.

5

Open Hearts, Open Doors

*Do not forget to entertain strangers, for by so doing some
people have entertained angels without knowing it.*

—HEBREWS 13:2

I n Charles Dickens's immortal and beloved *A Christmas Carol*, it is the rich man with the big house, Ebenezer Scrooge, who locks his door and heart tightly to others, content to count his solid gold and silver coins. It takes an ethereal ghost and the fear of what the afterlife—chains and all—might hold for him to awaken Scrooge to the dour and cruel miserliness of his ways. Soon after he sees the light, he is welcomed into the humble home of Bob Cratchett, where the air is cold but the hearts are warm, where he sees with his own eyes the richness of opening one's heart and home to others.

But my house isn't very big and my furniture isn't very nice.

Not sure about your gift of hospitality? If you have a smile, a warm heart, and a few kind words, no one cares about how simple your house is. It was the investor Charles M. Schwab who said: "Money will buy you a bed but not a good night's sleep, a house but not a home, a companion but not a friend."

Father God, remind me to open my heart and home to family, friends, and even strangers this holiday season.

A Most Beautiful Time of the Year

He has made everything beautiful in its time.

—ECCLESIASTES 3:11

A mericans spend almost $10 billion on Christmas decorations. Many of our streets turn into winter wonderlands each December, with lights twinkling, reindeer flying, and Santa dancing. And while some garish displays might earn grimaces from the passersby, others make us stop in our tracks and take in the view. Pale, twinkling lights gracing the eaves, a bright red ribbon adorning the door, are beautiful sights.

Bible scholar N. T. Wright says that our appreciation for beauty is one of the things that indicates our need for God—that our longing for beautiful things represents a longing for another world and the presence of God. Perhaps that longing intensifies at Christmastime, because at Christmas, we fill our homes with beautiful things.

There's something about Christmas that inspires beauty—striking, colorful images as well as music and literature that seem nothing short of divinely inspired.

This Christmas, slow down long enough to enjoy something beautiful. Let it fill your heart with joy and wonder at the inexpressible truths of Christmas. And let it make your Christmas season truly blessed.

Creator God, you have filled your world and my life with beauty. Thank you for inspiring me with your handiwork.

DECEMBER

7

The Peace of Unity

"My prayer is not for them alone. I pray also for those who
will believe in me through their message, that all of them may
be one, Father, just as you are in me and I am in you."

—JOHN 17:20-21

A CLASSIC DEVOTION FROM JUSTIN MARTYR (SECOND CENTURY)

Who then among you is noble-minded? Who compassionate? Who full of love? Let him declare, "If on my account subversion and disagreement and schisms have arisen in the church, I will depart, I will go away wherever you ask, and I will do whatever the majority commands; only let the flock of Christ live in peace under the authority of the [church leaders]."

Let us then also pray for those who have fallen into any sin, that meekness and humility may be given to them, so that they may submit, not unto us, but to the will of God. For in this way they shall secure a fruitful and perfect remembrance from us, with sympathy for them, both in our prayers to God, and our mention of them to the saints. Let us receive correction, beloved, on account of which no one should feel displeased. Those exhortations by which we challenge and encourage one another are both good [in and of themselves] and highly profitable, for they tend to unite us to the will of God.

God of peace, make me a peacemaker in my church who promotes love and harmony.

8

— *Big Gifts Come in Small Packages* —

*The kingdom of heaven is like a mustard seed, which a man took
and planted in his field. Though it is the smallest of all your
seeds, yet when it grows, it is the largest of garden plants and
becomes a tree, so that the birds come and perch in its branches.*

—MATTHEW 13:31-32

He wasn't supposed to live beyond infancy. But the tiny baby survived, even when he was floated down the Nile River in a basket. The man Moses grew to lead his people out of slavery, and, against impossible circumstances presented by nature and enemies, he brought them into God's Promised Land.

He was the youngest son of an inconsequential family that belonged to a small tribe in the hill country of an obscure nation. Yet David, a man after God's own heart, prevailed in combat against lion, bear, and giant.

In a dark and violent world, in a bleak and blighted village, a tiny life appeared. Jesus, the babe in the manger, brought light and hope to a world engulfed in strife—and forever changed the course of history. But the message of Christmas is that great things come in small packages. A grand and magnificent love broke into the world when Jesus was born. Enjoy the bright lights of the season. But don't lose sight that the greatest blessings come in the smallest packages.

My Lord and Savior, thank you for the greatest gift of all: the gift of Jesus.

Reconnecting with Loved Ones

And over all these virtues put on love, which
binds them all together in perfect unity.

—COLOSSIANS 3:14

The greeting card industry has been around a lot longer than Hallmark Cards. Ancient Chinese and Egyptian civilizations had a tradition among the wealthy of sending simple prepackaged blessings and well wishes to loved ones on papyrus or clay surfaces. It was in fifteenth-century Europe that handmade greeting cards became a common expression of affection and love.

Now our mailing lists might be electronic or found only in our social networks. In addition to paper, the cards we receive might be found on a friend's blog or arrive in our inbox as e-cards or highly designed family newsletters.

But the purpose is the same. Christmas reminds us to catch up with the people who have come and gone in life but for whom we still feel love, affection, and attachment. Our Christmas correspondence, no matter what form it takes, also stands as a living history of our lives.

Christmas reminds us that staying connected, even when our relationships are scattered, may be a challenge, but one that is more than worth it through the blessing of being connected.

Loving Father, thank you for all the people you have sent into my life to make my life richer and happier.

Childlike Wonder

He called a little child to him, and placed the child among them. And he said: "Truly I tell you, unless you change and become like little children, you will never enter the kingdom of heaven. Therefore, whoever takes the lowly position of this child is the greatest in the kingdom of heaven."

—MATTHEW 18:2-4

Even though little Cindy Lou didn't stop the Grinch from stealing Christmas, most Dr. Seuss readers still think it was her big brown eyes that pierced his heart and began his personal transformation, even before he heard the whole community come out and sing from his icy hilltop home.

Now if you've had enough of being a Grinch, if you've seriously been feeling like canceling Christmas this year, there is a cure.

It begins with humility. Not believing you are too sophisticated to stop and admire the tinsel and the toys. But the cure continues by spending time with children. Lost the wonder of Christmas? Maybe you need to watch a child enjoying the season. Kids approach Christmas activities with unabashed enthusiasm. Watching their excitement and outright glee over things as simple as sugar cookies and wrapping paper, you just might find your heart softening—or growing three sizes—and your cynicism melting. Best of all, what will replace your hard heart is a renewed sense of childlike wonder and joy.

Help me, O God, to see Christmas through the innocent and wonder-filled eyes of a child.

Generosity

The Lord Jesus Himself said: "It is more
blessed to give than to receive."

—ACTS 20:35

A young couple just starting out in the world lived together in New York City. Sure, they were poor, but they were in love, so all was well—until Christmas.

Della's pride was her beautiful hair. Jim's pride was a gold watch that had been owned by his father and grandfather. Jim's gift to Della was a set of combs she had admired. Della's gift to Jim was a platinum fob chain for his watch. All was wonderful, except the small detail that Jim had sold his watch to buy Della's combs—and Della had sold her hair to a wigmaker in order to buy his chain. But in his classic short story, "The Gift of the Magi," O. Henry wrote:

> The magi, as you know, were wise men—wonderfully wise men—who brought gifts to the Babe in the manger. They invented the art of giving Christmas presents. They are the magi.

The Christmas season is fun and exciting as we open presents—but it is even more joyful for the opportunity to share from our abundance with others.

Provider God, as Christmas approaches, help me to experience the joy of giving with lavish love and generosity.

12

The Blessings of Tradition

I remember the days of long ago; I meditate on all your
works and consider what your hands have done.

—PSALM 143:5

On September 21, 1897, Francis P. Church, an editor at the *New York Sun*, replied to a young lady about a Christmas tradition:

Yes, Virginia, there is a Santa Claus. He exists as certainly as love and generosity and devotion exist, and you know that they abound and give to your life its highest beauty and joy. Alas! How dreary would be the world if there were no Santa Claus! Virginia, in all this world there is nothing else real and abiding. A thousand years from now, Virginia, nay, ten times ten thousand years from now, he will continue to make glad the heart of childhood.

No, Christmas is not fundamentally about Santa Claus. But in an anchorless culture, traditions are essential. Oh, they can drive us a bit crazy, and might even feel a little bit boring at times. But they do point to the "unseeable" and help us experience anew the "supernal beauty and glory beyond."

Traditions are one of the sweetest blessings of Christmas.

Father God, thank you for Christmas traditions that remind me of your indescribable gift of Jesus Christ as Savior of the world.

Follow the Star

"Where is the one who has been born king of the Jews? We saw His star when it rose and have come to worship Him."

—MATTHEW 2:2

Sometimes a dream can change our lives dramatically! Consider Brad's story:

"From birth, it was expected that I would join the company my grandfather founded and be groomed for succeeding my dad as president one day.

"Then one Christmas, my wife and I went to serve a turkey dinner at an inner-city rescue mission. Something pierced my heart to the core that day. I couldn't sleep all night. All I could see when I closed my eyes was the despair of lost souls.

"I finally said something to my wife: 'I think God is calling me to work at the rescue mission.' To my amazement, she was 100 percent supportive.

"My family, particularly my dad, was a different story. It was my grandfather who eventually brokered peace between my dad and me. He said to him, 'Douglas, I followed a dream when I started this company, and nothing else would have made me happy. Your son is exactly the same way. He just has a different dream.'"

Dreams come in different shapes and sizes. But wise men still follow the star God has put before them.

Father, show me your will for my life and help me to follow the star that lights my way.

DECEMBER

14

What Can I Give Him?

*But when the kindness and love of God our Savior
appeared, He saved us, not because of righteous
things we had done, but because of His mercy.*

—TITUS 3:4-5

EXCERPT FROM A CLASSIC CHRISTMAS POEM BY CHRISTINA ROSSETTI (TWENTIETH CENTURY)

Our God, heaven cannot hold Him, nor earth sustain;
Heaven and earth shall flee away when He comes to reign.
In the bleak midwinter a stable place sufficed
The Lord God Almighty, Jesus Christ.

Angels and archangels may have gathered there,
Cherubim and seraphim thronged the air;
But His mother only, in her maiden bliss,
Worshipped the beloved with a kiss.

What can I give Him, poor as I am?
If I were a shepherd, I would bring a lamb;
If I were a Wise Man, I would do my part;
Yet what I can I give Him: give my heart.

**Father God, thank you for the gift of Jesus; in return I give
you my heart.**

Hardships Don't Last

Weeping may stay for the night, but rejoicing comes in the morning.

—PSALM 30:5

Mary. A peasant girl. Pregnant but unmarried. Subject by law and custom to stoning or, at minimum, a lifetime of shame. It doesn't get much harder than that.

Joseph. A respected leader in his community. Engaged to be married to a young woman he adored. His life turned upside down by a seeming betrayal and the whispers that he had been cheated on. It doesn't hurt much deeper than that.

A young couple. Just getting started in an already shaky marriage. Forced to travel at the very time when she most needed rest and warmth. An arduous journey atop a stumbling donkey. They arrived at their destination. But there were no more accommodations available. Couldn't they get a break?

Life can get bumpy for all of us. Just when we think we've arrived, we see the "no occupancy" sign lit brightly. For some, life gets even harder around Christmas. It is a reminder of mistakes, lost opportunities, and broken relationships.

Christmas reminds us that hardship doesn't last. God smiles on mother and child—and on us.

God of salvation, thank you that your eyes are always upon me; you always know where I am and what I need.

16

A Christmas Celebration

Rejoice in the Lord always. I will say it again: Rejoice!

—PHILIPPIANS 4:4

Christmas is most definitely a time for serious reflection and worship. But don't let anyone steal the joy of celebration that is part of the Christmas season from your life. Jesus, the Author of Christmas, the One we worship and celebrate at Christmas, was criticized sharply for attending parties: "The Son of Man came eating and drinking, and they say, 'Here is a glutton and a drunkard, a friend of tax collectors and sinners'" (Matthew 11:19).

One of Jesus's most famous stories was of a son that wandered far from home, squandering all the material and moral resources his father had given him. But when he did finally come to his senses and return to his family, the father's immediate response was to throw a huge party to celebrate having his son back home.

When we truly come home for Christmas, we rediscover that our Heavenly Father loves us so much He gave the gift of His son. That calls for a celebration!

Loving Father, thank you that when I was far away from you, you sent the gift of your son, Jesus Christ.

Forever Grateful

*Every good and perfect gift is from above, coming
down from the Father of the heavenly lights, who
does not change like shifting shadows.*

—JAMES 1:17

There is a simple attitude that determines in our own minds whether we are rich or poor, blessed or cursed, and fundamentally positive or negative about life. To make that enormous of a difference, that attitude must be incredibly powerful. And it is. That attitude is gratitude.

One person looks under the Christmas tree, finds a simple and thoughtful gift, and knows she is loved; all that another person can think about as he tears the glossy wrapping paper from the box is what he didn't get. She had a great Christmas morning and got absolutely everything she wanted; he had a lousy Christmas and didn't get anything good. The only difference was gratitude.

Whether there are gifts stacked to the ceiling with your name on them or you aren't sure anyone is going to give you anything, stop and give thanks to God. You'll receive a special blessing in your spirit and discover you have everything you need.

My heart is filled with gratitude this Christmas season, O Lord, as I think of all the blessings you have given me.

Life Is a Journey

Now faith is confidence in what we hope for and
assurance about what we do not see.

—HEBREWS 11:1

I t was about a hundred miles to Bethlehem. Maybe as many as eight or ten days by donkey and foot. She wasn't very old—a mere teenager, late in her pregnancy. The road ahead was full of rocks and steep grades, not to mention the danger of thieves. When they reached their destination, the book of Luke tells us, "the time came for the baby to be born" (Luke 2:6). And Mary gave birth to the baby they named Jesus.

Now, two thousand years later, we make our own journeys at Christmastime. Maybe you're racing around town in search of the perfect gift. Or maybe you're starting a thousand-mile drive home.

Maybe you love the scenery you're experiencing in life right now, or maybe you can't wait to get over a hill or around a curve. But if you're living life with purpose, even the bumpiest sections of the road have meaning and will lead you to the destination God has mapped out for you.

Gracious and loving God, thank you that you are on the journey of my life each mile of the way.

19

The Season of Joy

A cheerful heart is good medicine.

—PROVERBS 17:22

I t seems that a new one comes out every year. Starting with nearly every Thanksgiving weekend, theaters release a new Christmas movie—or three! Many of them land in cinematic obscurity shortly after New Year's Day and are only mentioned in trivia games. Others, like 1983's *A Christmas Story* or 1990's *Home Alone*, become instant classics and run seemingly nonstop on cable channels throughout December for years to come. Tellingly, most Christmas movies are not dark dramas, but family-friendly comedies.

The Christmas season is a time for reflection. It's a time for worship and giving to others and counting our blessings. But it's also a time to celebrate. Is it possible for Christmas to become too light and frivolous? Absolutely. But that probably won't be evidenced by the laughter when we enjoy being with others, but rather by the sullen quietness that comes from preoccupied separation.

Enjoy a few laughs this Christmas season—look for opportunities to share laughter with others—and you'll be enjoying one of the best blessings of the Christmas season.

Thank you, Heavenly Father, for the gift of joy and laughter as I spend time with people I love.

Angels Watch Over Us

Praise the Lord, you His angels, you mighty ones
who do His bidding, who obey His word.

—PSALM 103:20

Angels play a leading role in the story of Jesus's birth. They appear to Joseph in a dream and tell him of the coming child. The angel Gabriel appears to Mary to tell her she has been chosen by God. And then a heavenly choir proclaims the message of the Christ child to the shepherds. But we have to wonder if angels played a behind-the-scenes role in the events of Jesus's birth as well. Mary and Joseph's journey to Bethlehem would have been difficult and dangerous—doesn't it make sense to think that angels helped them find their way and arrive at just the right time? Under those circumstances, it seems that Providence was watching out for the young family—through the care of angels, perhaps?

Christmas—with all its little everyday miracles and blessings—has a special way of comforting us with reminders of the presence of angels. Be reminded this Christmas season that God watches over you and that His angels stand beside you right now.

Heavenly Father, you have watched over my life, and I am grateful and honored that you care that much about me.

The Birth of Your Savior

After Jesus was born in Bethlehem in Judea, during the time of
King Herod, Magi from the east came to Jerusalem and asked,
"Where is the one who has been born king of the Jews? We
saw His star when it rose and have come to worship Him."

—MATTHEW 2:1-2

A CLASSIC DEVOTION FROM SAMUEL WILLARD
(EIGHTEENTH CENTURY)

Let me invite you to come to the birth of your Savior: see the King
of Glory, veiled in obscurity and entering into the world under
a cloud. He is the Lord of heaven and earth entering into His
dominion, in the lowest and most obscure situation imaginable.

The Son of God was a great king; He could have commanded
all the world, and with a word built a stately palace, and
furnished it in magnificence for himself. But how would He
be our redeemer then? It was "for your sake He became poor"
(2 Corinthians 8:9). It was for this reason He was born. Was
not this condescension a disclosure of His great love? Let this
stable and manger make him exceedingly precious to us.

And if we enjoy any benefits in our birth, let us acknowledge
them to Him. For in the day of patience, God allows this favor
even to wicked men, yet God's people should understand that
all their mercies flow through Christ, and ascribe them to Him.

**Almighty God, the birth of my Savior is the most precious
gift in my life.**

22

Sing a Song at Christmas

He put a new song in my mouth, a hymn of praise to our God.

—PSALM 40:3

I t was early Christmas Eve in 1818 when the priests of St. Nicholas Church in Obernadorf, Austria, learned that the broken pipe organ would not be fixed in time for Midnight Mass. Joseph Mohr, the assistant priest, was at first saddened by the news, but then moved to action. He sat down and wrote a song that could be easily sung a cappella or with guitar accompaniment. That night, *"Stille Nacht"*—or "Silent Night"—was debuted at Midnight Mass and is now sung by millions of people each year in 180 languages.

Christmas is about music and singing—and not just listening, though you might not want to try belting out the Hallelujah Chorus from Handel's *Messiah* in public without a little practice.

Christmas puts all kinds of songs in our hearts and reminds us to sing. Most of the year, we put in our earbuds and have others do the singing to entertain us. But this year at Christmas, put voice to what is in your heart. You will be blessed!

Joyful, joyful, I adore thee, God of heaven!

A Season to Forgive

Be kind and compassionate to one another, forgiving
each other, just as in Christ God forgave you.

—EPHESIANS 4:32

It had been years since the two brothers had spoken. It was a son and nephew who broke the silence between them. He hadn't seen his uncle and cousins in years. He looked up at his dad and asked, "Where are Uncle John and Aunt Kathy? Why don't we see them anymore?"

His dad had no real answer. He knew he no longer wanted to be torn apart from his brother.

He picked up the phone. The conversation started icy and stiff. Finally, both brothers broke the silence, speaking at the same time: "I'm sorry for..." The ice was melted, and forgiveness was offered and received by both parties. Christmas saw two families celebrating the holiday together again.

Christmas is timeless and spurs us to think about eternal matters. It's also a time to reconnect with family and friends. For those two reasons, forgiveness is often the most important part of a meaningful Christmas. Yes, relationships can be difficult. But if Christmas teaches us anything, it's the power of love and sacrificial giving, expressed beautifully in the miracle of forgiveness.

God of peace, I ask you to work in my heart this Christmas season as I seek to reconnect some broken relations.

Prince of Peace

He will be called Wonderful Counselor, Mighty
God, Everlasting Father, Prince of Peace.

—ISAIAH 9:6

n 1863, Charles Longfellow enlisted in the Union Army. In late November, a bullet entered his left shoulder and very nearly left him paralyzed. He was taken home to recover. "Home" was with his younger brother, Ernest, and his father, the famous poet, Henry Wadsworth Longfellow.

As Henry nursed his son back to health that Christmas season, something began to happen in Longfellow's heart. He gave thanks every day that Charles had not been killed in battle, and his heart began to lighten and soften. Out of this experience he wrote the classic poem, "I Heard the Bells on Christmas Day," which was set to music and became a beloved Christmas carol. Longfellow's poem bemoans the tragedies of our weary world. But the last verse declares a renewed hope:

Then pealed the bells more loud and deep:
"God is not dead; nor doth he sleep!
The Wrong shall fail,
The Right prevail,
With peace on earth, good-will to men!"

In a world of conflict and strife, you, O Father, bring peace. Thank you for lifting my spirit this Christmas season.

A Prayer on Christmas Day

*Suddenly a great company of the heavenly host appeared with
the angel, praising God and saying, "Glory to God in the highest
heaven, and on earth peace to those on whom His favor rests."'*

—LUKE 2:13–14

God of joy,
  On this Christmas day, I look forward to special times
with friends and family, to celebrating your love and goodness
to us. Thank you so much for giving us the gift of Jesus. Help
me to have a heart filled with gratitude and praise as I am
reminded of that glorious night so long ago.

Many people do not look forward to Christmas and experience depression and feelings of aloneness. You know who I
have in my heart and mind. Give me grace to reach out to them
with kindness and encouragement.

Some people are unhappy during the Christmas season
because they don't know you and are still resisting your
grace. They seem to fight the Spirit of Christmas. I pray that
even the rebellious may feel the wonder of the story—and
truth—of Christmas.

Bless my friends and loved ones. Give us cherished moments
together that we will never forget.

In Jesus's name. Amen.

O Come Let Us Adore Him

Worship the Lord with gladness; come before Him with joyful songs. For the Lord is good and His love endures forever; His faithfulness continues through all generations.

—PSALM 100:2, 5

When John Wade penned the immortal words to "O Come All Ye Faithful," he beautifully captured a vision of that first Christmas, when mother and father, wise men and shepherds, and even beasts of burden simply "adored" the baby in a manger.

Can anything be more important for you this Christmas than simple worship? Worship is different from thanksgiving. Thanksgiving is expressing gratitude for what God has done for us. He has redeemed us and blessed us in countless ways. Worship, on the other hand, looks behind what God has done and expresses awe, reverence, and admiration for the attributes of God.

Where do you even begin to worship God this Christmas season? It can happen in a church service or the reading of a Scripture passage with your family or in a time of prayer or so many other ways. But maybe this is the year to reach back across the generations and simplify. Why not find a living nativity in your community and simply stand in wonder as you adore the baby in a manger?

Father God, you showed yourself to the world in a manger; I stand before you in awe.

A Baby Changes Everything

Glory to God in the highest heaven, and on earth
peace to those on whom His favor rests.

—LUKE 2:14

A mentally disturbed king. A tumultuous engagement. A new marriage. A pregnancy that generated whispers and rumors. An emperor's command. An arduous journey. The wrong setting to deliver a child.

But a baby is born, and this baby changes everything. Angels sing. Shepherds and wise men worship. A mother's prayer of praise is heard throughout generations. Salvation has come to a fallen people.

Love came down on Christmas day so many years ago and brought the greatest happiness the world would ever know. Peace came down on Christmas day to fill the hearts of men with all the sweet tranquility each Christmas brings again. Joy came down on Christmas day as angels came to earth heralding the miracle of our Messiah's birth.

No matter what circumstances surround you this Christmas season, never forget. A baby changes everything.

I praise you, Heavenly Father, for the gift of a baby.

Your Life Matters

But I have raised you up for this very purpose, that I might show you my power and that my name might be proclaimed in all the earth.

—EXODUS 9:16

When Simeon saw Jesus, he knew that day had come, and he proclaimed the coming Messiah and offered a blessing to Mary and Joseph.

This moment must have stood out in the young parents' minds as another confirmation of who their child really was. It would seem that God had placed Simeon in the right place at the right time.

Each member of the entire cast of characters in the first Christmas story plays a unique role, and each of them furthers God's plan in a way that only they can. God needed someone to bring His son into the world; He chose Mary. Mary needed a protector and provider; God gave her Joseph. The wise men brought gifts and adoration, and the shepherds spread the good news of the baby's birth. God had a plan to enter our world with peace and love, and He used ordinary lives to bring it to fruition.

What is God's special purpose for your life? How can He use you during this Christmas season? Pause. Pray. Listen. Be blessed.

Heavenly Father, thank you that my life matters and that you have a purpose for me today and in the future.

Be Prepared

*Because Joseph her husband was faithful to the
law, and yet did not want to expose her to public
disgrace, he had in mind to divorce her quietly.*

—MATTHEW 1:19

Christmas is full of surprises each year. But perhaps no one faced a greater surprise than Joseph did in the months before that first Christmas when Jesus was born.

What prepared Joseph to handle these surprises with such grace? We are told that Joseph was a righteous man. Righteousness, in the Old Testament world, was defined as being innocent and doing right. For Matthew, the most Jewish of the Gospel writers, it was being ethical and doing the will of God.

What's the best preparation for any surprise that comes your way in life? Righteousness. Living a life of faith and becoming more and more Christlike. The great English preacher of the nineteenth century, Charles Spurgeon, encourages us with this thought: "Have your heart right with Christ, and He will visit you often, and so turn weekdays into Sundays, meals into sacraments, homes into temples, and earth into heaven."

Are you prepared to see Jesus? Is your heart ready to be part of the miracle of salvation for yourself and others?

Heavenly Father, work in my heart today to give me a righteousness that will allow me to do your will in every area of my life.

Focus on Christ

*There is but one God, the Father, from whom all things came
and for whom we live; and there is but one Lord, Jesus Christ,
through whom all things came and through whom we live.*

—1 CORINTHIANS 8:6

December is a month that draws our attention back to Christ. We are reminded that Christ was with God the Father from the very beginning of eternity (John 1:1); that His appearance as Savior and Redeemer has been anticipated and prophesied for centuries (Isaiah 9:6–7); that His birth as the baby Jesus has brought salvation to the world and to each one of us (John 3:16–17).

Because the scenery and images are so different, we usually think of Christmas and Easter as two very separate events. After all, one observance is about a birth and the other about a death. But in the divine picture of life, the birth of Jesus is woven together with His death and resurrection. All are acts of grace from God that brought us salvation.

As the Christmas season comes to a conclusion, don't forget the lessons and blessings of the birth of the Savior. Nothing will keep your heart and life in perfect alignment more effectively that keeping your focus on Jesus today and all the days to come.

Lord Jesus, I am so glad I know you. In the coming new year, help me focus on you.

Another Year

See, the former things have taken place, and new things I
declare; before they spring into being I announce them to you.

—ISAIAH 42:9

Another year has come and gone. How will this one go down in the books for you? As years continue to come and go, are we growing and making a difference in the time God has given us?

The psalmist has this simple but profound prayer on behalf of himself and you and me: "Teach us to number our days, that we may gain a heart of wisdom" (Psalm 90:12).

Consider writing down a highlight of your year before you forget, and before you even begin thinking about goals for next year. Do this thoughtfully and prayerfully. List your main events and the things on your heart and mind. It doesn't have to be long or carefully worded. Just get it on paper. Then ask God to convict you in areas that need to change. Let Him affirm you in areas where He is pleased with your life. Let this account of your year challenge and encourage you to live your best life yet in the days ahead.

God, as I sit down to take stock of the year, I want to thank you for your blessings and ask for your guidance. Help me to make this year count for you.

Mark Gilroy has had a long, varied, and successful career in publishing, from his first paid creative assignment as a newspaper sports writer while in college, to serving as head of gift, specialty, and backlist publishing for Thomas Nelson, the world's largest Christian publisher.

Mark has had a leadership role in numerous publishing phenomena, including God's Little Devotional Book and Jesus Calling—two series that each sold more than 10 million copies and touched countless lives.

Mark won't claim he has done it all in the world of publishing, but he has packed boxes, edited manuscripts, made sales calls, created marketing plans, directed design and illustration, started companies, consulted, agented the works of others, and written advertising and catalog copy. He's authored, compiled, and ghostwritten books that have landed on an array of bestseller lists and sold millions of copies.

Gilroy and his wife Amy reside in Brentwood, Tennessee. Their six children are Lindsey, Merrick, Ashley, Caroline, Bo, and Zachary—the youngest has now headed off for college, so he and Amy are officially empty nesters.